THE CHRISTIAN FAITH

AND ITS

CONTEMPORARY RIVALS

RICHARD B. CUNNINGHAM

BROADMAN PRESS
Nashville, Tennessee

Dewey Decimal Classification: 291
Subject Headings: CHRISTIANITY AND OTHER
RELIGIONS // RELIGIONS
Library of Congress Catalog Card Number: 87-28940

Printed in the United States of America

Unless otherwise indicated Scripture quotations are from the Revised Standard Version of the Bible, copyrighted 1946, 1952, © 1971, 1973. Quotations marked (KJV) are from the King James Version of the Bible.

Library of Congress Cataloging-in-Publication Data

Cunningham, Richard B.
    The Christian faith and its contemporary rivals / Richard B.
Cunningham.
        p.   cm.
    Bibliography: p.
    ISBN 0-8054-6705-X :
    1. Apologetics—20th century.   I. Title.
BT1102.C78 1988
239—dc19   87-28940

To
Eric C. Rust and Henlee H. Barnette
Friends, Teachers, Colleagues

Preface

Christians are called to bear witness to the saving gospel of Jesus Christ to every person within the human family. The witness takes many forms—lives that evidence the indwelling presence of God, serving, preaching, teaching, and defending. Christian apologetics has been one major instrument from the apostolic era until today in the church's effort to understand the Christian faith and to advocate and defend it to people both inside and outside the church. Christian apologetics takes seriously the doubt or struggle with unbelief among Christians and the inquiry about or challenges to the faith from non-Christians.

Christian apologetics is necessarily an intellectual task, although it involves profound spiritual sensitivity and interpersonal skills when it engages people in the flow of everyday life. The more sustained and penetrating intellectual work of apologetics will normally be done by Christian theologians or philosophers as they grapple with the intricacies of numerous specific apologetic problems and the large-scale conceptual encounter of alternative worldviews. It is imperative, however, in our complex modern societies that Christian ministers and laypersons appropriate and translate the more academic treatment of apologetic issues into the actual arena of dialogue with ordinary people in everyday life.

My intention in this book is twofold. On the one hand, I have attempted to treat the selected alternative worldviews with sufficient theological and philosophical depth that the book may offer an apologetic resource for academics, theological students, and ministers who want to develop a basic understanding of some of Christianity's major rivals and how to respond apologetically to them. On the other hand, I would hope that the discussion of these views may also be appropriated by literate laypersons who desire to be effective interpreters and defenders of the Christian faith in the many varied structures of modern society.

In my judgment, Christian apologetics can never be a substitute for a simple Christian witness or straightforward preaching or teaching of the Christian faith. It can, however, complement other disciplines and ministries as the church encounters the multilayered structures of modern society. Today, as in the apostolic era, personal witness, preaching, and teaching remain central in the mission of the church. But in the modern global community, in which there is an immediate exposure to and clash of cultures, religions, and worldviews throughout the world, apologetics has taken on a greater sense of urgency and importance. That is particularly true at the level of the apologetic encounter between rival world views. That is what this book is about.

I dedicate this book to Eric C. Rust and Henlee H. Barnette, my retired colleagues at The Southern Baptist Theological Seminary, the two people who have most directly influenced my own professional work in apologetics. Eric Rust has been my close friend, most influential teacher, and colleague in Christian philosophy for many years, the dominant shaper of my own way of doing theology and interpreting the Christian faith to the world. Over the years, we have discussed numerous areas of theology and various apologetic issues. Henlee Barnette, an ethicist, is one of my great teachers and friends. He first suggested to me in 1963 the possibility of doing a dissertation on C. S. Lewis, which initiated for me an ongoing interest in bridging the gap between professional theologians and the practical theological and apologetic ministry of the church. For years, he has been one of my greatest encouragers. These two valued friends share profoundly my concern for an apologetic ministry in our contemporary world.

Contents

1
Christian Apologetics in the Contemporary World

A distinctive mark of human beings is that they organize their lives around sets of fundamental beliefs. Wherever humans have lived in different geographies and cultures, they have inevitably developed basic convictions, ways of valuing, and interpretations of the mysteries surrounding them that attempted to make sense out of life and to provide the organizing principles for their individual lives and particular social settings. Such interpretations can take the form of practical everyday beliefs or highly sophisticated systems of thought called *worldviews*. In the course of human history, these basic approaches to life have converged into certain broad patterns of understanding existence that provide the options within which most people interpret their lives.

In earlier historical eras when limited travel and communications placed the larger world beyond a vast and mysterious horizon, cultures existed in relative isolation, and their dominant interpretations of life remained largely unknown to each other. The majority of people in the world rather naturally adopted a philosophy of life or worldview from the dominant tradition within which they lived—normally some prevailing religious worldview. For the most part, one's options in expressing ultimate concerns or adopting worldviews were quite limited.

Such comfortable parochialism has changed with the advent of the modern era. Due to our global military, economic, and cultural entanglements and the impact of the missionary activity of several world religions, formerly isolated systems of belief and worldviews have been thrown into a planetary melting pot. The encounter between rival worldviews, religious and secular, occurs throughout the world and is intensified by rapid travel and communications. A new element in our present situation is that the world's religious and non-religious options are now more widely available to people than in earlier generations. By far the majority of modern people still adhere to some religious worldview. Christians are found in sizable numbers in most nations on earth because of Christian missionary efforts. As a result of the massive population shifts of modern history, many Buddhists, Muslims, Hindus, Shintoists, and other non-Christian religious people now live in the traditional Christian nations of the West.

Religions, however, are only part of the current options in worldviews. With the sweeping secularization that has occurred in twentieth century, a substantial portion of the human family—one billion or more—no longer adheres to any of the great religions or recognizes any reality that transcends the universe itself. Nevertheless, these nonreligious people—at least in the traditional definition of religion —continue to orient their lives around systems of belief, philosophies of life, or formal worldviews that present secular, nonreligious options to contemporary humanity. They may be self-conscious naturalists, atheists, secular humanists, Marxists, nihilists, or something else. In the case of many other nonreligious people, their systems of belief may not be consciously spelled out in detail, and they might not even attach a name to their approach to life. Yet their outlook may fall broadly within an easily identifiable pattern of belief or worldview. Even in a pluralistic world, we humans remain creatures of ultimate concern who struggle to find significance for our lives, if nothing more than to attach ourselves to some value within the universe itself.

Christian Apologetics in a Pluralistic World

The Christian church now lives and ministers in this new global community—a small pluralistic world where the clash between cultures, systems of belief, philosophies of life, religions, and worldviews has great impact upon the way Christians understand their own faith and define their world mission. In earlier historical eras, most Western Christians, living in predominantly Christian cultures, had little knowledge of alternative worldviews or opportunity to dialogue with adherents of other views or even to weigh those views for themselves. The church's missionary activity was usually left in the hands of professional missionaries who often went to foreign cultures without understanding or appreciating the prevailing religions or general worldviews of particular people. In sharing the good news of Jesus Christ primarily through preaching, many missionaries did not come to understand how their message was being heard by people with quite different views.

The Christian apologetic task today is defined by our new setting in a pluralistic world. It is directed to many people with enlarged cultural horizons within the church as well as to those outside the Christian church who may be deeply committed to an alternative view of life. The Christian encounter with rival ideologies occurs within the Western countries where Christianity has dominated, as well as in other places in the world. Rivals to the Christian faith are advocated in many areas of modern life—in the universities, television and radio, literature, the arts, politics, economic theories, and social life, as well as through the missionary activity of other world religions. As a consequence, many contemporary people are exposed to a far greater variety of possible systems of belief and worldviews than were people in previous generations. The challenge of contemporary alternatives to the Christian faith is not exclusively in relation to non-Christians. In our time, many Christians themselves are for the first time examining the appeal of alternative approaches to life and reevaluating the Christian faith in light of their exposure to new ideas.

The church is at a juncture in history where it is increasingly important for ministers and many laypersons to better understand the alternative belief systems and worldviews that challenge the Christian faith's proclamation of Jesus Christ as the way to truth, reality, and God. The mission of the church to people who hold alternative religious or other kinds of beliefs is no longer the special task of missionaries alone. The average Christian has not wrestled with the challenge of entering into dialogue with alternative points of view, a responsibility we have gladly delegated to professional missionaries or theological specialists.

Dialogue has become increasingly essential in the encounter between Christianity and its modern rivals. The people of our world have a right to ask for the reasons one should choose to be a Christian rather than to opt for a religious or secular alternative. We—ministers and laypeople—need to be able to give reasons "for the hope that is in us." And we need some understanding of the people we talk with.

Many questions are important in developing a knowledge of alternative beliefs and formulating specific Christian responses to individual worldviews or systems of belief. What do people believe who are committed to some alternative system of belief? What is the inner appeal of that view? What are its implications for life itself? Is there anything there from which Christians can learn? Is there any common ground between the other view and Christianity? Where is the alternative view vulnerable to a general critique or a Christian critique? Does Christianity more adequately address the basic values of the alternative point of view? These kinds of straightforward questions must be faced in any open arena of dialogue with people who hold other points of view.

My purpose in this book is to examine selected prominent alternatives to the Christian faith and analyze important dimensions of dialogue that can facilitate the Christian apologetic task. That intention determines the nature of my analysis. I am not simply engaged in a detached scholarly analysis and comparison of belief-systems or worldviews. The modern study of religions is contributing greatly to our understanding of the other great religions of the world and to giving all the people of the world a more sensitive appreciation for cultures and religions different from their own. The church is indebted to many scholars who are opening a wealth of objective, descriptive insight into other religious and secular worldviews that is potentially important to the apologetic task. Certainly my hope is that my own descriptive analysis of the various alternative views would be judged by other scholars to be objective and accurate. I am convinced that one can engage in creative apologetic only when one has genuinely gotten inside the skin of people who hold other belief-systems and appreciates their ultimate concern and depth of commitment. But my immediate purpose in understanding them is to facilitate the Christian apologetic task of presenting and defending the ultimate claims of the Christian faith in relation to all alternative beliefs and worldviews.

In our human quest for ultimate truth and reality, it is an important step for an individual to come to understand in critical and objective fashion the great alternative worldviews available to the human family. However, dispassionate and detached knowledge alone, even if encyclopedic in scope, does not settle the question of truth and value for a person or lay claim upon one's life. Unless one is willing to be a relativist, judging all belief-systems and worldviews to be equally true and valuable, at some point in the human quest, one must make discriminating judgments between alternative expressions of ultimate concern. Are some beliefs true and others false? What are the criteria for truth? Do some worldviews better meet criteria for truth? Do some worldviews contribute more to the quality of life than do others? Do some worldviews better correlate with the whole sweep of human experience than others? If so, how do we know? These are important questions as one begins to reflect about our ultimate commitments. A good place to begin is with some thought about how basic beliefs and wider worldviews actually take shape within our human experience.

The Existing Human Individual

Formal patterns of interpreting life emerge inevitably from the human situation. That is because, with all our individual uniqueness, humans struggle at common points in our creaturely existence. All humans have a few fleeting years to make sense out of life and find fulfillment within their individual lives. In the words of Martin Heidegger, the individual is thrown into existence without any explanation of his whence or whither.[1] One did not ask to be born or choose the genetic code that creates the particular person one is. One simply finds oneself existing, without definition, in the world, born to a particular set of parents in a particular social setting.

When the individual first attempts reflectively to define oneself and understand life, one immediately encounters one's own finitude. We are born and we die. We did not choose to be born and we cannot choose not to die. Death is life's starkest inevitability, and it is unpredictable. We will die, and we do not know when! That unknown end to one's finite existence injects urgency into each individual's human quest. The pressure of finitude is intensified by my sense of insignificance when I measure myself against the vastness of the universe. As preoccupied as I am with myself, I am forced to define myself in relation to a universe that existed long before I came to be and will continue long after I am dead. What is the origin, nature, and goal of a universe that can produce a reflective creature like myself and other human beings?

An individual is an existing self headed toward death after a few years of life in a vast cosmic process. That is dilemma enough! But it is compounded by the fact that the process of life will not wait for me to discover answers to life's problems and mysteries. I live on the razor's edge where my immediate present slips irretrievably into a frozen past and the inbreaking future determines my next present moment. Time moves on—inexorably, rapidly, and irreversibly— into a future yet to be decided or determined at many levels. Our human awareness of time distinguishes us from other creatures who, except at the level of survival instincts, have little awareness of the future or of an impending death.

In consciousness of my future, I discover my freedom. Within the limitations of my own particular natural and historical contexts, I find myself partly determining my personal future through my own choices between future alternatives. In exercising my freedom and finding myself having to live with the consequences of my choices, I experience my accountability for the decisions that affect major aspects of my life.

As finite, free, and responsible individuals who are thrown unexplainably into the world, it is no wonder that human beings exist in anxiety. Deluged by a flood of questions about existence and forced to make momentous choices within boundaries I did not choose and cannot alter, I live in anxiety—with guilt about past choices, insecurity about my present situation, and uncertainty about the impending future. At every point in life, I am not satisfied with everything I have chosen in the past or with many elements of my present situation. A universal characteristic of every individual and culture is the brokenness, estrangement, and alienation we experience in relation to our noblest vision of our best selves, the highest values we hold, the quality of life we want to live, and the ground of our being or ultimate reality. Within the confines of our individual estranged life situations, we struggle to find reality and meaning.

Humanity is characterized by a quest for ultimacy, even when at times it is unrecognized, that may be described in different ways. We are creatures of ultimate concern, wrestling with the dimensions and aspects of life that concern each of us ultimately, define our self-understanding, and structure our approach to life. We opt for some chief way of valuing out of which various subsidiary values emerge. Our ultimate concern and chief way of valuing are expressed in extensive patterns that allow us to organize everyday life and to make sense out of life's great mysteries.

Our existential questions may be practically expressed or theoretically and formally constructed. Who am I? Where do I come from? What is life about? How should I live? What is the nature of the good? What is reality? Where can truth be found? What is wrong with me? How can I surmount my sense of estrangement? What happens at death? Does my life have any lasting significance? Since the individual human being is only a part of a whole historical human social order on a tiny planet in a vast universe, the understanding of one's individual life requires setting our lives into relationship with the whole cosmic process itself, forcing us to probe the origin, nature, purpose, and goal of the universe. In any extended intellectual reflection, the human individual is compelled to deal with one's own individual existence, the nature of being (ontology), and the overall structure of reality (metaphysics). For that reason, our individual quests coalesce in formal worldviews.

Many philosophers and theologians have proposed that there are actually only two great questions in life. The most basic is, Why am I "I" and not "not-I"? The second asks, Why is there something and not nothing? Answer those two questions and one has the fundamental solutions to all other questions. The first question is the existential question, the mystery of the individual existing self: Why do I exist, and why am I the distinctive person that I am? The second is the great ontological question of why anything at all should exist. And since something does exist, why should it be this particular universe within which we find ourselves, a universe so structured that it produces intelligent, reflective creatures like human beings—creatures who emerge out of the natural process and proceed to inquire about the nature of the process that has produced them? Is nature its own explanation, or is there a reality that transcends and produces nature? What is the nature of being that underlies everything that is? Answers to questions like these give rise to integrated, comprehensive models of existence called worldviews, interpretations of existence and being so integrated and comprehensive that they call for the ultimate allegiance of individual human beings.

The Emergence of Worldviews

In different ways and at varying levels of intensity, humans have asked the great questions about life. By far the majority of human beings have been born into a particular geographical and cultural setting that provides a generally agreed upon way of interpreting existence. In the process of living and being educated within a given culture, the answers to the great questions are assimilated naturally just as one adapts to certain foods, styles of clothing, folkways, and mores. The average person accepts the givenness and truth of available options in interpreting one's life both existentially and ontologically. Without grasping all the intricacies or sophistication of their own particular worldview, most people take their own solutions for granted and live out their commitments in the practical arena of everyday life. They leave it to the major thinkers to develop the contours of a full-scale worldview that is carefully integrated at the highest intellectual level.

Everyone holds certain fundamental convictions about themselves, the world they inhabit, the nature of life, values for their lives, and what for them is ultimately real—convictions that powerfully shape the way people interpret their individual lives and live practically on a day-to-day basis. At the bedrock level, one's basic convictions take the form of beliefs. We commit ourselves to things we believe to be true or to be of value. Whether religious or nonreligious, these beliefs seize one's allegiance in an absolute way. They are not merely matters of the head, ideologies that can be conceptualized in a clear-cut set of intellectual assertions. They tap into our deepest level of feelings and volitional capacities. Beliefs are normally attached to key symbols—God, or flag, or humanity, or universe, or matter, or economic history, or something else—symbols that elicit profound feelings and a commitment of will to direct our lives. These basic beliefs begin to coalesce into systems of belief and on into formal worldviews that, whether as practical everyday beliefs or highly developed worldviews, impact the whole of a person's life. In the course of human history, these basic approaches to life have converged into certain broad patterns of understanding existence that provide the options within which most people interpret their lives.

In one's concern for the Christian encounter with its contemporary rivals, one must not forget that average people in a society have not likely spent the time or do not have the intellectual gifts to work out the inner logic and full implications of a worldview that shapes their lives at a very practical level. Yet they often do tend to affirm and utilize in their own way the intellectual's more rigorous conceptual development of their lived worldview. It is therefore important for Christians to grasp something of the way that worldviews take shape, the inner logic and appeal of major contemporary worldviews, and how to dialogue effectively with people who are committed, in either a practical or an intellectually sophisticated way, to a particular conceptualization of life.

A worldview, simply put, is a model for understanding existence, a conceptualization inclusive of all dimensions of reality from the existing individual to the universe itself, one that integrates every aspect of life into an intelligible whole. One might argue, with some justification, that there are as many worldviews as there have been individuals in history. No two people ever agree on everything, and every way of conceptualizing reality has the stamp of uniqueness about it. Every worldview, therefore, is relative to the individual who holds it. Conceding that claim, it is also the case that there are historically only a limited number of options in interpreting reality. The varied individual perspectives fall naturally into general family groupings of worldviews. So, granting that there may be many versions of worldviews like naturalism, secular humanism, Marxism, Hinduism, Christianity, and others, there is also enough common ground among the versions to allow some dialogue between the alternative points of view. Any critical evaluation of worldviews must focus on the wider family groupings.

Worldviews do not develop in a vacuum. They conceptualize the way that particular groups of people experience reality. There is a preconceptual set of components of any great worldview. One of the reasons for the variations in worldviews is the fact that people are different, living in widely varied geographical, cultural, and historical settings, with their individual biographies affected by their social experience. Those factors probably build a metaphysical bias into our experience of reality itself, influencing the way we feel about the universe, life, other people, and ourselves before we ever think conceptually about reality. The universe appears to be friendly or unfriendly, nature real or illusionary, people of surpassing value or expendable, life a venture or a trial. It may be that we become intuitively aware of transcendent value and depth meaning to life—or perhaps of meaninglessness and valuelessness—long before we ever have the concepts to express what we already know. Michael Polanyi has argued that we often tacitly know things prior to conceptualizing them and that we always know more than we can tell.[2] A consequence is that the deepest convictions of people about their own particular worldview may not be so easily made explicit in defense of their formal point of view. It may also be, as a result of this preconceptual grounding, that one becomes open to change only when one's own worldview begins to break down, proves inadequate, or even fails at critical junctures of one's life.

Whatever the case, people do select explicit ways of conceptualizing their deepest convictions. So a worldview takes shape in a conceptual model that yields specific responses or answers to the major questions of existence, including those about the individual and the universe. This conceptualization of reality provides the basic content of a given individual's particular explicit worldview or practical beliefs that reflect a tacit worldview. Worldviews are not simply intellectual abstractions detached from life. Individuals translate their worldviews, often unconsciously in the case of tacit worldviews, into the organizing principles for understanding one's life, living practically day by day, and determining one's values. In one's set of beliefs or formal worldview, there is an obvious intellectual or conceptual component and some degree of intellectual affirmation of fundamental concepts. Yet a worldview involves more than an intellectual act. It requires a fundamental trust that this model—and not another—is the best guide to truth, reality, and individual living. In real terms, the individual invests one's life on the basis of one's worldview, committing oneself to live one's years in light of this particular understanding of the way things are.

Major worldviews normally have certain identifiable structural elements within them. In some way they will usually address the question of the origin and goal of the universe—if only to say the universe is a happy or tragic accident within purposeless reality or to say that there is no explanation for the universe. The great religions often have ways of expressing their views in the form of creation stories and stories about the end of the universe that embody their particular understanding of the universe.

Worldviews deal with the classic questions of philosophy and theology about the nature of existence, in particular those relating specifically to the nature of the real, truth, value, and beauty, all of which are integrally bound up with the whole question of meaning within life. What is real? Where can truth be found? What is good and of value? What is the nature of beauty? Widely varied answers have been given to these kinds of questions in the history of Western and Eastern philosophy. Is reality composed of one or of many kinds of being? Is reality material or mental or both? Is reality confined to the universe or is there a reality that transcends the universe? Where can truth be found? In formal logic? In scientific investigation? In other possible ways? What are good and evil? How should I live? All these questions, and others like them, have perplexed the greatest minds in history.

Beyond the formal classic questions, worldviews address numerous broad concerns. Any worldview that has formal credentials and practical application in life provides an interpretation of nature, history, and the multiple facets of human life. We are born into and remain dependent upon nature. We are inescapably involved in the historical process, trying to find meaning and purpose within it. We struggle with the full range of pressing human questions about the nature and purpose of life, the values by which we should live, and the solutions to our human dilemma. If it is to have persuasive credentials in the marketplace of worldviews, any worldview must have some interpretation of these major dimensions of human experience.

One needs only to glance at the history of human thought and experience to realize immediately the sweeping variety of worldviews that people have held in the history of the human race. Think of just the high watermarks of Western thought—Platonism, Aristotelianism, Thomism, naturalism, materialism, idealism, nihilism, Marxism, and a wide variety of Jewish and Christian religious worldviews. There are the classic religions of the East, including many varieties of Hinduism, Buddhism, Confucianism, Shintoism, and others. Islam has produced various rich cultures and worldviews from Africa through the Middle East to Southern Asia. There still remain influential in the world the varieties of traditional religions of technologically underdeveloped cultures that have never taken on the conceptual integration of a world religion.

Not all worldviews are religious by any restricted technical definition of religion. However, many worldviews are religious or align themselves closely with formal religions. When one specifically examines religions as worldviews, many distinctive religious elements characterize formal religions, such as sets of beliefs, cultic organizations, rituals, ways of behavior, and implications for social existence. Yet a religion is not necessarily the same thing as a worldview. When a religion develops into a worldview, the core of the view is the theological or religious conceptualization of the particular religion. However, the theological perspectives will usually be fleshed out in relation to the whole range of human experience, incorporating and relating to insights out of many intellectual disciplines and human experience—philosophy, history, science, culture, world religions, and other areas. In fact, a major religion could be compatible with various differing larger worldviews. A worldview cannot be an island of religious insight insulated from the wider experience of existence. It must attempt to incorporate all dimensions of human experience in relation to the universe taken as a whole. When a religion refuses to extend itself to embrace the wider sweep of human experience, it may remain vitally important to its religiously parochial adherents who deliberately choose to understand all reality within the limited parameters of their strictly religious system of belief. But it will not have general credibility in the larger human arena where alternative worldviews contend for the ultimate allegiance of human beings.

Tests for a Worldview

Modern human beings are increasingly able to choose from among a number of viable worldviews the particular interpretation of existence that fits their own understanding. Exposed to various options, people today require some kind of criteria or measuring rods when evaluating one worldview against another. This need for justification of a proposed worldview, including a Christian worldview, profoundly impacts the way that Christians proclaim and interpret their faith in our contemporary setting. How can one make intelligent judgments between rival faiths that command the allegiance of large numbers of people?

It is important to recognize that an integrated system of belief or a worldview cannot be approached in a piecemeal way. Each worldview has its own kind of internal logic that impresses its adherents as being basically coherent. People are often deeply convinced of the truth of their own view of existence, profoundly committed to the truth as they understand it, and frequently live out their commitments in noble ways. One can fully understand a worldview only by getting inside the view, grasping something of its inner persuasiveness, and applying it within one's own life. If that is the case, then there is always a limitation in one's ability to make an objective intellectual judgment about the internal persuasiveness of worldviews other than one's own. Any worldview requires something like a leap of faith—an affirmation of a set of beliefs that goes beyond what is provable. There is always some risk in committing oneself to any particular worldview, a risking commitment that parallels faith within the Christian context. This existential dimension of a worldview places a limitation on any comparative analysis of worldviews, particularly of religious worldviews. Yet if one is to make an intelligent choice between them, one must be able to make some judgments, however imperfect, about the truth and value of rival worldviews.

There are some traditional philosophical tests for truth, claims of various kinds that can be utilized in evaluating rival worldviews. Taken alone, no one test proves overwhelmingly persuasive in establishing the truth of a particular worldview. Even when weighed together, the tests cannot establish with absolute conclusiveness the superiority of any one worldview over others, certainly not to devout or dedicated adherents of other worldviews. Too many factors beyond an objective intellectual assessment are involved in such an evaluation. A worldview is too tightly bound up with the inner self—mind, feelings, and will—and the whole of life for it to be assessed in the same way by adherents of other worldviews. Nevertheless, the tests do help in establishing some relative degree of credibility and adequacy for alternative worldviews. Let me suggest some tests that are useful.

A first is the test of coherence. Taken as a whole, is a particular worldview internally coherent? Is it free from contradiction? Do its major insights mesh together in a consistent whole? In using this test, one must be careful not to be too constructed by the cold rigors of formal logic. Religions, in particular, often insist that logical coherence be defined and utilized in such a way that allowance is made for paradoxical truth, truth that at one level may appear to be contradictory but that at another level so juxtaposes insights that the tension between them opens new levels of truth otherwise not attainable. By any standards of coherence, however, one ought to be able to distinguish paradox that illumines and nonsense that obscures the truth. Is the worldview an integrated whole, so that all truth within the system is related to and logically follows from or leads to all other truth?

A second test is correspondence with the facts. Now it may be disputed at times what exactly the facts are in our human experience with which any worldview must square. But it remains the case that no worldview will be persuasive that insists on flying in the face of established facts. Those facts would now include confirmed scientific facts about the nature of the universe, from the subatomic to the astrophysical aspects of the cosmos, and what we now understand about the nature of the biological process and of human life in particular.

A third test is comprehensiveness. Is a particular worldview comprehensive of everything within human experience? Can it in principle address every aspect of existence? Are major areas of human experience or of the larger universe left out of the worldview? Can it relate human life to other forms of life, to the whole energy continuum, to everything that is—including any possible transcendent reality? Does the view have implications for society, politics, family, ethics, and other areas of human life? It must not be guilty of Shakespeare's accusation, "There are more things in heaven and earth, Horatio, Than are dreamt of in your philosophy."[3]

A fourth test is a worldview's applicability to life. Life, after all, is to be lived. What does a worldview say to the everydayness of my individual life—to the eating, sleeping, working, playing, laughing, crying, hurting, achieving, failing, making love, raising children, worshiping, and dying that fills the pages of actual life? Does the worldview help me to organize, center, define, function purposefully within, and fulfill my own particular life? A worldview ought to inform in intelligent ways an individual's own peculiar daily existence, setting the individual's experiences of life in a universal context.

A fifth test is the universality of a worldview. Is the heart of the worldview applicable in principle to all kinds of people in all cultures in all ages? Are there enduring principles that reveal the core reality at the center of existence, principles that, however reinterpreted in ongoing history, contain insight into the way things actually are? In a universe characterized by the relativity of space-time, surely truth and reality as a whole are not relative to a given observer. Whatever is real, it is real. Whatever is the truth about the way things are, it is the truth in all times and places. Though we will always imperfectly grasp the truth because of the limitations of our finite minds, the truth is what it is, just as reality is what it is. If that is the case, a particular formulation of the truth at some point in human history remains true, even though it may be enriched in later generations, or new truth might be brought by implication out of the old, or it might find varied application within the peculiarities of a new culture or historical context. But the truth ought to be applicable in all situations at all times—if it is actually the truth.

Tests like these are helpful in evaluating worldviews and in giving Christians insight into the credibility of their own faith in the encounter with alternative worldviews. The tests, however, cannot be used with mathematical precision, so that a given worldview achieves so many credibility points in a comparative chart of worldviews. Ultimate concerns that are expressed within established worldviews do not function like that. In evaluating alternative worldviews and rival faiths, the best case for a particular worldview will not persuade everyone. Many subtle factors enter into our ultimate commitments. Honest, sincere people will differ in the way they express their ultimate concerns and in the worldviews to which they commit themselves. Christians ought always to respect the integrity of the commitment of non-Christians to their perspectives, knowing that the ground of ultimate concern is always sacred.

At the same time, Christians should equip themselves for serious engagement with alternative worldviews, be prepared for caring, sensitive dialogue with adherents of other points of view, and not hesitate to make a sustained case for Christianity as the most defensible among all available worldviews in the contemporary era.

The Christian Encounter with Its Contemporary Rivals

My concern in this book is with the Christian apologetic encounter with modern rivals of Christianity. One purpose is to help my fellow Christians and other seekers after truth to be better informed about both Christianity and prominent contemporary alternative worldviews and to develop a deeper understanding of the nature of Christianity's superiority as a worldview. My criticial analysis of Christianity in relation to other major worldviews is also designed to contribute insight and facilitate the skills of my fellow Christians in the art of defending and advocating the Christian faith in our contemporary world. In a practical way, I would hope to provide Christians, both ministers and laypersons, with specific arguments and interpretations of Christianity that will enhance their ability to dialogue creatively with people who hold alternative points of view.

A contemporary defense of the Christian faith requires that one have a clear understanding of the basic dimensions of rival outlooks and worldviews as well as the core of one's own faith. Why, for example, should an intelligent person choose to be a naturalist and hold that the universe is self-explanatory and self-originating? What are the reasons for such a view? Who are prominent people who advocate such a view? What kind of influence do they have in society today? Where are their voices to be heard? What are the strong arguments in support of a naturalistic worldview? Is there anything within naturalism that a Christian might affirm? What are the distinctive differences between a Christian worldview and a naturalistic worldview? Where exactly is a naturalistic worldview vulnerable to a Christian critique? How can the Christian go about making an intelligent case for Christianity to the naturalist? I will address questions like these to a variety of prominent worldviews in the chapters that follow.

The Christian faith has several choices about how to relate to rival ultimate commitments or worldviews. It can adopt a relativistic stance and assume that all roads lead equally to truth and to God, even when their followers reject God. Or it can become syncretistic and appropriate ideas and values from other worldviews and religions into a new more universal and widely informed worldview. At the opposite pole, Christianity can become insensitive and self-assertive, assume that nothing in other worldviews or religions is of consequence or value, and callously disregard the deep commitments of adherents of alternative worldviews and religions.

My own approach rejects all those options. My treatment of rival worldviews is developed on the assumption that in the apologetic encounter we should affirm as much of an alternative view as is possible with integrity, acknowledge common ground where it exists, and then bring a perceptive and reasoned critique from the Christian perspective to the inadequacies of alternatives to Christianity. In many cases, it is then possible to demonstrate how Christianity takes up the legitimate insights and values within the alternative worldview and transposes those to a new level around the integrating center of all reality, truth, and value—Jesus Christ. In an apologetic encounter, it is essential to know both the common ground and the distinctive differences that must not be compromised between Christianity and its modern rivals.

Such freedom in the encounter is based upon the conviction that belief systems do not happen in a vacuum or by accident or as intentional distortions of the truth. When large numbers of people follow a certain way of life and commit themselves to a conceptualization of that way, it is usually because they have grasped a kernel, or even a large slice, of the truth about existence. When certain values or points of view become rival gods to the Christian God, there are obviously good reasons that prove persuasive to large numbers of people. From a biblical perspective, the substitution of any value for the primary commitment to the God of Jesus Christ is idolatry. One needs to remember, however, that in many cases a person's submission to an alternative highest good is not capricious or perverse or rebellious against the truth of the Christian revelation. Even idols, to use that symbolism, are simply personifications of important values in life that are elevated beyond their appropriate level and are not subjected to the God who has revealed Himself in Jesus Christ.

Jesus Christ must always be the touchstone for truth in the Christian encounter with rival faiths. As the way, the truth, and the life, Jesus Christ is the final criterion by which the Christian judges and rejects or affirms other values. The Christian faith encompasses a vast array of good things in life. Although these values may become rival gods when made central in other worldviews, many can be affirmed as enduring values by the Christian when they are subjected to the lordship of Jesus Christ and transposed into their proper sphere and balance within a Christian worldview.

The scheme of my discussion is simple. Chapter 2 provides a succinct statement of the Christian faith as it has been held historically by the mainstream of the Christian church and then extends that theological core into central dimensions of a Christian worldview, one with which, hopefully, the majority of Christians might find broad concurrence. The ideas developed in this chapter will serve as a continuing point of reference and source for the Christian apologetic dialogue with modern rivals to the Christian faith in the remainder of the book.

The dialogue with contemporary rivals to Christianity begins in chapter 3, where I discuss modern atheism and the major arguments that atheists make against the existence of God. Although atheism takes different forms and is not a singular worldview, it is a forceful modern rival of Christianity and an underlying assumption of various other more comprehensive secular or naturalistic worldviews. The following chapters deal with selected influential alternatives to the Christian faith. My basic criterion for treating these particular views is that the view presents a formal interpretation of life or worldview that is widely held in the contemporary world. In chapters 4 through 7, we will deal successively with the secular or nonreligious worldviews of naturalism, secular humanism, Marxism, and nihilism. Chapter 8 will focus on the Christian encounter with world religions. In the concluding chapter of the book I will offer some suggestions on the dynamics of the Christian apologetic dialogue with rival faiths in the contemporary world.

The structural development within each of chapters 3 through 8 will follow a broadly similar pattern. First, I will state the particular alternative view to Christianity as objectively and fairly as possible, noting some of the prominent formal advocates of the perspective and assessing its impact among its adherants. I will then explore any common ground between Christianity and the alternative worldview, indicating where possible how the key value or values of a particular alternative view can be related to a Christian worldview. Finally, I will bring both a general critique and a Christian critique to the overall claims of the alternative worldview.

Each chapter may be read independently of the others, if one chooses, because I have developed within each chapter the heart of a Christian interaction with that particular alternative to the Christian faith. As a result, there is some similarity, along with distinctive emphases, in the lines of argument and interpretation of specific Christian ideas to be found in several chapters. At the same time, there is an overall pattern of apologetic response to rivals to the Christian faith that emerges only in the total sweep of the book, one that represents the convergence and mutually interlocking support of a variety of specific points of dialogue with individual worldviews.

My hope is that the dialogical interaction will provide my fellow Christians with a sensitive appreciation for the ultimate commitments of many non-Christians and with basic critical arguments that can facilitate the church's apologetic encounter with Christianity's modern rivals.

2
Christianity:
The Key to Existence

Christianity centers its understanding of existence upon Jesus Christ, based upon the belief that He is the revelation and redemption of God, the Savior and Lord of the world, and the creative cause and goal of the universe itself. It is not an overstatement to say that for most Christians in history, Jesus Christ Himself is Christianity. As *the* distinctive element of Christianity, He marks it off in relation to other world religions and worldviews. The central confession of the Christian church is that "Jesus is Lord," an affirmation that binds Christ's church together in oneness in the earth and is, the church has preached, the only prerequisite for a human being coming to know the living God.

Beyond its common confession, how does one describe and analyze Christianity, with all its diversity throughout history and in the particular confessional configurations of today? Although variety is not a problem peculiar to Christianity, its great diversity makes it difficult to provide an interpretation of Christianity that all Christians would find acceptable. The approximately one billion confessing Christians throughout the world are divided into many churches and denominations. The major branches, which are broken into many subgroups, are Roman Catholicism, Eastern Orthodoxy, and Protestantism. Having dominated the West for two millennia, Christianity now has adherents throughout the world. There are few countries in the world where there are not professing Christians. For the first time in history, in recent years Christianity is on the brink of becoming the dominant religion of some Asian nations. As the one truly universal religion, Christianity transcends geographical barriers, national identities, cultural distinctives, and rival religious allegiances. Devout Christian believers are found with every kind of individual human distinctive. What links believers throughout the world is their common confession, "Jesus is Lord."

The Origins of Christianity

Christianity developed from the first Christians' belief that their crucified Lord was raised from the dead on Easter morning in ancient Palestine. Seized by that conviction, they moved aggressively into the first-century world, preaching that Jesus is the Son of God and the only one through whom all people must be saved. Jesus was a Jew. He himself lived and taught as a Jewish rabbi and affirmed the heart of Hebrew religion, particularly around the confession that there is only one God whose name is Yahweh. When His followers were awakened to faith at Jesus' resurrection, they drew upon the wealth of Hebrew Scriptures to understand Him in light of the ancient prophecies of the coming Messiah. As they interpreted His mystery to the first-century world, they enlarged and extended those Hebrew insights to cast the historical Jesus on the scale of eternity and the whole cosmos, portraying Him as the Word by which the eternal God created the world, the creative force that works within the ongoing creative process, and the very goal of the creation itself. By the end of the apostolic era when most of the present New Testament documents had been written, Jesus was seen as the focal point of the whole creative process, the turning point in human history, and the present reigning Lord of history who will return to judge all human beings at the end of history. The apostolic witness within the New Testament remains the church's contact with the historical life of Jesus and the inspired revelation surrounding His life.

Originating in the relationship of the first believers to their risen Lord, the Christian faith is fundamentally a personal relationship of trust in Jesus Christ, a new way of life that, when interpreted, provides an expanding insight into the mystery of existence. When theologically developed, Christianity ultimately comprises a comprehensive, integrated existential worldview that encompasses everything from the life of every individual human being to the vast expanse of the universe. Even as a worldview, it is not basically an intellectual construct but a way of living that centers one's life in the worship of God, involves one in the Christian community, focuses one's life on a consuming purpose to serve Jesus Christ through loving and serving people for whom He died, and makes strong ethical demands on one's life. The peculiarities of the Christian life-style may vary somewhat from culture to culture or era to era, but the central mark is the commitment to love all humans as we have been loved by God. Such love is made possible by the personal presence of God within the life of the Christian believer. Christianity is not simply a worldview to be intellectually affirmed; it is a way of life that must be lived. For that reason, the only way an individual can finally test out the claims of Christianity or the truth it asserts is by commitment to Jesus Christ as Lord and living out the truth to which one is committed.

The Theological Core of the Christian Worldview

How can one describe what most Christians believe at the conceptual level? That is presumptuous for any one person. Yet there is an identifiable central flow of beliefs that most Christians throughout the history of the church have held with only slight variation, a core of belief that cuts across denominational, cultural, national, and church boundaries. With some humility and a willingness to be corrected by others, let me attempt to state views that most Christians have historically affirmed in one or another version.

At the heart of Christianity is its belief in creation and redemption. It is a story of God creating a good world, with the pinnacle of creation being humans with whom God wills to have relationships. This crowning glory of His creation rebelled, broke fellowship with God, and stands under divine judgment. As a God of love, God desires the salvation of all human beings. So, some thirty five hundred years ago the redeeming God chose a people to enter into a particular covenant with Him as He reveals Himself to the whole earth through their religious experience. The story of God's elect people, Israel, is one of faithfulness, rebellion, repentance, and renewal. Within their history, a hope emerged for a messianic figure who would finally redeem His people into a right relationship with God.

That Hebrew hope was fulfilled, Christians believe, in the birth of Jesus. After a brief public ministry in Palestine, He was crucified and resurrected for our sins, so that the incarnate Christ is the one through whom the world is reconciled to God. He is the reigning Lord of history who will come at the end of history to judge all human beings and deliver His redeemed followers to God for eternity. The ultimate issue of life depends upon our response to the God of love who has acted on our behalf in Jesus Christ. In repentance and faith, Christians experience reconciliation to God, receive the gift of God's Spirit within their lives, and are taken into God's ultimate purposes in the universe. His followers enter into His church and live out Christ's will for humanity through a life of love in the ministry and mission of His church. In the Christian worldview, the Christian believer discovers and experiences in a personal way the very divine purpose for the universe and for human beings.

God and Creation

The Apostle's Creed represents a touchstone of Christian confession that at its heart states beliefs most Christians insist on preserving. The Apostle's Creed begins, "I believe in God, the Father Almighty, Maker of heaven and earth." Those words echo the opening refrain of the Christian Bible, "In the beginning God created the heavens and the earth" (Gen. 1:1), a creative act that the New Testament centers in Jesus Christ. Christians affirm that God is the sole eternal reality. God is a personal God of love who reveals Himself to us as Father, Son, and Spirit, a revelation that produces Christianity's Trinitarian affirmation that God is one being in three persons. Within God there is an eternal giving and receiving love between Father, Son, and Holy Spirit.

God is self-existent. He is not dependent upon any other reality for His own being and inner life. He does not need the universe either to be God or to fulfill His own creativity. When God wills to create the universe and its living creatures, it is an act of sheer grace. Because God freely chooses to create the universe through His own divine power, He is sovereign over the created order. He is omnipotent, omniscient, and omnipresent. At every moment of the creative process, God is both radically transcendent to and immanent within the universe.

Christians affirm that God is creator of the heavens and the earth. Nothing comes to be without being called into existence by God, and everything remains ultimately dependent upon God for its existence. Most Christians have expressed this belief by the idea of creation out of nothing, an image that points to God's bringing finite existence out of nothingness in a primal act of creation. In saying that the world is created out of nothing, Christians specifically affirm that the universe is not eternal alongside God as either a neutral or evil entity that eternally sets limits to the infinite being of God. The universe is not created out of some kind of chaotic energy mass that has eternally existed. Without the creative activity of God, absolutely nothing other than God would exist, the universe would not have come to be, and even now it would collapse into nothingness again. God creatively orders being against the ever-present threat of nothingness. Creation out of nothing also underlines that nature is not divine. God did not create the universe out of His own being. The cosmos is other than God, a created and finite entity that does not share in the divine life but depends absolutely for its existence upon the creative power of God.

The great creation stories of the Hebrew and Christian Scriptures picture the world as essentially good. At each stage of His creative activity, God was pleased and exclaimed that the world was good (Gen. 1:1-31). The world was the stage upon which God acted out His own drama of creation and redemption. However marked the fallen world is by the evil within it, it remains essentially good and represents a substantial dimension of God's own purposes in creation. Christians have properly viewed the world as a gift of God to be enjoyed, not an evil prison to be escaped. In its original state, before the invasion of sin, the world represented the perfect will of God.

A part of God's original intention is reflected in the regularity of the natural order. He created a harmonious, predictable universe, one whose regularities are vital to human happiness and fulfillment. Nature's laws are an element of His design for human beings and other creatures. Biblical faith has affirmed that the universe is quasiindependent from God, in the sense that, although it is absolutely dependent upon God for its existence and natural laws, God gives nature an independence within that absolute dependence. He will normally abide by the regularities that He Himself has created within the routine course of nature, even when at times that is harmful to His human creatures. Without a stable world order human life, as God designed it, would be practically impossible.

The world itself is integral to God's purposes. The cosmos is a permanent element in the eternal plan of God, so that God is redeeming the universe itself. That conviction gives Christians a basis for strongly affirming the goodness of the world, the importance of this earthly life, and the value of all human relationships and experiences to the eternal becoming of the children of God. Unlike worldviews that make the universe ultimate or others that take a negative view toward the world and life, Christians celebrate the beauty of the universe and the joy of life. The world is a great value but not the highest value in human experience.

Humanity and Sin

The focal point of God's creative activity is in human beings. Genesis pictures humans as made in the image of God, a mysterious symbol that likely means many things. It is a way of portraying that humans, who have continuity with all other created life, also are set off from other created life. Of all the creatures in the world, humans alone are made in the image of God, with a capacity to know God, to fellowship with God, to reflect something of the glory of God in the earth, and to embody at a creaturely level something like the personal life within the being of God Himself. When the Bible pointedly applies the symbol of the image of God to human life together as male and female, it underscores the fact that we are human only in relationship. Humans reflect something of the inner Trinitarian life of God—the true personal image of God—only when we live in love in community. God Himself takes delight in His personal relationships with His human creatures and in the personal relationships humans have with each other.

A critical aspect of our bearing the image of God is the freedom and responsibility that God bestows upon us. Because God chooses to enter into personal relationships with humans whom He can love and who can love Him in return, He gives us maximum freedom within the limits of finitude. Only as love is freely given is it truly love. So the Bible pictures God as choosing to be loved only as His human creatures choose to love. Love can never be coerced or programmed. Consequently, freedom and responsibility for life are essential elements of what it means to be a person. In all relationships—human and divine, human and human—the integrity of personality must be respected, so that we protect the freedom of the other within the limits of the general good of society, even when that freedom is used in unwise ways. The image of God, which reflects the nature of God Himself, determines the very foundation of the Hebrew and Christian ethic.

Another dimension of the image of God is the responsibility it gives humans to enter into the creative activity of God Himself within the world of nature and society. The Bible describes that role as a mandate to replenish and subdue the earth, which is a picturesque way of indicating the high status that humans have. In both Genesis 1 and 2, humans enter into the ongoing creative activity of God in the world as they shape and direct nature to further accomplish His purposes, a role that today has been extended into highly sophisticated technologies that can enhance the quality of life upon the planet. When used within our creaturely limits, our freedom is one of the crowning marks of our being made in the image of God to share in His own creative work.

Tragically, humans have never been content to remain finite and to live their lives in dependency upon and to the glory of God. Humans, from the first humans onward, have lived in rebellion against their own Creator, which is the fundamental problem within the human family, the planet, and the universe as a whole. The most profound picture of the rebellion of every human being is found in Genesis 3—5. The first humans attempted to use their freedom to transcend the limits of their finitude, an act of rebellion against God that the Bible calls sin. In attempting to be God, humans lose their authentic status as human beings. Genesis portrays God reacting to human sin in judgment. He turns the first humans out of paradise, the ideal state that He has willed for humanity. Humans now live in a world infected by the virus of sin, a world in which people live for themselves without acknowledging accountability to God, a world in which our alienation from God issues in alienation from our own authentic humanity and from our fellow human beings. The judgment of God upon our sin is that without salvation we are eternally separated from our Maker and Redeemer. As Paul states it, "For the wages of sin is death" (Rom.6:23). From the primal, existential rebellion of every human being, the tragedies of human history flow. Our human problem is that we have lost contact with the ground of our being, the relationship to the God who defines our own humanity. If we are to discover the meaning of our own existence and the purpose of the universe, then we must in some way rediscover God and relate ourselves to Him as creatures made in His image.

Jesus Christ and Salvation

The core of the Christian gospel to the world is the good news that God has reconciled the world to Himself in Jesus of Nazareth. Jesus was not born in a historical vacuum. The Christian Bible begins the story of God's redeeming love from eternity itself. From before the creation of the world, God wills the redemption of human beings in Jesus Christ. After the sinful fall of humans, God has continued to reveal Himself in many different ways—in the beauty and regularity of nature, in human conscience, and in human reason. Yet our human awareness of God in those media is always too limited to provide sufficient light for our understanding. So God chose a small group of people to be His special vessel of revelation and redemption for all the people of earth. Beginning with the call of Abraham and the Exodus of his Hebrew descendants out of slavery in Egypt, God revealed Himself in the historical life of the people of Israel over a period of many centuries. A small nation often caught between the warring conflicts of larger neighbors and periodically occupied by conquerors, Israel developed the highest insights in the ancient world about the nature of God and the mystery of life. Often they proved unfaithful to their special covenant with God, which resulted in various kinds of divine judgment. Out of the ebb and flow of their own history and experience of God, a hope began to develop that focused on the future coming of a messianic king who would lead His people Israel into a kind of paradisal existence that would correct the prevailing evils of present history.

The Jewish hope was fulfilled when Jesus was born of a young virgin girl and grew up in a small Galilean town. He worked there as a carpenter and became a master of the Hebrew Scriptures. At about age thirty, He began a brief public ministry in Palestine in which He preached the coming kingdom of God, performed miracles, taught about life within the kingdom, and gathered around Him disciples and followers who repented and entered into the kingdom He preached. His ministry climaxed in a rapid flurry of events over a period of a week in Jerusalem, where He had gone to observe the Passover feast. Accused of claiming to be the king of the Jews, He was crucified and buried in a borrowed tomb. Three days later He was resurrected from the grave in a transformed body and encountered various groups of disciples over a period of forty days. Then He was exalted before the observation of some disciples into the heavens, where He reigns as the Lord of human history.

The bare outline of His life is simple to sketch. The mystery of who He was, what He taught and did, and His continuing presence among His followers has consumed more thought and filled the pages of more books than any other figure in human history. His brief life had such an impact upon His followers that they were convinced that He was the incarnate Son of God, God wrapped in human flesh. Beyond any question, He has reshaped the course of history more profoundly than any other person. For good reason, His life marks the watershed of history.

Who was Jesus, and why is He so important to Christianity? Christians believe that Jesus was both God and man in one integrated person. Many symbols in the New Testament point to the mystery of the incarnation. Jesus was called Messiah, Son of God, Son of man, Suffering Servant, Word of God, Divine Wisdom, Savior, and Lord, among other titles. No human image can adequately express who He was. Christians are convinced that God actually became man in Jesus, so that the eternal Son of God took on human flesh, walked among us, and experienced life as a real human being. The closest portrait that we have of what God is like was in the life of Jesus. He is both the revelation of God and the redemption of humanity. In His life, teachings, preaching, and way of relating to people, we have imaged before us what it is to be an authentic human being and how life should be lived. He sets the standard by which all of us are measured.

Christians believe that the death and resurrection of Jesus has peculiar significance for our salvation and reconciliation to God. In some sense, Jesus so closely identified with sinful humanity in His submission to an unjust death, He took all our sins upon Himself. In bearing the judgment upon sin on our behalf, He made atonement for sinners before God, opening a path of reconciliation to God for believers who identify with Him and His way of life. Christians have tried to express the nature of Christ's saving death with various symbols and theories. All recognize that the mystery of His atonement for sinners transcends all our best efforts to explain it. All are agreed that in repentance and faith, believers experience the benefits of His saving death and the power of His resurrection within their lives.

Consequently, Jesus Christ is at the center of the Christian worldview. Christians affirm that He is God in the flesh and that the Son of God who became incarnate in Jesus was eternal and was engaged in creative and redemptive work in the world before He became a human being. His creative activity transcends His incarnate life. He is the creative power behind the universe itself, the one in whom the creative process of the universe coheres, and the very goal of the universe. He continues to be present in human history in the person of the Holy Spirit who makes Him known within the lives of believers. The Christian church has preached that Jesus Christ is the way to God for all people, the Savior and Lord of the whole human race.

Christians believe that it is imperative for persons to repent of their sins and to commit their lives in faith to Jesus Christ as Savior and Lord. In the act of belief, Christians consciously experience reconciliation to God, forgiveness of sins, the gift of God's Spirit in their lives, and the beginning of a process of growth in becoming at a finite level something of what Jesus Himself was like. Faith is a trusting relationship to the person of Jesus Christ whom Christians publicly confess to be Lord of their lives. The normal way that Christians have symbolized their confession is through the rite of baptism by which they enter into the Christian church.

The Christian Church and the Life Everlasting

The Christian church understands itself as the body of Christ on earth, the people of God, who carry on Christ's work within the world. The church is a sphere of existence where the ideal future life of God's people begins to take root within human history. It is a new humanity where people are reconciled to God, to themselves, and to each other, and where they begin to learn how to love within a fellowship of love. The church is a redemptive fellowship where Christians are nurtured in how to live the Christian life and strengthened to embody the Christian ethic. It has a world mission and ministry of serving people and sharing with them the good news of Jesus Christ, calling people to believe in and follow Him. The conviction that Jesus is the Savior of the world propels the Christian church on a mission that takes Christians into encounter with all rival ideologies and worldviews throughout the world. The church lives out of the conviction that Jesus Christ is the way, the truth, and the life for all people.

There is a Christian hope for the future of history and for life beyond history. Christians believe that their salvation will culminate in an eternal life in the presence of God beyond death. In one way or another, Christians have usually affirmed that at the end of history, Jesus Christ will return to render judgment over every human being who has ever lived and over history and the world. In the climactic event of history, believers and unbelievers will be separated for eternity. Those who have committed their lives to Jesus Christ will be taken into heaven to live with the redeemed and God for eternity. At that point, God will have redeemed the whole cosmic process to Himself, which is the purpose and goal of the universe and human history.

Wider Contours of a Christian Worldview

The core of a Christian theological understanding of existence has many implications for a wider worldview—for understanding the universe, human history, human beings, the purpose and goal of life, the nature of the good, the source of life, and so on. In dealing with the ultimate meaning of existence, the Christian faith is capable of correlation with all knowledge and human experience into a comprehensive worldview that embraces the whole sweep of existence. It addresses life's great mysteries from the individual human being to the origin and goal of the universe. It offers answers to our deepest existential anxieties. Christianity prescribes a solution to our individual human struggles and our social alienation. The answers to our deepest questions and the solution to the our existential dilemma are fundamentally wrapped up in the person of Jesus Christ, who is the heart of the Christian faith.

Nature

Christianity holds that the universe is not self-explanatory or inclusive of all reality. Everything within the universe is contingent; it depends on a transcendent cause for its very existence. The God who brings the universe into existence, though He is immanent in the universe at every point, transcends the created order and is not just another—even if more powerful—entity or contingent reality within the universe. God is the ultimate explanation and cause of the universe. In contrast to the universe, God is His own explanation in that He exists necessarily; it is His own inner nature to be eternally. God can be fully God without the universe, but the universe cannot exist or be as it is without God. As humans pursue ultimate truth and a final explanation for the universe, they must always move to heights and depths beyond the visible universe in order to encounter the God who transcends the universe even as He manifests His presence within the universe. The ultimate value and the only proper subject of our human ultimate concern is the eternal God who has revealed Himself in Jesus Christ. Ultimate allegiance to any lesser value is idolatry, the substitution of a creaturely value for the living God.

Although nature is not its own explanation and is totally dependent upon God for its existence, nature claims a high value in the Christian perspective. Nature is the creative work of God, representing awe-inspiring beauty and giving glory to its Creator in its heavenly spectacle. Unlike some religions and worldviews that regard nature as an illusion or the world of matter as evil or nature as the ultimate value, Christianity celebrates the reality and goodness of creation, revels in its order and beauty, and enjoys life within the created world, and yet it rejects the view that nature is the highest good or the final reality. Because the universe is God's creation, Christians affirm the reality of the world, the importance of our earthly lives, the sanctity of all natural processes, and the place of the natural world in the divine plan of creation and redemption.

The Christian understanding of evil grows out of that general perspective. Everything that God has created was originally good. Any evil that exists is an original good gone wrong or one of the unavoidable limitations within any possible created world. Some evil results from the level of independence that God grants to the way nature operates within the regularities He has built into the universe. Most evil arises out of the moral choices of human beings who are given freedom as a part of God's willingness to have relationships with created persons. Throughout history, God has aligned Himself with the suffering that results from sin and evil. In the incarnation, He suffered from within the human situation the ultimate consequences of evil within the universe.

The Christian affirmation of the reality of the world provides the historical basis for the emergence of modern science and its effort to study and understand the way that nature actually operates. In the Christian view, modern empirical science's theoretical explanations of natural phenomena or the universe as a whole are possible only because of the regularities and developmental processes that God has structured into His universe. Every new discovery and development within science ideally ought to enlarge the Christian's wonder at the creativity of God. Science, for the Christian, can never discover anything within the universe that was not willed there by the Maker of the heavens and the earth.

The Christian worldview, based upon Jesus Christ as its cornerstone, is capable of open-ended expansion and enlarging its own horizons as we utilize the gifts of intelligence to better understand the Creator's universe. Christians know that however much we come to understand through our natural intelligence about the structures and processes of the universe, science can never through its own empirical methodology resolve the ultimate mystery. The final explanation for the universe and the operations of nature can be found only in the eternal creator God. Christians, more than others, understand the transcendence and depth of the material world that modern science probes in its investigations. Because of the Christian's confidence that this is God's world, Christians can affirm the important and legitimate role of scientific research as an essential part of our coming to understand in a comprehensive way the mystery of existence. All truth, including all confirmed scientific truth, can be correlated with the ultimate truth that has been manifested in Jesus Christ. For this reason, Christianity takes up the results of science and places those empirical insights into a more profound and comprehensive worldview.

History

The Christian worldview also addresses the matter of human history. Just as there is a divine purpose operating within nature, there is a divine providential purpose working itself out within history. Christians believe there is a creative interplay at work between humans and God as God lovingly directs the human story into higher levels of creative achievement and more humane, just, and loving relationships within society. Most Christians admit that the divine activity is often difficult to discern through the tragic episodes of human history when many of history's chief actors manifest little awareness of God and many of history's chapters fall vastly short of God's ideal will for His human children. Yet it is essential for Christians to affirm that God is at work, that events do not transpire without His awareness or beyond His influence at some level, and that God is little by little moving history toward His ideal future goal for humanity.

History is important to Christians. It is not a grand illusion to be denied or an evil state to be fled. History is an arena of divine activity, where God moves among the nations of the world in judgment and redemption. The leaders of nations are His servants, even when they are not aware of Him or explicitly deny Him. In the checks and balances, the ebb and flow, of history, God is slowly working out His will for history itself. So Christians are called to enter vigorously into the central thrust of history and to be engaged in a wide range of occupations and tasks vital to the welfare of the human family. Secular history is the stage within which the divine-human drama is being acted out.

Consequently, most Christians have not withdrawn from the secular historical process but enter into it with their ultimate allegiance focused upon God as they cooperate with Him in His struggle to move the whole story toward His own ultimate goal. Christians can enter positively and joyously into the full range of tasks within the world—in politics, education, medicine, farming, the arts, industry, business, and other vocations. Any task vital to human well-being can be done to the glory of the God who is concerned about history. Because God is the chief actor in the human historical process, individuals and nations will be held accountable for their faithfulness in living out their history according to the will and to the glory of God. History is not an illusion to be surmounted, an evil to be fled, or the highest good demanding our ultimate allegiance. History does matter—precisely because its basic script is authoried by God and is intended to be acted out to His glory!

Human Life

Human life also is affirmed within a Christian worldview. Human beings, like the rest of the universe, are not happy accidents in an accidental, purposeless process. While in continuity with the rest of nature, humanity is the culmination of the earthly process of development designed for the emergence of intelligent life made in the image of God, a species that can have knowledge of, fellowship with, and live to the glory of God. Standing at the apex of the chain of biological life, humans occupy the highest status among all living creatures within our own nexus of life on this planet.

The Christian worldview provides an understanding of individual human beings and of society as a whole. The Christian view of humans is intensely realistic, taking into account both body and spirit in the unity of personhood. Humans actually are embodied creatures. Without our bodies, the very material stuff of our personalities, we could not exist at all or be who we distinctively are as individuals. Biblical Christianity does not disparage our material dimension but affirms the whole range of our bodily needs and drives—for food, water, sex, work, play, exercise, aesthetic pleasures, and others. Still, personhood is more than body. The human spirit, drawing upon its intelligence, volitional capacities, and affective sensitivity, gives to the human individual a distinctive reality not found in any other creature on earth. As body and spirit, we are persons made in the image of God. Authentic human life requires a recognition of both aspects of our personhood. Christianity never becomes so focused upon the spirit that the body is denigrated nor upon the body that the spirit is denied. In its insistence that we are both material and spirit, Christianity rejects both a cynical materialism and an anti-material spiritualism. At the highest level, this heady spiritual-material Christian understanding celebrates the body as the temple of God, the embodied life of the believer within which the Holy Spirit resides.

Authentic humanity, in the Christian view, involves an essential social dimension. We are fully human only in relationships with other human beings as well as with God Himself. Such a view gives the highest significance to the individual but rejects a ruthless individualism that runs roughshod over the rights of society or a regimenting social order that crushes the rights and worth of each individual within it. We are most truly human only in open, loving relationships with other human beings. One result of sin is the loss of the delicate balance between the individual and society, the ongoing conflict between the individual and society, and the varied historical efforts to balance out the two values.

Christians believe that Jesus Christ perfectly models authentic human nature, both as an individual and as a social being. The church itself represents an inbreak of the new humanity that God originally willed for the human family and will recreate in fullness at the end of history. Nothing is more important within the created order than an individual human being, however insignificant or even despicable in the eyes of society. Yet the individual is never authentically human, in the fullest sense of the word, without being rightly related to society as a whole in loving, genuine human relationships. One responsibility of Christians in the world is to help make actual, as far as possible within their own histories, the ideal humanity that God wills for human beings, in delicately balancing out the worth of the individual and the good of society as a whole. Christianity may be compatible with various systems of social order, but it will always struggle against tyrannies that oppress individuals or rugged individualist systems that neglect the needs and rights of the whole society. Within those outer acceptable limits, Christianity can live creatively within different social systems.

The nature of the good life is defined by the personal interaction between God and His human creatures and between human beings. As the confessions have put it, the highest good of human beings is to love God and enjoy Him forever. In Christian thought, one's love for God is best expressed in love for one's fellow human beings. The love of God and love of humanity are inseparable for humans. Life is fundamentally defined by the personal, Trinitarian being of God Himself—as a giving and receiving of love within personal relationships. The moral standards by which we live should reflect the holiness of God expressed within the limits of the created order. Within a fallen world, those standards are expressed by the quality of life Jesus advocated for His followers within the kingdom of God. Both holiness and love should characterize the lives of people redeemed in Jesus Christ.

Eternal Hope and Historical Responsibility

The eternal worth of human beings produces the Christian hope that a loving God will give eternal life to those who love Him and attempt to do His will through faith in Jesus Christ. There are religious views that teach the natural immortality of the human soul. Other worldviews hold death to be the final word for humans as with all other life. Some worldviews teach that individual human life loses its distinctive character at death and is reabsorbed into some kind of all-encompassing ontological reality. Christians, however, formulate their eternal hope for human destiny around the love of the God who creates people in His own image and recreates us in redemption in the image He has revealed in Jesus Christ. If God loves the individual so much, then a logical extension of such love is that God will preserve for eternity the very human beings for whom He gave His only Son. Thus, while death is a mark of finite existence, it is not the final word over human life. Human beings matter so much that God will resurrect believers at the end of history, transform them into a new kind of embodied existence, and take them into His unmediated presence in a perfect kind of life for eternity. What is redeemed eternally is the very distinctiveness of the individual as an identifiable self. The Christian gospel—that God so loves each of us so much that He gave His only Son on our behalf—implies that such love will not let us go at death and allow annihilation to be the concluding epitaph over human existence.

Christianity links the individual's potential eternal future to one's responsibility in historical life. The decisions people make, the alternatives we pursue, the values by which we live, the goals we attain all have eternal consequence. Ultimacy is attached to human life. As we utilize our freedom to actualize future possibilities in our individual lives, those choices enter into a ledger of accountability that determines our eternal future. For that reason, Christianity takes our lives with utmost seriousness. At every step of our individual journeys, we move with our daily choices either closer to or farther away from the kind of life and history that the eternal God wills for His human creatures. Such ultimacy blankets daily life with an eternal significance and makes each moment a kairos in the unfolding of the divine plan for all human beings. The Christian's affirmation of worldly life is based upon the eternal potential that life in this world embodies—the possibility for finite creatures like ourselves to become the eternal children of the living God. Each individual bears a weight of eternal glory!

Tests for a Christian Worldview

As a worldview, Christianity offers explanations for the universe, human life and destiny, the nature of the good, the purpose of human life, and the meaning of human history. It provides a basis for understanding the material world, a set of ideas for structuring human relationships, and a solution to the human dilemma. It responds to our deepest existential anxieties—the struggle with meaninglessness, the pain of guilt and self-condemnation, and the threat of fate and death. Christianity corresponds to all the known facts of our experience in the world. It is comprehensive, coherent, applicable to life, and in touch with the deepest human longings. It transcends and supersedes all ideologies, transposes the highest insights of other worldviews, and brings an integration to the loftiest aspirations of the human race. Jesus Christ Himself becomes the final criterion for evaluating the adequacy of all worldviews.

When measured by the standard tests for claims to knowledge and truth, Christianity is impressive. It passes the test of realism, in that it corresponds to all the facts we now know about life and the universe. Christianity provides intelligent answers to the highest aspirations and most urgent questions of human beings. It takes a realistic look at the prevailing evils in the world, refuses to minimize the tragedies of our human situations, and yet insists that the very real evils do not have the final word in history. It accommodates the full range of scientific knowledge and sets the scientific worldview into a larger frame of reference that deals with origins, goals, and purposes for the world of nature.

Christianity is internally coherent. Based upon the elegant simplicity of its theistic view of God, it provides the irreducible explanation for why there should be a universe at all and why individuals are who they are in their individual distinctiveness. Some of the core ideas of Christianity, most specifically those surrounding the incarnation, are inherently paradoxical, and yet there is an inner coherence at a higher logical level that transcends the limits of our broken and finite logic. To thinking Christians, those central paradoxes are the key to unlock the mystery of existence. The greatest challenge to Christianity's logical coherence is the problem of evil. Though no Christian has adequately solved that problem, various Christian defenses have at least developed a variety of ideas that soften the severity of the problem of evil in relation to the omnipotence and goodness of God.

Christianity is also comprehensive. To be sure, many Christians live out a simple religious faith geared to the pressures and needs of their everyday lives. They do not reflect particularly upon many of the great philosophical and theological questions that have occupied intellectuals over the centuries. Many Christian intellectuals, however, have extended the basic theological dimensions of Christian thought to incorporate the fuller range of human experience, examined its claims in relation to numerous alternative worldviews, and developed a comprehensive worldview that includes every aspect of our existence in this kind of universe. Developed in this way, Christianity becomes the integrating key to all knowledge and experience drawn from ordinary everyday life, culture, science, philosophy, theology, world religions, and all other areas. Not every person recognizes such an integrating genius in Christianity. There are parochial Christians who never relate their religious faith to their worldly experience, and there are non-Christians who never grasp in Christianity the integrating factor that links together all life's richest experiences and values. Yet, at its best as a carefully constructed worldview, Christianity embraces the whole universe and universal human experience, with Jesus Christ at the center.

When Christianity is put to the test of life, it proves true and fulfilling for Christian believers. The reason is basic. As a worldview, Christianity is, above all, a way of life to be lived in practical terms and not merely an intellectual set of concepts to be believed. In the life of faith, believers are reconciled to God. They are reunited to the very source of their being, to the creative agent of the creation itself. Faith roots the life of believers in the ground of being Himself, empowering believers to live out the kind of authentic human life that God has originally willed for the human family, a life that is impossible to live to the fullest degree without being in touch with the very power of God himself. Christians discover that the life of faith works, enabling them to live at levels of personal integration, fulfillment, loving relationships, peace, joy, right actions, and purpose that they were not able to achieve by their own natural powers and abilities. No Christian ever attains perfection within this life. Still, even in recognizing how far they fall short of God's ideal will for their lives and their own highest potential, most Christians claim to be better persons within faith than they would be without faith.

As a worldview, Christianity is both narrow and broad. Its essential commitment to Jesus Christ is narrow. *He* is the way, the truth, and the life. No one ultimately can come to God except through Him. Yet Christianity is so broad that it can embrace the truth wherever it is found, based on the conviction that because this is God's universe, all truth is God's truth. Consequently, even while preaching the narrow way that is found in Jesus Christ, Christianity can be open to and affirming of the truth that might lie in alternative worldviews, confident that such truth can be related to the full manifestation of

God in Jesus. There is an inner imperative within Christianity to share the good news of our redemption in Jesus Christ with every person in the whole world. To do less is to turn Christianity into something other than its biblical understanding. Nevertheless, in its world mission, Christianity can respect the ultimate commitments and religious visions of all human beings as it presents to them the distinctive revelation and redemption of God in His son, our only Savior, Jesus Christ. Certainly one of the imperatives for the Christian world mission today is to encounter modern alternative worldviews, understand their inner logic and appeal to their serious adherents, and be prepared to demonstrate in serious dialogue the universal claims of the Christian worldview. One can understand Christianity only if one grasps its imperative for world mission that grows out of its conviction that Jesus Christ is the Savior and Lord of the whole world.

3
Atheism:
Life Without God

"The fool," writes the ancient psalmist, "says in his heart, 'There is no God'" (Ps.14:1). That statement would have been a truism to many people during the great ages of religious faith. It is no longer so self-evident to many modern people who, for a variety of reasons, reject or profoundly doubt the existence of a God of any kind. Since the Enlightenment in the seventeenth and eighteenth centuries, unbelief and disbelief have rapidly accelerated in Western and some Eastern societies. Various factors have been at work in the modern era producing increasing numbers of atheists. Friedrich Nietzsche thought the trend so irreversible that he powerfully imaged the collapse of the believability of God's existence as the death of God, a death so decisive that it would require a restructuring of the very foundation of Western civilization.[1]

Conceptual atheism (an intellectual unwillingness or inability to affirm the existence of God) and practical atheism (living as though God does not exist) claim many adherents in the contemporary world. A disproportionate number of the intellectual and cultural shapers of the nineteenth and twentieth centuries have publicly professed atheism as their credo. Many ordinary people who do not believe in the existence of God may have arrived at their conclusion without any struggle with the traditional rigorous intellectual questions or problems about the existence of God. Many more people live at the deepest existential level of everyday life as though God does not exist, even though they may formally acknowledge at the level of mind the cultural ideas of God within their society. Although atheists constitute a distinct minority in today's larger society, they include a number of formidable advocates.

48

Atheists do not believe in God, and yet individual atheists reach that conclusion for very different reasons. There are likely emotive, volitional, and relational, as well as intellectual, reasons why practical atheists do not believe in the existence of God. Among people who are atheists for intellectual reasons, there are rather different intellectual arguments for why a given atheist denies the existence of God. Atheism as such is not a worldview, yet it can be a vital element of various different worldviews. Atheism is characterized not by what it positively asserts about reality but by its rejection of any kind of divine being as the explanation for existence or the foundation of a worldview. Before one ever raises the question of what is the most persuasive among alternative worldviews, atheism forces the crucial questions of whether or not there is a God, of how we should go about addressing such a question, and of what kind of arguments would be pertinent to securing an answer. In reaching a negative judgment about the existence of God, the atheist will normally link his atheism to a larger worldview that interprets reality without a foundation in any kind of God. Atheism and the more comprehensive worldview are not the same thing. Consequently, a Christian's apologetic defense in relation to atheism is a basic component in the dialogue with a number of larger secular or naturalistic worldviews.

Many Christians do not grasp the diversity within atheism and the variety of reasons why individual atheists reject the existence of God. Among Christians, there is often considerable ignorance both of atheists as persons and of the nature of the atheist posture. Consequently, some atheists at times suffer unwarranted misunderstanding and prejudice from some religious persons or communities. Certain religious attitudes toward atheists and atheistic positions are incorrect or misplaced. Religious opponents of atheism have often assumed that atheism deprives life of all meaning and purpose and plunges people into sadness and aimlessness. Critics sometimes argue that atheism leads to such evils as social disintegration, personal immorality, and cultural ruin. However, an honest appraisal of actual atheists reveals that is not necessarily the case. There are all types of atheists just as there are of religious believers. Many atheists are, in fact, superb, sensitive, caring, engaged human beings who affirm a wide range of important human values, but they refuse to link those values to an affirmation of the existence of God. The question of the character of atheists or their style of life is not basic to the question of whether or not there is a God, or whether their varied reasons for rejecting the existence of God are valid or not.

The critical issue between Christianity and atheism is quite simple and clear. Is there or is there not a God? If there is *not* a God, then atheism is not only an honorable position, it is the only legitimate point of view. If atheism is correct, then life would be better structured on some nonreligious basis. The atheist addresses *the* most crucial question of life—even if, as Christians believe, he arrives at the wrong answer. Of all the modern challenges to the Christian faith, atheism, which is basic to many nonreligious worldviews, forces crisply the question central to religious faith: Does God exist? The atheist's honest questions and serious arguments against the existence of God deserve a candid and intelligent response from the Christian. The encounter with contemporary atheism requires that a Christian first know something about atheism and the kinds of arguments that atheists make against the first affirmation of the Apostle's Creed: I believe in God!

The Atheist Posture

Atheism is both ancient and complex. Although atheism undoubtedly is more widely prevalent in modern societies, it has roots in early human cultures and has taken several broad approaches to the question of God. People are atheists for a variety of reasons. Before we examine a series of the typical arguments employed by different major modern atheists, it is helpful to become aware of the historical roots and types of atheism.

Types and Roots of Atheism

What exactly is the atheist posture? In popular understanding, an atheist is a person who *denies* the existence of God. That basic definition allows several levels of the denial of God. The general posture of not affirming belief in God can be formulated as a conclusion of an argument or as a presumption without argument. Atheism as a conclusion represents a strong form that forcefully denies the existence of God. Atheism as a presumption represents a weak form that is more neutral in its view of God's existence.[2] The stronger form embodies what most people consider atheism to be, in the sense that it explicitly denies the existence of God for any one or several of a variety of reasons or arguments. After examining the evidence on both sides of the question, the strong form of atheism *concludes* that the weight of evidence makes it more probable that there is not a God. It makes a rigorous positive case for atheism, much as theists make for the existence of God.[3]

The second broad form of atheism *presumes* rather than concludes that there is no God. This more neutral form of atheism does not so much deny the existence of God by force of argument as it presumes that there is no God until the theist proves otherwise. Philosopher Antony Flew calls this position "Stratonician atheism" after its originator, the Greek Strato. This approach argues that the burden of proof is upon the advocate of a particular position—in this case that God exists.[4] Much as in a court of law where one assumes the accused is innocent until a case is made for guilt, the presumptive atheist contends that there is no reason to assume a God exists unless a reasonable case is made for His existence. Otherwise there is nothing to deny or nonexistence to prove. He is willing to listen to the evidence from the theistic believer, to engage in a cross-examination of the case for God, and to present contradictory data. He feels no need, however, to prove that there is no God. As a result, he presumes there is no God until a persuasive case is made for theism.

This weaker form of atheism is close to the kind of agnosticism proposed by the great scientist T. H. Huxley who first coined the term "agnostic" in 1869.[5] The "a" in agnostic negates the Greek word *gnosis* (knowledge) and means literally "without knowledge." In the twentieth century, agnosticism has come to be differentiated from atheism and is usually viewed as the suspension of judgment on religious claims because of a lack of sufficient evidence on either side to warrant saying that there is or there is not a God. Huxley's point, however, was that one must follow reason to its limit without any other consideration and then refuse to hold to the objective truth of any proposition that cannot be logically justified by good evidence. In the Huxleyan version, consequently, one might be agnostic about the current results of the rational investigation of the question of God and yet contend that the presumption of atheism is the most neutral view of the world until the existence of God can be demonstrated on the basis of persuasive evidence. One could then choose to remain open to the possibility that theists might be able to produce solid evidence for their belief that God exists. Until then, one would be quite as justified in assuming that God does not exist as that unicorns do not exist until it is proven otherwise. Of course, one could carry agnosticism on to a position closer to ancient skepticism and conclude that the subject of God is unknowable in principle and that no *objective* intellectual judgment can ever be made about the existence or nonexistence of God. But in either case, the natural starting point for the question of God is the presumption of atheism—a presumption that one need not objectively verify. The presumptive atheist shares with the more assertive atheist a number of major arguments against theism, though the two types pose somewhat different apologetic problems for the Christian.

The Western roots of atheism lie in the earliest period of Greek philosophy. The early Milesian philosophers Thales, Anaximander, and Anaximenes, while formally speaking of God, were materialists, and their use of the term *God* was simply a religious way of speaking of the world process itself. The tendency toward atheism was given impetus by philosophers like Parmenides and Heraclitus and received full expression in the materialistic philosophies of Democritus, Epicurus, and Lucretius.

During the Middle Ages when Christianity dominated Europe, few atheists were to be found. But with the Renaissance affirmation of reason and the consequent development of the scientific method, the ground was seeded for the growth of atheism in the following centuries. In the seventeenth and eighteenth centuries, atheists frequently suffered social ostracism and civil penalties if they took a public stand. The vast majority of people held to a theistic view that the universe was created by God and that its meaning and value are given by God. Most held that the fundamental task of human life is to acknowledge and glorify God.

With the growth of modern science and its rapidly accelerating discoveries about the universe, various dimensions of traditional religious belief were called into question. The Newtonian universe of absolute time, absolute space, infinite extension, and mechanical causation began to provide alternative ways to explain the universe. The result was that many educated people in the nineteenth and twentieth centuries have no longer accepted the existence of God as a self-evident fact. In particular, certain scientific discoveries have raised serious questions about the nature of God as traditionally conceived.

Another critical factor in the nineteenth century that contributed to the growth of atheism was the view held by various influential thinkers that religion fundamentally alienates human beings from themselves—a theme that found powerful statement in the writings of Feuerbach, Marx, Schopenhauer, Nietzsche, Lenin, and others. Coupled with the theme of alienation was the explosive growth of rigorous rationalistic approaches to any and all questions of truth, meaning, and value. The result was the eruption of atheism in the nineteenth and twentieth centuries.

The task of Christian apologetics is to understand and respond to the atheistic case against theism as a first step toward making a positive case for Christianity. There are several ways to do this. Many books on atheism focus on the specific thought of prominent atheistic intellectuals of the nineteenth and twentieth centuries—Feuerbach, Comte, Nietzsche, Marx, Freud, Sartre, and others. Of course, the vast majority of atheists are not students of the writings of major thinkers like these. Yet the viewpoints of great intellectuals have a way of trickling down to ordinary people who in a less sophisticated way find a rationale for their own atheism in simplified versions of the intellectual's more erudite arguments. So rather than examining the extended thought of individual atheists, we will summarize a number of the most important typical lines of modern arguments against theism.[6] Where appropriate, we will refer to a major philosophical advocate of that particular argument. Any given individual atheist will likely utilize several of these arguments in his own case against theism.

Atheistic Arguments Against Theism

The major atheistic arguments against the claims of theism may be conveniently grouped into perhaps seven general categories, within which there are subsidiary arguments. There are arguments based upon the logical incoherence of theism, the presumed exclusive authority of the scientific method, the problem of evil, theism's alleged dehumanization of humanity, psychological projection, theism's passivity to social injustice, and the lack of awareness of God on the part of many modern people.

Logical reasons against the existence of God.—First, many people reject belief in God for purely logical reasons. Two lines of argument are currently quite prominent. Some contemporary analytical philosophers frequently probe the question of God at two levels. The first relates to the logical coherence of the "concept" of God itself, and the second raises the question of whether or not there is an actual divine being who corresponds to the concept. These philosophers insist that if the theistic concept of God is not itself logically coherent, it is irrelevant to attempt to apply the concept to any possible divine being. These objections are rooted in the very nature of language and the necessities of logic.

Various philosophers have argued that the theistic concept of God is itself inconsistent and logically incoherent.[7] This objection is not directed specifically to the matter of the existence of God. It rather contends that before addressing the question of the existence of God, we must first be clear concerning what kind of God it is about whose existence we might wish to inquire. The theist, these thinkers argue, attempts to ascribe attributes to God that are either inherently contradictory or cannot be reconciled with certain harsh facts in the world. Theism holds that God is personal, immanent, and transcendent, perfectly good and all-powerful, and so on. These atheists point out that theists often do not mean the same thing when they use words like these and that they cannot consistently and coherently assert at the same time all of the theistic attributes for God. So one problem is that the term "God" itself has no clear, unambiguous, univocal meaning, so that the same word means the same thing in every context for everyone. For example, when the theist says that God is personal, he does not mean that God is all that a human person is. All human persons are identified with bodies, but God is said to be a spirit without a body. The problem is that we know what an embodied person is, but we have never seen a disembodied person and do not know what a personal spirit is.

Similarly, some philosophers have challenged the logical meaning of saying that God is love, or perfect goodness, or all-powerful. In relation to the problem of evil, some philosophers hold that there is an irresolvable contradiction in asserting that the creator God is both omnipotent and benevolent in relation to the massive amount of evil in the world. These logicians insist that it is futile to ask if God exists when one cannot define the attributes of God in a logically coherent and consistent concept.

Today's atheistic thinkers often take another logical tack. They argue that even if one allows that a logically coherent concept of God can be formulated, it has yet to be conclusively demonstrated that the "concept" describes any *actual* being. This type atheist is convinced that all rational proofs for the existence of God fail. Many atheists see the failure of rational proof as fatal to the theistic position. At the point of proof, atheists feel quite secure. For them, it is only when a religious person asserts that there is a God that the question of the existence or nonexistence of God even arises. Appealing to a law court analogy, these atheists insist that the burden of proof rests upon the one who affirms the existence of God. One should properly assume that there is no God unless there is good reason to think that there is. Atheistic thinkers contend that there is no logical necessity to go beyond what we clearly know for an explanation of existence. What we know is the universe. If there should be any reality beyond the world of nature, its existence must be proved. There is not an equal imperative to prove that there is no reality transcending nature.[8]

Arguments against God's existence based upon science.—A second line of argument against theism is scientifically oriented. It holds that theism is incompatible with the scientific method and the scientific view of reality. In a variety of ways, this view argues that there is no need to go beyond the world of sense experience and the scientific approach to knowledge of that world for answers to the questions of human existence and of reality in general. Scientific positivism, as this restricted view is called, builds an exclusive fence around the scientific method as the only legitimate way of knowing any aspect of reality.

Auguste Comte (1795-1857) was historically a major philosophical influence in the direction of positivism. Comte prroposed that all individuals, as well as the human race, in history go through a three-stage development in relation to the natural world. At a first primitive level, humans imaginatively attempt to explain natural phenomena and events through the activity of supernatural beings. At a more sophisticated second stage, humans attempt a metaphysical explanation through abstract and unobservable principles within nature itself. The highest stage is the scientific, in which humans abandon the search for ultimate explanations of the origin and destiny of the universe and focus on the natural causes of observable events. Science aims at formulating natural laws that can be experimentally verified. History has now moved into the age of science, which has superseded theology and metaphysics. Comte's atheism is of a negative type. He was methodologically committed to positivism and, consequently, viewed all theological or metaphysical questions as inappropriate. He had no metaphysical concern to demonstrate the nonexistence of God in the fashion of classical atheism. Comte simply assumed that the concept of God is a useless and unnecessary hypothesis in a scientific age that can explain all natural phenomena through natural causes. Comte believed that the only appropriate religion for a scientific era is a new religion centered upon the worship of humanity.[9]

In the twentieth century, logical positivism has shared some common ground with Comte in focusing upon the proper use of language. Positivists have argued that the only factually informative statements about reality are statements about our sensory experience of the physical world that can be empirically or scientifically verified or falsified. Thus all theological, metaphysical, or valuational statements are quite literally "non-sensical." Although there are few strict logical positivists in our contemporary scene, many current analytical philosophers still assume that the only statements that refer factually to how things are in reality are scientific or empirical statements.[10]

At a much more sweeping level of thinking, many people today assume that the scientific method is the only valid way to arrive at knowledge of the world or of any reality. This popular exaltation of science is often called "scientism." If one wants to raise the question of God, it must be addressed and answered empirically, if at all. Some advocates of this restrictive view would be open to the scientific proof of the existence of God, but at the same time they think that nature itself contains sufficient principles to explain itself. At best, "God" is scientifically an unnecessary hypothesis.

Some scientifically oriented atheists aggressively resist Christianity for the sake of science and human knowledge. They contend that theism, because of its dualistic view of the natural and the supernatural, inevitably attempts to block scientific research and a sound natural explanation of nature. They point out that the Christian church has historically most often resisted virtually every major scientific advance. Churches have repeatedly denounced the most brilliant research scientists—Copernicus, Galileo, Newton, Darwin, and others. Some institutional expressions of Christianity oppose any scientific truth that conflicts with their understanding of the world derived from their own limited view of Scripture or tradition. Hence, Christianity, including its view of God, is inherently antiscientific.[11]

Arguments based upon the problem of evil.—A third formidable argument against the existence of God grows out of the presence of the disproportionate amount of evil and suffering in the world. The argument may be formulated either logically or existentially. It may take the form of a carefully developed case against the logical coherence of theism or the form of a prophetic protest against God for having made this kind of world. Theologians have long recognized that evil presents the most difficult barrier to theistic belief, because it seems to indict the basic claims that theists make for the nature of God. "Theodicy" represents the theological effort to justify a theistic God in the face of evil.

The logical dilemma is well known: If God is all-powerful and perfectly good, evil would not exist. Evil does exist. If God is all-powerful, then He is not perfectly good, because having the power to do something about evil, He is not good enough to do it. On the other hand, if God is loving and good, then He is not all-powerful, because in willing the good of His creatures, He does not have the power to eliminate evil. Therefore God cannot be both perfectly good and all-powerful. The God of theism is logically incoherent and does not exist.

Atheists are not impressed by the efforts of religious people to justify God by abandoning a belief in either His goodness or his omnipotence. More pointedly, they find theistic efforts to preserve both God's omnipotence and goodness to be logically incoherent. For example, when the theist attempts to attribute all moral evil to human free will, the atheist will argue that God could have made persons who will always choose the good and not do evil. God's failure to do so is not consistent with His being both omnipotent and good. Thus, they argue, theism fails to justify its own claims about the nature of God.[12]

Evil for many people, however, is more of an existential or experiential than a logical problem. The amount and intensity of human suffering have accentuated the problem for many twentieth-century people. Observing the brutality of humans and the evils of nature, Albert Camus thought that the order of the world is shaped by death. We live in a world in which everything is permitted. The solution is to reject belief in God and to struggle defiantly as tragic heroes against the order of death, knowing that we are fated to defeat.[13] Similarly, Jewish rabbi Richard Rubenstein asks, "How can Jews believe in an omnipotent, beneficent God after Auschwitz?"[14] Numerous atheists think that we live in a heartless, indifferent, unfeeling world without any divine power to call upon beyond our own resources.

Arguments based upon theism's dehumanization of humanity.—A fourth line of argument rejects the idea of God for the sake of humanity. This argument contends that theism alienates individuals from their authentic selves and from freedom and responsibility for their own lives. This central theme has several variations. Ludwig Feuerbach was the major nineteenth-century influence on this line of thinking. He gave powerful expression to a psychological projectionist view of religious beliefs and argued that the concept of God fundamentally alienates humans from their own best qualities and possibilities. The individual is aware of his own limitations and imperfections but also of the infinite perfections of reason, will, and love that are the essential nature of the human species. But the individual ascribes his own imperfections to the human species and then externalizes and projects the perfections of essential humanity into a transcendent but nonexistent object called God. In attributing his own best qualities to God, man is alienated from his best self and diminishes his own worth and possibilities. The proper course now is for humans to recognize that their talk about God is, in fact, talk about the highest qualities of humanity and that theology is actually anthropology. Modern Christianity, asserted Feuerbach, should recognize that there is no being called God and transform itself into a true philosophy of man.[15]

Jean-Paul Sartre, the French existentialist philosopher, rejected God for the sake of human freedom, which he took to be the only self-authenticating value in life. The human is totally autonomous and free to determine his own nature and values—a quality that is essential to a human being human. There is no universal created human nature to which individuals must conform or universal values to guide an individual's choices. Thus we should abandon belief in God and live responsibly in radical freedom in a valueless world.[16]

Arguments that belief in God is psychological neurosis.—A fifth type of atheist argument contends that religious beliefs are basically expressions of psychological neurosis and projections of purely human wishes or needs upon the universe. Feuerbach originated this type of psychogenetic explanation of religious beliefs. As already observed, Feuerbach held that individuals project their own best characteristics to a superhuman being called God who actually does not exist. In Friedrich Nietzsche's version of this, God is the projection of man's consciousness of his own power and love, by which man robs himself of the best that is in him. God cannot live anywhere except in the human mind, and the best way of getting rid of Him is not be refuting the proofs of His existence but by showing the psychological origins of the idea of God.[17]

Sigmund Freud developed perhaps the most influential expression of this argument. Freud regarded religion as an obsessional neurosis of humanity. God is nothing more than a wish-fulfillment, the projection of the parental image from the warmth and security of the nursery upon a harsh and indifferent world. God is a psychological adaptive mechanism. Freud conjectured that the ancient Greek Oedipus myth represents the universal human experience of repressed infantile sexuality and ambivalent feelings toward the father that are the source of religion. In a complex process, sons have ambivalent feelings of love and admiration and of jealousy and resentment toward the father, particularly in competing for their mother's affections. Coupled with their sexual desires for the mother, humans repress their sexual feelings and psychologically project their conflicting attitudes into the idea of God and various religious rituals.[18] Religion, for Freud, is an illusion, an unjustified wish-fulfillment of people who wish to view nature as harmonious with their own needs and desires. So they revert to their childhood and invent an all-powerful father who orders everything in life to the individual's benefit.[19]

An argument based upon theism's passivity to social injustice.—A sixth argument is that religion produces social alienation, making people passive to social evils and injustice and resistant to social change. Karl Marx is the most prominent among numerous advocates of this argument. We will examine Marx in detail in a later chapter. Here let us spotlight the key elements of Marx's case against God. He contended that religion represents one of the individual's ways of coping with economic alienation and one of the capitalist's instruments for continued economic enslavement of the proletariat workers. Religion is a form of consciousness that most reflects our work-alienated human condition and fundamentally alienates the individual from himself and society. Humans, Marx asserted, make religion. It is a psychological illusion with a self-serving purpose. Religion is an opiate designed to ease the pain of reality for individuals who live in a world dominated by economic injustice and the enslavement of the masses of people by capitalists. Capitalists, in turn, use religion, with its otherworldly focus, as an instrument to keep people content despite the injustice and unhappiness of their present lives. By encouraging submission to the status quo, religion cooperates with economic injustice. Christianity has, consequently, justified slavery, serfdom, and the modern capitalist oppression of the proletariat. Social slavery is simply an expression of the fundamental demand of Christianity—namely that the individual must abandon autonomy and enter into a master-slave relationship with God. Therefore, Marx insisted, the criticism of religion is the basic premise of all social criticism.[20]

A variety of non-Marxists also argue that religion, particularly Christianity, is passive toward social evils. Such criticisms are at times directed toward the institutional churches.[21] They point out that institutional religion has often been socially conservative and supported any political and economic status quo, however unjust it might be. Other critics focus on theism itself and charge that passive social attitudes are inherent in theism's view of God. In their hope that only God can at some future point change the quality of life in the world, theists often abandon responsibility for life in the world.[22] Other Christians think that social wrongs can be set right only in a future heavenly life and are indifferent to economic inequality, political oppression, social injustice, military conflict, and a vast range of other human problems in today's world. These types of atheists reject God for the sake of humanity.

Arguments based upon an unawareness of God in some humans.—A final objection to theism is the fact that vast numbers of people live without any conscious awareness of God. This objection can be directed toward the character of God or to the experience of human beings. In focusing upon the idea of God, these atheists point to the logical incoherence in the theist's claim that an omniscient, omnipotent, and loving God created humans for fellowship with Himself, and yet did not bother to give His human creatures sufficient evidence of Himself for them to understand His presence and purpose. As Nietzsche observed, it would be a cruel God who could be so indifferent to the struggling confusion of humanity about the nature of ultimate truth.[23]

This objection can also take an existential or experiential direction. Many noble human beings have no awareness of God. In fact, some experience the absence of God even when they have sought Him. For some people the absence proves liberating from any transcendental interference with their human autonomy. For others, the absence of God may plunge them into an impassioned quest for meaning or into resignation or heroism in the face of the nothingness of existence. Whatever the reason, many people have not experienced the reality of God. So as a practical matter, for them God does not exist.

A Christian Response to Atheism

The major arguments of atheists against theism pose serious problems and technical issues that require extended responses from a Christian thinker. I will address some of those in the following chapters. My purpose in this chapter is not to answer exhaustively all the arguments from atheists or to make a comprehensive and convincing extended case for a theistic understanding of the existence and nature of God. That would require one or more books. Rather I have in mind the Christian who is concerned to know how to begin to respond to the atheist posture. With that purpose in mind, I will suggest in brief fashion the constructive elements in the atheistic arguments, their key points of vulnerability to theistic criticism, and constructive ways a theist could respond to specific arguments. Then I will chart the broad options that Christians have traditionally pursued in making a positive case for theism. My own view is that the best case for the existence of God must be developed within the larger contours of a comprehensive case for Christianity. I will do that in later chapters dealing with secular or naturalistic worldviews.

A Christian Response to Atheistic Arguments

Before one embarks on the endeavor of making a constructive case for God's existence, one should take seriously and at some level respond to the problems raised by atheists concerning the existence of God. Let me suggest some ways to respond to the seven atheistic arguments we have discussed.

A response to the logical challenge.—First, there is the challenge to the logical coherence of theism. The Christian might begin by admitting that in our talk of God there is inevitably some lack of clarity and precision simply because the only way we have to talk about the infinite God is through finite language. We attempt to say more than our broken and earthbound language will directly permit. For that reason, religious language for the most part is used analogically or symbolically. The words we use for God do not mean literally the same thing when applied to God that they do when directed toward finite levels of experience. Our religious assertions are loaded with qualifiers and have an odd twist about them when measured by ordinary language usage.

The Christian view of God has been refined over many centuries by keen intellects who in correlating terms such as omnipotence, benevolence, and other attributes have qualified them in ways that theists themselves at least do not find to be logically incompatible within the divine nature. Paradox is an important category for theological language. Theists hold that paradox is not contradiction and that it opens up levels of meaning that are not accessible to the usual patterns of formal logic. This is not to say, however, that the concept of God is incoherent. Even from the standpoint of strict logic, first-rate philosophical minds have argued on both sides of the question of the logical coherence of theism.[24] That debate in itself may be a clue that there is a higher or unique kind of logical coherence in the Christian concept of God that is convincing to the philosophical minds of faith that do grasp it.

Then there is the question of proofs for the existence of God. The fact is that most Christians are not threatened by the possibility that the rational proofs do not conclusively prove that God exists. Few Christians have ever believed in God because of rational proofs. Of the Christians who have accepted the validity of arguments for the existence of God, most have simply found in them a broad rational correlation with what they believe through faith and revelation. In fact, Christians themselves have developed many of the classic objections to the validity of rational arguments for God's existence. Still, many Christians do find that the arguments demonstrate at the level of reason a possible case for God that makes good rational sense out of faith. Unlike atheistic thinkers, most theists do not think that the world provides a sufficient reason for its own existence, and they contend that there is, therefore, a pressing need to establish some explanation of the existence of the universe.

That task to theists, however, involves more than the approach of formal logic. The atheist ought to be curious about why there is among theists such a strong compulsion to believe in God quite apart from the positive or negative results of logical argumentation. For Christians, there is a lived dialectic beyond a logically argued dialectic. If a person chooses to believe in the existence of God only if persuaded solely by rational argument, it is likely that few will ever believe. (As important as rational thought and correct logic are, the mystery of God as He touches human life cannot be satisfactorily addressed in logical syllogisms alone) If the atheist logician is ever to believe, it is more probable that he will encounter God as a whole human being in the concrete situations of life, not restrictedly as a skilled logician asking tough-minded logical questions.

A response to scientific positivism.—In responding to atheists who contend that theism is incompatible with the scientific method and the scientific worldview, one must admit that some religious people do indeed resist the scientific method and its findings and that some interpretations of Christianity do conflict with certain scientific views. All Christians, however, should not be measured by antiscientific Christians. Most Christians affirm that science is the best method for gaining knowledge of the natural world. Christians have no compulsion to resist science unless it oversteps its own proper bounds.

The scientific method by definition applies to the general order and interconnection of events and processes *within* nature. In being methodologically limited to questions within nature, science cannot legitimately address the question of why nature exists or of whether any reality or God transcends nature. Those are religious and metaphysical questions. The positivistic atheist is unjustified in insisting that the existence of God be capable of scientific verification. If one could by examining nature scientifically verify God's existence, then God would be nothing more than a spatiotemporal entity within nature. By definition, God would then be a finite God, a part of the natural order. But that is precisely the kind of God Christians do not believe in. The Christian God transcends nature, although He is also immanent within nature. At best science could establish the existence of some kind of finite creative force within nature, one composed of the same basic stuff as the rest of nature as it directs the evolutionary process. Such a finite God is not the God of the Christian faith.

The scientific positivist's view that the world is a closed causal system is an absolute presupposition that is itself not derived from the scientific method. No scientific hypothesis can be verified at more than some level of probability within the system of nature. There is no way to establish any degree of probability for nature taken as a whole. Therefore, the view that the God hypothesis is not compatible with the scientific worldview is itself an unproved assumption. Science cannot prove either that there is or there is not a God. Any attempt to do so, and thus to reduce all knowledge to scientific knowledge, is to overreach the legitimate limits of the scientific method.

It is worth noting that highly disciplined scientists have viewed in sharply differing ways the question of the compatibility of God with science. Admittedly, some scientists do consider the God hypothesis to be incompatible with their commitment to a restrictive scientific methodology and their naturalistic worldview. Yet other scientists see science, as it unfolds greater depths of mystery within the universe, driving reflective minds to ask ultimate questions about the origin, nature, and purpose of the universe, questions that science alone cannot answer. They are drawn beyond science to religion and metaphysics. When comparable outstanding scientists take opposite views about the scientific method's implications for the question of God, there is a clue that the difference is due not to the clear necessities of the scientific method itself but to factors beyond the empirical method—namely, whether the particular scientist takes a narrowly positivistic or a more holistic approach to understanding life's basic issues.

When set in the broader context of life, science cries out for the more comprehensive vision of religion. Intelligent religion has no problem assimilating the results of science into an ever-increasing understanding of God's creativity and of the nature and purposes of life in this world. Science is the best method for understanding *how* nature operates and how things work, but religion provides the reason for why there should be a universe for science to investigate and the ultimate explanation for the origin, nature, and purpose of human life.

A response on the problem of evil.—The problem of evil is the third atheistic argument we have noted. Most Christians recognize that evil, both in logic and in life, presents the single greatest obstacle to belief in a personal, creator God. Most committed Christians will concede that evil and suffering do count against our claims for an omnipotent, benevolent, personal God, and yet they insist that evil does not count *decisively* against His existence or character.[25] Few theists believe that any fully satisfactory explanation of evil has yet been developed. Nevertheless, certain apologetic defenses can at least reduce the problem to tolerable intellectual dimensions for the life of faith, leaving one with the hope that ultimately in God's future the mystery may be clarified in relation to God's eternal purposes.

Many apologetic arguments attempt to mitigate the problem of evil. The most constructive efforts insist that we view evil in the larger purposes of God, which require that He limit Himself in creating this kind of world. The meaning of divine attributes like omnipotence and goodness must be qualified in relation to God's personal purposes for the created universe and for human life. God creates a world with its own built-in laws and regularities and humans who have free will, both of which are essential to fully personal life. Given these factors, evil then becomes a possibility. Yet all Christians agree that God is never directly responsible for evil. Numerous treatments of the problem of evil are too technical and diverse for a brief discussion here. Christians with apologetic interest should become familiar with them if they want to defend the Christian faith in the face of this challenge. Several useful extended treatments of the problem of evil are listed in the notes to this chapter.[26]

If Christians have difficulty with the problem of evil, atheists ought to have even more of a dilemma with existential evil. If what the atheist calls evil and suffering are merely brute facts in a purposeless and indifferent universe, then he must not engage in any moral agonizing about those experiences. If the atheist chooses inconsistently to make a *moral* judgment that suffering is evil and not merely unpleasant or inconvenient to the individual, then it becomes apparent that he measures evil and good by some standard of value, which in turn opens up the possibility of some transcendent good by which we call suffering "evil." That implication then points one to at least the possibility of God. It further follows that if one makes such moral judgments, then one must explain not only evil but good. If there is no God, then the atheist has a problem of explaining why there is so much good in the world. Where does goodness come from if there is no God? It takes great faith to believe that a blind mechanical universe can produce the noblest spirits and self-sacrificing acts of the human race.

A response to the rejection of God for the sake of humanity.—A fourth atheistic argument rejects God for the sake of humanity. As noted, one version of this argument holds with Feuerbach that humans are alienated from their own essential selves through their projecting the human race's best qualities into the idea of God and then assuming a negative attitude toward their own human existence. In response, one might admit that some Christians have taken a negative view of human nature, but certainly not all Christians hold such attitudes. Yet if, for the sake of argument, one were to concede that all Christians hold negative attitudes toward human nature, it would not naturally follow that God is nothing more than a projection of the best of human nature upon the universe. If Feuerbach's assumption were accurate about Christianity alienating humanity from itself, then one might be forced to admit that Feuerbach proposed a reasonable cure and that humanity's eyes ought to be turned back from God to the human family.

To the contrary, Feuerbach's judgment was not correct. Christian theology holds that humans are made in the image of God. When humans live as God created us to live, we embody in ourselves the very qualities that Feuerbach contended we wrongly project into the idea of God—reason, will, love, and goodness. Christianity recognizes that there is an inner conflict within every individual between one's vision of what one's best self can be and what one, in fact, is. The problem is that we are alienated from our best selves not because we have projected our own best qualities into God but because the individual is estranged from God and from the divine qualities we are meant to embody at the human level as creatures made in the image of God. True humanity can be achieved only in relation to the God who has created us. Properly understood, the image of God should lure us on to our best selves in relation to God. There is no theological reason for such a fundamental alienation from our own human nature as Feuerbach supposed.

Christians can respond in a similar way to the atheistic charge that the belief in a sovereign creator God is inconsistent with the dignity, freedom, and responsibility of humans. The Christian can agree with the atheist that human freedom and responsibility are essential values that ought to be maintained. Admittedly, certain versions of

Christianity do strip people of their freedom and responsibility and subject people to domination by external forces and structures. Yet one cannot judge the intention of Christianity itself by perverted interpretations of it. Certainly for biblical religion, human freedom is essential to responsible human living.

The critical issue here is what is the true meaning of freedom. Atheists assume that no *created* being can be fully autonomous and free. Christians dispute that assumption. According to Christian thought, freedom means self-determination within certain creaturely limits. Christianity maintains a tension in the relationship of the sovereign God and His free, responsible creatures. Creaturely freedom always exists within the limits of its own nature. Even God, by definition, is not free to be everything (He is not the world) or to do everything (for example, He cannot do what is logically contradictory or what violates His own nature). Freedom at its highest is the freedom to be what by nature we are. In the case of humans, it is freedom to be human creatures made in the image of God who are dependent upon Him and yet free and responsible. Even if humans were not dependent upon God, we would, of necessity, live within certain types of social structures and physical limitations. Humans can never be absolutely free. It is precisely in recognizing our creaturely dependence upon God that we are most free to be ourselves and to achieve our highest dignity as the pinnacle of the creative process, creatures made in the image of God.

The atheist himself has a problem in justifying on a naturalistic basis his affirmation of the dignity and worth of humans and his confidence in human autonomy. If there is no creator or ultimate purpose in the universe, then humans are hardly worth noting in a universe as vast and indifferent as ours. How can humans have freedom in an accidental, mechanistically determined, purposeless universe? For that reason, many careful scientific observers argue that freedom is an illusion and that humans are determined in their actions by sociobiological factors. If the atheist thinks that the Christian has a problem justifying the dignity and freedom of humans in relation to God, he needs to look at his own dilemma of attempting to establish those qualities in a mechanistically determined, closed causal universe. This kind of atheist is rightly drawn to affirm the value of humanity—but for wrong and insufficient reasons that he cannot sustain.

A response to the view of "God" as wish-fulfillment.—Of all the atheistic arguments, the easiest for the Christian to deal with is the argument that the idea of God is merely wish-fulfillment, a projection of our psychological needs and wants upon the universe. The Christian ought to begin by admitting that psychological projection does occur and that it demonstrably happens at times within religion just as in other areas of experience. Even if one could establish that the idea of God is fundamentally a projection of an image of our earthly father upon the universe, that would not settle the question of whether or not there is a God. The fact that a small child can in his imagination battle a bear projected out of the depths of his own unconscious does not prove that bears do not exist. To assume that one can explain away a reality by demonstrating the origin of the idea is to commit what in logic is called the genetic fallacy. When measured by other types of psychological projection, the idea of God is most striking in its universality. If the concept of God is nothing more than a psychological projection, then as a psychological projection it is in a class by itself.

Even more critical for the integrity of the projectionist argument, projectionist theories have a built-in, self-destruct mechanism. Unfortunately for the atheist, the argument works both ways. If the Christian's belief in God is a psychological projection, then it logically follows that the atheist's disbelief in God is a psychological projection. If the Christian believes in God because he wishes there to be a God, then the atheist does not believe in God because he wishes there not to be a God. To complicate the dilemma even more, there is also such a thing as fear-fulfillment as well as wish-fulfillment, which extends the logical possibilities even further. The debate about projectionist theories comes to a standoff. The argument about the existence of God must be settled on some basis other than psychological theorizing.[27]

From the Christian perspective, there is an intriguing possibility concerning projection. Is psychological projection an inherent human structure? If one accepts the God hypothesis, one could argue that God might make such a psychological mechanism a natural constituent of human personality and then use it as one of the instruments through which He opens up to human beings an awareness of Himself.

An extensive critique of projectionist views can develop a number of decisive arguments against the projectionist position. It is certainly not scientific. In its concentration on the neurotic expressions of religion, it knows little of healthy religion. It makes major unjustified psychological assumptions. It is likely that even some of the psychological insights are not defensible. So the Christian can with some confidence defuse the threat of this frequently advocated argument.

A response to the accusation of theism's social passivity.—A sixth argument holds that theism produces social alienation and passivity in the face of social injustice. The argument may be directed toward institutional religion or toward the theological views of Christianity. The Christian would best admit, first of all, that historically and today there are otherworldly forms of Christianity and that some institutional expressions of the Christian church have been guilty of sanctioning unjust status quos in society. The history of the church is dotted with examples of complicity with unjust structures. At the same time, there is another side to the picture of Christianity. Its founder, Jesus, was radically committed to the poor and the social outcast and in opposition to unjust power structures and brutal social processes. The church itself has been chiefly responsible for many of the sweeping social reforms of the Western world. Yet even if one grants substantial weight to this criticism, the argument is irrelevant to the question of the existence of God. It is at best a judgment on some Christian believers, but it does not illuminate the question of whether or not there is a God. The existence of God is not affected by good or bad religion. Adherents of various ideologies, including atheists themselves, are capable of supporting unjust social systems.

A second form of this argument that directs social criticism against Christian theology is even more off base. Its indictment of the God who fundamentally alienates humanity from itself is certainly not the God of the Bible. The Jewish-Christian God is the God of the enslaved and oppressed. He is the God who promises to right all wrongs in a future age dominated by love, justice, equality, and peace, an age in which present human distinctions no longer exist. But He is also the God who acts within history to bring those future possibilities into the present age. Any religious institutional view of God which conflicts with that picture is a deviation from the biblical view of God. Even more, Christian thought holds that although the ultimate social revolution depends primarily upon the activity of

God, Christians are called into partnership with God in helping to achieve His historical purposes.

A response to the argument from humans who are unaware of God.—The final argument for atheism we have outlined is that vast numbers of people live without any conscious awareness of God. When this argument is directed toward the character of God, in the sense that a gracious God would make Himself more evident to people He holds accountable for relating to Himself, the Christian must take note of several theological matters. One is that because God wants to be loved freely by His human creatures, He creates enough distance in His creatures' awareness of Himself that He does not overpower them and crush their free self-determination in relation to Himself. Another factor is that humans have misused their free wills to rebel against God, with the result that the available knowledge of God is obscured by human preoccupation with the spatiotemporal world.

The Christian recognizes that large numbers of humans, although knowing the concept of God, have no personal awareness of God. But their unawareness may reflect more upon their lack of capacity or even of desire for God than upon the reality of God Himself. Christians can agree with this type of atheist that what is important is not to affirm some "idea" about God but to experience the reality of God in our lives here within the real world. Belief in God is useless unless it touches us where we live.

In fact, there are conflicting data concerning humanity's experience of God. It is of great importance that hundreds of millions of people across thousands of years, living in varied cultures and religions, have reported experiences of God in deep personal intimacy. Within the same religious traditions, the experiences are often described in strikingly similar terms. It is certainly credible to assume that there is a possibility that such diverse experiences point to a God beyond the experiences, however differently He may be conceptualized among the great religions. A majority vote cannot settle an issue like this. It does highlight, nonetheless, a possibility that the atheist or the unbeliever has looked for God, maybe even the wrong kind of God, in the wrong places and in wrong ways. In the final analysis, there is a way for the atheist to test out the claims of people who believe that they have experienced the reality of God by trying the path of belief for himself.

Making the Case for the Existence of God

Even if a Christian is successful in rebutting or weakening the force of specific atheistic arguments against the existence of God, the checkmating of arguments is not the same thing as making a persuasive case for the existence of God. How can such a case be made? Can one prove that God exists? Interestingly, Christians have never been in agreement about whether or not one can *prove* the existence of God or whether such proof would even be desirable. One of the longstanding points of debate within the Christian church has been the question of what are the proper approaches to establishing some knowledge of God.

Virtually all Christians have agreed that the supreme mode of knowledge about the existence and nature of God is in the Judeo-Christian revelation. Here in the story of God's saving activity within human history, particularly in Israel and the Christian church, is the clearest disclosure available to the human family. The essential elements of God's historical revelation are interpreted and witnessed to in the biblical revelation. Many of revelation's highest insights about the God of Jesus Christ cannot be reached by human reason. Many revelatory insights that can also be discerned through human reason cannot be attained with unquestioned clarity without the help of the biblical revelation.

Christians generally hold that the knowledge of God made possible through the witness of revelation is not just knowledge *about* God but is an awareness *of* God at the most personal level. A personal knowledge of God comes only through a leap of faith that includes but transcends our best rational insights. This faith is an act of personal trust in the divine person, a commitment of one's whole life to God through belief in Jesus Christ. The Christian's life in Christ, although it never provides conclusive evidence beyond logical dispute about the existence of God, does give enough assurance that the Christian is willing to wager one's life on the God who is revealed in Jesus Christ.

At this point, Christians do not agree on whether other approaches to establishing the existence of God are possible or even desirable. In more classical Christian theological reflection, this is the point of debate about natural theology—whether we can know something of the existence and nature of God through our natural human faculties and capacities without appeal to supernatural revelation.

One Christian tradition has held that one can indeed philosophically demonstrate the existence of God through logical proof. Some Christians have held that one or more of the traditional arguments for the existence of God can provide rational *certainty* of the existence of God. Others, in particular some contemporary Christian thinkers, have contended that reason can establish a high *probability* case for the existence of God through inductive arguments similar to those used in the empirical sciences. These arguments are too extensive and involved to discuss in this chapter. However, the reader will find suggestions in the notes about where to engage such arguments as developed in different ways by their particular advocates.[28]

The fact is that the majority of nonreligious philosophers in the modern era have held that the traditional arguments for the existence of God are either fatally flawed or, at best, not persuasive. This rather common judgment should raise some question about whether rational argument alone or even to some degree will persuade contemporary atheists. My own view is that it is important for contemporary Christians to face and become familiar with the philosophical questions about the existence of God. Philosophical knowledge is vitally useful in engaging atheists who raise logical and philosophical questions about the existence of God, if nothing more than to be able to point to philosophically vulnerable dimensions of their particular arguments. There are people who will be helped by a constructively reasoned case for the existence of God and who may find one or more of the traditional arguments to be persuasive.

It is likely, however, that atheists, of whatever kind, will not be persuaded by logical argument alone. Yet if rational argument can be utilized to open up at least the possibility that atheism may be wrong and theism right, then, at a minimum, the easy confidence of the atheist in the truth of atheism would be unsettled. One might even provide some atheists with sufficient reasons to enable them to make a leap of trusting faith into a personal relationship with the living God. It is likely that for most atheists, reasons for believing in God will flow more from their grasping a patterned gestalt on the centrality of God in the Christian holistic understanding of existence. One's persuasion then is likely not from this or that particular argument but from seeing or fathoming the totality of the Christian picture of reality in such a way that it makes sense of the great questions of life. A person's gestalt then receives further confirmation in the experienced presence of God in one's life of faith. From the Christian perspective, God, in the final analysis, is not merely an intellectual problem to be resolved but a living presence to be encountered. The knowing of God then develops in the doing of faith.

4
Naturalism:
Nature as Ultimate

There are modern people who doubt the existence of God, but few question the reality of the world. For good or bad, the world is undeniably with us. We are born into, live our lives within, and die in the world. As living, intelligent organisms, we observe the processes of nature all around us—natural things coming to be and passing away, the cycles of day and night, the seasons of the year, and organisms being born, developing, degenerating, and dying. As integral parts of the natural processes, we humans, even while children, begin to ask our first questions about ourselves and nature. Despite all the changes within nature and the fleeting temporariness of all individual things and organisms, the universe as a whole seems to go inexorably on, assimilating every change within its overall pattern of uniformity. So we make a discovery! If everything within the universe, as Heraclitus observed, seems to change, then the universe as a whole is always there embracing the changes.

How are we to understand human existence and the wider life process in this kind of universe? Most people throughout human history have considered the universe to be related in one way or another to a supernatural realm of some kind. Theistic religions have taught that the universe is the handiwork of a creator God who transcends the world. What if one no longer believes that kind of God, or any kind of God, exists? What if there is no ultimate explanation for the universe or life? Even in a universe thought to be running on its own, people still must live their allotted number of years and attempt to discover some meaning for their everyday lives within a natural cosmic process. When religious or transcendent explanations for the universe are no longer persuasive, naturalism is a perennial option for human beings. Naturalism calls us to make peace with a world of nature operating under its own exigencies. If life has any meaning, naturalists insist, it must be found *within* the universe, not in reference to anything outside of or beyond or supernatural to the universe.

Naturalism is the worldview which holds that nature is a self-enclosed whole, an integrated all-inclusive system beyond which nothing else exists. Anything that is exists within nature itself and is, therefore, a wholly natural reality. Naturalism explicitly denies any form of supernaturalism. However, one might symbolize anything beyond nature—God, transcendence, depth, beyond, above, below, or whatever—nothing supernatural exists outside of the system of nature. Nature does not require any supernatural being, force, or power to explain the existence of nature. Nature is self-originating, self-sustaining, and self-directing. Nature as a whole is its own explanation and constitutes the orderly closed system within which all particular natural and historical events occur.

As a general worldview, naturalism is neutral and open about what kinds of reality may or may not exist within nature and what may be the essential character of the basic stuff of nature itself. Naturalists could define the substratum of nature as matter, mind, life-force, will, or something else. The critical issue for naturalism is not so much *what* the basic stuff is as that it is *natural*. This basic naturalist posture may be linked with other ontological views that do attempt to define the basic character of the being of nature, and in that case the naturalist may also be a materialist, vitalist, dualist, or even, in a certain sense, an idealist. Based upon a broad definition of naturalism, a naturalist might even believe in a limited kind of immanental natural God, if by that term one means, as certain emergent evolutionists do, that there is an immanental purposive force within nature that is directing the process forward to higher levels of actualization. It is, however, a purely natural force to which he applies the term *God*.[1] For purposes of dialogue with the naturalist, it is important to distinguish naturalism within its normal limits from additional ontologies the naturalist may be committed to. In principle, he could be wrong about the ontological makeup of nature and yet be right about nature constituting all that there is.

Contours of Contemporary Naturalism

A powerful contemporary movement, naturalism also has ancient roots in Western civilization. The early Greek materialists were naturalists. Contemporary naturalists often claim affinity with one side of Aristotle's thought. In the modern post-Renaissance era, naturalism has flourished in Thomas Hobbes, the French materialists, eighteenth-and nineteenth-century British scientific naturalists, Marxists, and an array of twentieth-century American naturalists.[2] Naturalism is in the modern "air."

The Influence of Naturalism

Naturalism heavily impacts Western life and culture, both in overt expressions and in disguised forms. In the modern era, naturalism has tied itself closely to science, with which at times it has had a reciprocal relationship, influencing the outlook of many scientists and, in turn, receiving impetus for its own worldview from a number of developments within science itself. A certain percentage of practicing scientists uncritically presuppose a basic naturalistic background for their scientific work, an attitude that for many may be more tacitly assumed in the back of their minds than consciously formulated as the conclusion of a rigorous philosophical thought process. Perhaps as a consequence of the impressive practical and theoretical successes of modern science, some scientists are induced to go beyond the legitimate judgment that science is the best way to understand the empirical world to assume that all existing reality falls within the realm of scientifically investigable nature—which is a naturalistic philosophical view that cannot be justified within the strictures of the scientific method itself.[3] Philosophical naturalism influences a segment of individuals in the human sciences as well as in the natural sciences, particularly in Freudianism and behaviorism.[4] Naturalism has a captivating attraction for many scientific laypeople, who in a similar way erroneously equate scientific empiricism with philosophical naturalism.

Within contemporary nonphilosophical disciplines, many intellectuals hold naturalistic assumptions, even though they might not have worked out all the fine points of a consistent naturalistic philosophy. Nonetheless, they go about their intellectual work with the assumption that the universe is a closed causal order beyond which nothing else exists. Naturalistic philosophers provide the philosophical justification for a view held by a notable number of scientists, psychologists, sociologists, historians, economists, political theorists, artists, writers, and others.

Naturalism has penetrated American education, particularly through the enduring influence of John Dewey and other naturalistic educational theorists who have stressed the importance of a natural scientific explanation of all human experience, including the natural world, body, mind, emotions, and the full range of other experiences within the world.[5] It may even be argued that the United States constitutional provision of the separation of church and state has contributed to an increasingly naturalistic and secular interpretation of all human experience because of the prohibition against providing theological sanctions for ethics, human existence, and the universe itself. In the absence of a theistic interpretative framework for life, naturalistic assumptions may be unconsciously, even unintentionally, transmitted in the legitimate course of teaching otherwise neutral ideas. Naturalism will settle into a value vacuum. Naturalism is frequently a tacit assumption behind the explicit advocacy of a radical secular view of life which insists that life should be lived without reference to anything beyond nature and history.

Earlier forms of naturalism have become focused in a powerful American movement of philosophical naturalism. The fountainhead of American naturalism was the transplanted Spaniard George Santayana.[6] The single most influential force was John Dewey, whose numerous writings influenced a wide range of philosophers, educators, and scientists. Among the more prominent American naturalistic philosophers are Sidney Hook, W. V. Quine, Morris Cohen, Roy Wood Sellars, George Herbert Mead, and John Herman Randall, Jr.[7] A number of British and American analytical philosophers also assume a naturalistic point of view.[8]

Elements of a Naturalistic Worldview

Different types of naturalists hold in common a number of assumptions and implications of their general view. The fundamental assumption is that nature is all there is and that any existing reality—from subatomic particles to the stars and planets to living organisms to human life to mind—is a natural part of the spatiotemporal process in the universe. All things come to be and pass away solely from natural causes. Naturalists do not necessarily define the basic nature of the universe as matter and then reduce all other realities to matter. However, spiritual or mental entities are natural in the sense that they arise within the all-encompassing system of nature. Naturalists explain mind, spirit, purposiveness, beauty, ethics, and other unique human dimensions through the same principles that explain atoms, stars, rocks, seas, and organic life. Human life is merely another product of nature.

Naturalists vigorously oppose any effort to divide nature into sharply contrasting realms of whatever kind—nature and supernature, matter and mind, or body and spirit. Ever since Descartes split the world into two distinct spheres characterized by the two irreducible and mutually exclusive substances of mind and matter, modern philosophy has struggled with the distinction between mind and matter. Cartesian dualism has tended to dominate modern philosophy, so that most philosophers have made either mind or matter primary. Naturalists, in contrast, insist that mind and matter must be reintegrated into one coherent system of nature.[9]

Nature, naturalists further contend, is a *system* that integrates *all* the natural processes within it. Nothing within nature exists in isolation, not galaxies or planets, not individuals or social groups. Nature is more than the sum of its parts. A rational pattern holds all things together, so that nature is intelligible. All individual things or parts *within* the system are integral to the intelligible pattern and are potentially explainable. Natural cause and effect apply to everything within the system. Unfortunately for questions about ultimate origins, causation as an explanatory category is confined within the system of nature and cannot explain how the *system* as a *whole* came to be. Naturalists are forced to accept nature as a brute fact for the simple reason that they have no way of investigating the cause of the system as a whole.

The intelligibility of nature produces a key feature of naturalism that John Dewey called "the principle of continuity," which highlights that each level of nature arises naturally out of the lower.[10] Everything is interconnected. There are no gaps, breaks, or levels within the natural process that require a nonnaturalistic explanation. The naturalist attempts to explain everything in terms of natural laws, including not only physical reality but human life, both individual and social, and all realms of human experience and value. This continuity means that nature is regular and predictable.

Because nature is intelligible and operates by predictable causation, naturalists insist that the scientific method is the key to understanding all areas of human experience. Science attempts to understand natural things by identifying their natural causes and then testing all explanatory hypotheses by drawing out further implications and applications. Since for naturalists nature is all there is and science is the only proper method for understanding nature, some naturalists contend that the unlimited extension of empirical science to all fields of human inquiry is the "nerve of the naturalistic principle."[11] For them, the principle of continuity means "that all analysis must be scientific analysis."[12] This includes not only the natural and human sciences but also areas traditionally excluded from scientific analysis or where the applicability of science has not yet been demonstrated. As John Dewey put it, to stop short of the universality of application could never be more than a "half-hearted naturalism."[13]

Scientific positivism is the technical name and "scientism" the more popular label for this exclusivist and Promethean view of the unbounded scope and power of science to explore any area of reality —politics, history, philosophy, ethics, aesthetics, psychology, sociology, economics, and others. Naturalism and positivism often go hand in hand. Positivism asserts that science is the only valid way to arrive at cognitive knowledge that genuinely grasps in rational concepts the way reality actually is in every realm of inquiry. Granted that people may find noncognitive meaning and values through other kinds of experiences, the positivist still insists that the scientific method is the only way to attain cognitive knowledge that, at least, roughly conceptualizes what a given object of knowledge is actually like. Whenever a scientist or anyone else insists that a belief or truth must assert its scientific credentials if it is to be considered knowledge, positivistic science is clearly at work. Like the majority of scientists, however, many naturalists are careful not to attach finality to any scientific theory but to regard it as a temporary instrumental theory by which we move on to new levels of understanding reality.

Naturalists recognize that the scientific method cannot be used to explain why there is a universe at all. Because science works only within the system of nature, it cannot deal with ultimate explanations for the system as a whole. In the commitment to strict scientific knowledge, the naturalist quite self-consciously cannot provide a sufficient reason for the existence of the universe. Naturalists even disagree on whether the universe had a beginning, although most assume that energy has always existed in some form. Beginning or not, nature requires no explanation beyond itself. Naturalists bow before nature as a brute fact that is self-originating, self-sustaining, and self-directing. That is enough to know! As Bertrand Russell has argued in classic fashion, any higher cause, like God, that explained the existence of the universe would itself have to be explained by a higher cause or be left unexplained. If a hypothetical higher cause like God must be left unexplained, why not stop with a known universe that remains unexplained?[14]

Another distinctive view of naturalism is that the universe is morally neutral. It has no moral character or purpose even in evolving humans who devise moral standards and pursue a life of values. Their moral and valuation character, however, is nothing more than an accidental dimension of human evolution. Despite their distinctive status at the peak of the earthly evoluationary process, humans, when measured by everything else in the vast cosmos, are only one more integral component of nature. Distinguished by their intelligence level, humans are nevertheless in continuity with all lower life forms, indeed, with all inorganic processes, which are taken up into a new level of complexity in human life. Simply put, all aspects of human life—biological, psychological, societal, purposive, valuational, and all else—are quite as natural within the universe as the whirling of the galaxies, the orbiting of the planets, or the intricate movements of the atom.

Not surprisingly, naturalists forcefully resist supernatural or nonnatural interpretations of human life. No soul can in any sense be distinguished from the behavioral patterns of a particular human organism.[15] There is no prospect of human immortality or any type of survival beyond an organism's natural death. Humans, as natural, are morally neutral with some destructive tendencies and some potential for constructive living. Naturalists reject theological views of human depravity. Most, however, do not believe in the natural goodness of humans—as some Christian critics accuse them. Many naturalists argue that theistic views of human depravity work against the natural resources available to humans for the betterment of human life, such as science, industry, commerce, politics, judicial processes, and ordinary human affections, emotions, and sympathies.

In spite of their rejection of transcendent values or absolute moralities, naturalists develop various types of naturalistic ethics that are tied to basic human needs or enlightened self-interest or some other natural dimension of experience. Whatever the basis for morality, the values are generally regarded as having evolved out of humanity's long experience of struggling to survive in the world, adapt to the environment, and cooperate in social structures. Morality is important, but human moralities have no divine sanction and express no moral structure within nature itself. Morality is essential but accidental.

Many of these general naturalist assumptions and their implications pose a serious challenge to the Christian faith. In excluding all transcendent realities, naturalism specifically eliminates God from its worldview—if God is anything more than a name for nature itself (pantheism) or for human ideals (John Dewey) or for a naturally evolved purposive drive within the evolutionary process (emergent evolutionists).[16] Without any supernatural reality creatively at work, there is no eternal purpose for the cosmic process and human life. There is no doctrine of creation or of providential purpose within the historical process. No absolute moral and spiritual values hold humans accountable for their lives. We are strictly on our own. Certain traditional religious categories such as miracles and prayer are eliminated from life. Humans are nothing more than accidental by-products of a blind evolutionary process, and all that is distinctively human will be lost in the eventual heat death of the universe. The concluding epitaph is that there is no lasting purpose in human relationships and no ultimate goal of human history.

Philosophical Partners of Naturalism

Naturalism has a variety of philosophical partners. The same thinker often holds philosophical views that go beyond a general naturalistic position. Materialism and naturalistic evolutionary optimism are two views that have had numerous prominent adherents and advocates. Secularism is a less radical and doctrinaire outlook that frequently has tacit naturalistic assumptions built into its immanental approach to existence. Before critiquing naturalism as a whole, it will be informative to take a brief look at these three selected variants of naturalism.

Materialism is among the oldest philosophies in Western civilization. A number of early classical Greek philosophers—Thales, Parmenides, Leucippus, and Democritus, to name a few—were materialists. Materialists have been scattered through the history of philosophy from the seventeenth century until today. Among some types of modern philosophers like logical positivists Rudolph Carnap and Otto Neurath and analytical behaviorist Gilbert Ryle, materialism is a working assumption.[17] In the sciences, some advances in biology, biochemistry, and molecular biology now indicate that certain organic functions are not different in kind from chemical and molecular processes. The physiological basis of many mental experiences is now better understood. Subtle changes in the electrochemical system of an organism can alter mental activity, emotions, perceptions, memory, anxiety, and much else. Behavioral psychologists often work with naturalistic assumptions.[18] A new scientific thrust is now under way with sociobiology in which much social behavior is interpreted as rooted in the biological makeup of a given organism or organisms.[19] In the rapid advances in computer technology, cybernetics (the abstract theory of machines) is enabling the construction of machines that can simulate mental activity.

As a result, contemporary materialists appeal to some impressive new data to support the old idea that all things are at their base material. Materialists view matter, or now energy, as the fundamental stuff of the universe. Their working motto is, "Everything that is, is material." More moderate materialists view matter as primary but may grant that mind has a secondary or dependent reality that cannot be exhaustively reduced to its material base. For all materialists, since everything is ultimately grounded in the material, everything can be explained on the basis of *physical* laws. Nothing possesses exclusively nonphysical or mental properties. In this regard, materialism is an extreme form of naturalism. One ought to be clear that while all materialists are naturalists, not all naturalists are materialists.

Naturalistic evolutionary optimism is another expression of naturalism. This contemporary philosophical view applies a biological evolutionary model to the historical process and self-consciously commits itself to some form of secular humanism. Evolutionary optimists regard biological evolution and human cultural evolution as two phases of the same continuing process. When humans emerge in the evolutionary process, certain new qualities—in particular, speech and conceptual thought—appear that allow the human species at least partially to take charge of its own evolution. In the judgment of Julian Huxley, a foremost proponent of this view, the next stage in evolution is sociocultural. Humans will socially evolve further in the arts, sciences, religion, and society. In particular, humans can now utilize science as an instrument to extend their own human progress and to shape nature itself. In Huxley's view, nothing in that future process is inevitable, but humans have the capacity to assume responsibility for their own future—if they choose.[20]

Secularism is another widespread version of naturalism that has become a far more dominant mentality than naturalism proper. More of a mind-set than a doctrinaire ideology, secularism is the often unconsciously assumed philosophy of masses of ordinary people who are part of the scientific-technological milieu of the twentieth century. Secularists live in a dedivinized world without any sense of ultimacy or transcendence. Secularism is a modern reaction to the domination of Western culture by the Christian church, with its focus on God, human dependency on God, faith, the division of secular and sacred, and eternity. Secularism is a magnet that draws not only people for whom religious faith is no longer relevant but also many who are religious by profession and yet live practically as secularists in the world.

In contrast to people in past ages who lived in a world that pointed hierarchically to God and in which God was the primary actor, secularists are no longer conscious of God or eternity or the sacred. The secularist's universe is quite as closed as the naturalist's. His preoccupation is history, not eternity. His instruments of adjustment to his world are science, technology, and rationality and expressly exclude faith. His basic value is personal autonomy, not the dependency on a supernatural being as advocated by theists. The secularist takes responsibility for life in this world without much thought for more ultimate questions about human existence or the nature of the universe. Everything—technology, politics, education, history, society, and ethical values—is dedivinized and pursued apart from any transcendent ground or point of reference. Even though secularists may not always be conscious theoretical naturalists, they concentrate exclusively upon this natural life in a closed spatiotemporal world.

Religion is so irrelevant for many secularists in our scientific technological era that it does not even warrant serious discussion. In treating
religious questions with such benign neglect, secularism presents one
of the most difficult challenges to the Christian faith.[21]

The Inadequacy of Naturalism

As attractive as naturalism is to many people, it has numerous
inadequacies as a worldview—if one measures it by the basic questions that most people ask about the universe and the meaning of
their own lives. Naturalists—including, oddly enough, even some
philosophers—have often not developed a thorough philosophical
rationale for their assumed metaphysic. They want to shift the burden of providing a metaphysical rationale to those who reject naturalism for another worldview. Other than professional philosophers
in their ranks, naturalists are normally specialists in a limited intellectual or academic field—scientists, historians, legal experts, political
scientists, or litterateurs. Even if experts in their particular fields, they
might naively and uncritically assume their naturalism. Not uncommonly, nonphilosophers can be impatient with the difficult philosophical task of establishing a defensible rationale for naturalism. As
most philosophical naturalists recognize, all major tenets of naturalism are quite vulnerable to philosophical challenge. Their validity is
not at all so self-evident as some nonphilosophical naturalists might
like to think.

One fundamental problem is that naturalism is a classic example
of circular argumentation or question-begging in which one merely
concludes what one begins by believing about the universe. The
naturalist only purports to conclude what in fact he has already
presupposed—that nature is a self-enclosed system that embraces all
existing reality. Assuming that nothing exists outside of nature, the
naturalist excludes without proving the supernatural, the nonnatural,
the divine, the miraculous, or anything else that is not an integrated
part of the spatiotemporal process. By a priori definition, nothing—
an entity, an event, a reality—can be outside the self-enclosed system
of nature.

Therefore any new discovery or experience that might appear to
be evidence against the assumption that nature encompasses everything—even one that appears to be an absolute novelty or to be
unexplainable within the natural principles of the system of nature—

is confidently regarded as a previously unknown part of the natural system. The new discovery, if sufficiently confirmed, requires only a slight revision of some particular statement of natural laws. If the event cannot be expressed in a revised natural law, it is viewed as a mistaken perception and not as the actual case in reality. In this way, no new discovery or evidence of a nonnatural order can possibly shake the naturalist's absolute confidence in nature as a closed causal system. Hence, the self-protected circularity of reasoning! Naturalism never concludes more than or other than what it has assumed without any examination of nature. The point is that despite the naturalist's contention that science is the only valid way of knowing, the naturalist's basic assumption that governs his approach to the universe itself is not established on the basis of the scientific method. Even if this assumption should be correct, it is beyond the capacity of science to *prove* conclusively that nature is a closed causal order beyond which nothing else exists.

In responding to this criticism, naturalists attempt to minimize the problem of absolute presuppositions. Every philosophical system, knowledgeable naturalists reply, begins with certain absolute presuppositions that cannot be proved by the philosophical system itself. If absolute presuppositions are unavoidable, there are better and worse presuppositions. The naturalist's are minimal and therefore are superior to those of the supernaturalists or nonnaturalists. Sidney Hook, for one, argues that even though the assumptions of naturalism are not necessarily true, they are more reasonable than their alternatives.[22] In responding to the charge that naturalism begs the question when it rules out the supernatural before it ever examines nature itself, Hook recognizes that all philosophers are to some extent involved in a circularity of argument. There "is no such thing," he asserts, "as strictly logical justification of first principles in science or common sense."[23] Any attempt to justify basic assumptions can only take a general form of seeking verification for one's assumptions and procedures whenever one can. On this basis, the naturalist can satisfactorily demonstrate the reasonableness and coherence of his position to rational people, even though admittedly he cannot conclusively demonstrate the validity of his basic presuppositions.

Naturalism, using this procedure, claims to be critical and self-correcting of its own position. The problem, a nonnaturalist would argue, is that any correction or modification by naturalism of its own point of view must derive from its own naturalistic presuppositions and method. Naturalism remains comfortably impregnable to any evidence of reality within or beyond the universe that cannot survive its own restrictive type of scientific verification. Unless naturalists are willing to widen their own criteria for what is real, then there is little chance that they will take seriously nonempirical evidence for any supernatural reality.

Given their strict naturalistic framework for interpreting the universe, naturalists have difficulty dealing with a number of important philosophical problems and elements of human experience. One of these is the problem of how to establish a basis for the self-existence of nature. Naturalists cannot explain *how* nature is self-existent; they can only presuppose that it is. A self-existent nature confronts us as a brute fact from which we begin to think, but we cannot explain how it came to be. Naturalists like to observe that theists have a similar problem with the self-existence of God. Yet the Christian can argue that there is a major difference in the two ultimate realities. God, in the theistic perspective, is not simply an unexplainable brute fact in a way that parallels a naturalistic universe. The universe of the naturalist may be a brute fact, but God in His self-existence is His own explanation. To state it pointedly, a personal God who necessarily exists is a more persuasive explanatory idea than is an impersonal primeval energy mass that necessarily exists. No strict philosophical argument can be posed that will finally resolve the difference in the two positions. However, common sense might say more to this dilemma than could any number of rational arguments. To common sense, the idea of an eternal personal God who creates the finite universe is a more illuminating concept than that of an energy mass that just happens always to have been and always will be. To believe that nature is self-existent demands at least as much faith as belief that God created nature.

The naturalist, further, has difficulty explaining how and why new and higher levels of realities and values such as mind, personhood, morality, the appreciation of beauty, and the search for truth emerge if nature is nothing more than a blind and accidental process. Informed theists are aware that recent mathematical research on chance and necessity has made strides in demonstrating how natural necessities can statistically emerge out of pure randomness.[24] Theists will grant that these higher values could *possibly* be chance by-products of a blind, irrational process, but there is a big difference in admitting that they *might* have accidentally emerged and asserting that they, *in fact,* did so.

The existence of the mind is not the least of the problems for the strict naturalist. He finds himself in the strange situation of using his own rational mind to argue that the universe is an irrational process, in the sense of lacking any purposive element within it. No naturalist has yet successfully explained why mind should emerge from a mindless process and then proceed to think about the process that produced it. The problem is so great that C. S. Lewis has suggested that "rationality is the little tell-tale rift in Nature which shows that there is something beyond or behind her."[25] It is one thing to *describe how* these new realities emerged but another to *explain why* the process has occurred.

The difficulty is compounded further when the naturalist tries to explain the appearance of general order—Remember that nature is a system!—and the apparent purposive striving forward of nature as if toward some future goal. Admittedly, Hume proposed various credible alternative explanations for the appearance of order.[26] In current scientific thinking, what is called the anthropic principle asserts that any universe which produces sentient life that can recognize the order in the universe must be the kind of universe whose order can be conceived by the kind of pattern-discerning intelligent life it has produced.[27] But there is a circularity in this line of argument which seems to say that a universe that produces intelligent life is the kind of universe that will produce intelligent life. Most thinkers hold that no conclusive line of argument can be developed either way on this question. In such cases, an intuitive hunch might be the best source of making a choice. With that criterion in mind, a theist might grant the possibility that some goal-oriented teleological force can arise out of a blind, irrational, accidental process, but note that it takes considerable faith to believe that to be the actual case.[28]

Naturalism also has existential limitations. It can provide no satisfying answers to many of the deepest human questions about the nature of existence, both of the cosmos and the individual human self. Two great questions have traditionally vexed the minds of most sensitive and reflective human beings. Why is there something and not nothing? Why am I "I" and not "not-I"? On these two questions hang most other great questions of life. Why is there anything at all, and why should there be a creature bearing my particular name? The naturalist says, "Sheer accident!" In all honesty, everyone has experienced intuitive moments when existence appears to be a cosmic accident. But for most human beings, there are too many flashes of awareness of "something more" to life to allow one to be easily content with the naturalist conclusion. There remains the deep-rooted instinct that there are transcendent dimensions to human existence.

Ethics and morality pose another major problem for naturalists. Whatever basis an individual naturalist chooses for his ethical views, it is an arbitrary selection of a key value within a nonmoral and nonrational natural process. Naturalists vary in their proposed foundations for ethics, including such ideas as basic survival needs, enlightened self-interest, cooperation with the ongoing forces of nature, living for the good of posterity, or even a frank view that ethical do's and don'ts are merely emotional expressions of one's personal moral preferences. At a minimum, two problems emerge for the naturalist. One is the need to provide a rational justification for his own particular basis for ethics. The other is to live consistently with his own naturalistic viewpoint.

Naturalists can often explain rather easily how certain patterns of morality might have developed in given societies, but it is another matter to explain why one should obey one's own pattern of morality. Naturalists usually act as if some patterns of moralities are better than others. A naturalist might, for example, argue that one should not commit murder on the grounds that indiscriminate killing does not contribute to human survival. Unfortunately, that does not answer the question of why it is *morally* important for humans to survive if there is no moral character to nature and humans are merely the highest accidental creatures to emerge. In fact, naturalists regularly violate their own rules and consistently express rigorous moral convictions such as that people *ought not* engage in war or allow other humans to starve or violate the ecological balance of the planet. Despite their philosophical view, they talk as if these are not arbitrary preferences but are somehow absolute moral canons that no one should be able to violate.

Finally, naturalism cannot explain a great wealth of data related to human religious experience—except by the device of explaining away. That includes a range of experiential data—such as miracles, prayer, and religious experiences of various kinds—that to those who experience these realities are not easily reducible to a naturalistic explanation. In addition, there is the phenomenon of the universal belief in God in all human cultures, if not in all individuals. Not least, there is the fact of the human race's aspiration for the eternal, the desire to root human existence in some more ultimate sphere than the brief years that an individual lives. In responding to those data, the naturalist often lapses into reductionistic explanations related to such things as wish fulfillment, hallucinations, or something else. By the very naturalistic assumptions and empirical commitment of naturalism, the naturalist has already ruled out of court—often without ever seriously examining the evidence—the possibility that religious experiences could yield some clue to the existence of a reality that transcends the natural order and is the basis for explaining the existence and character of the natural order itself.

Christian and Naturalistic Worldviews: A Critical Comparison

The Christian view of the world and ultimate reality conflicts sharply with the naturalist's. The two views grow out of irreconcilably different foundations. In contrast to the naturalist, the Christian holds that the universe is not self-explanatory. Christians are convinced that the Christian doctrine of creation is the best and most comprehensive explanation for the mystery of the universe, not only for its existence but for its nature as science unravels it today. The Christian faith provides cogent explanations for realities and levels of experience within nature—for the emergence of life, mind, persons, values, a sense of purpose, and the universal idea of and hunger for God.

Ironically, the Christian view allows the Christian to affirm a number of values important to the naturalist, but for different reasons and with differing interpretations of some of those values. Among other things, the Christian can agree with the naturalist that nature is a system, that it is intelligible, that it generally operates according to natural laws, that there is continuity in the life process, and that science is the best way of coming to understand the natural world around us. The Christian, however, has a different perspective upon all these natural facts and values because he holds that nature and everything within it is *created*.

In valuing the world, the Christian's understanding of the world begins with God, not with the world itself. In fact, the Christian holds that one can never fully understand the world unless one sees the world in relation to its creator. The world is contingent. The eternal personal God is the sole self-existing, uncreated, necessary, ultimate reality. Nature requires God for its existence, but God does not need nature. God is not merely a finite power within nature; He can exist in His own way of being without nature. Without the world, God would still include within His own being all that He needs to be fully God. From the very start, the Christian view of God commits one to a belief in the supernatural, in a transcendent divine Being who is not bound to nature but who is Himself the ultimate explanation for nature. When God creates the universe, it is by an act of free choice, not by some inner compulsion or external necessity. God chooses to share existence with finite creatures.

Christians affirm an absolute creation, normally in a view called creation out of nothing. According to this view, not only is the universe absolutely dependent upon God for its existence, but it is not eternal and began with a first moment of time. It was called into existence out of nothing. This idea is important because it denies that there is any realm of matter or primeval energy eternally alongside God in any kind of tension or conflict with God. God is more than a designer of an already-existing world of nature; He is the Creator who called the primeval energy mass into existence. Without the creator God, there would be nothing at all, no world and certainly no intelligent human creatures asking questions about themselves, the world, and God. Creation out of nothing also affirms that the world is not divine. God did not create nature out of His own being. Nature is finite, not infinite. It is creation, not a part of the Creator. It is other than God, not divine. Everything other than God that exists is the creation of God and must therefore be distinguished from God. The Christian certainly concurs with the naturalist that everything which now exists within the spatiotemporal dimensions of the universe is indeed natural in the sense that it is an integral part of the complex that we call nature. But the Christian holds that even after its initial creation, nature does not exist on its own. Creation is an ongoing process, and God is active within the processes of nature as He upholds the existing order and continues to create within the changing and evolving course of nature.

The Christian can therefore agree at one level with the naturalist that the universe is a cosmos, a system, a unified whole. The Christian, like the naturalist, is not interested in a fragmented view of reality. It is basic to the biblical view that the universe is an ordered creation that has been brought out of chaos. Its order is intelligible, and humanity has the task of understanding and managing elements of the processes of nature. In fact, the Christian believes that the universe is not only capable of yielding up the secrets of how its own natural processes work but also of revealing clues about the existence of the Creator Himself. As the ancient psalmist sang, "The heavens are telling the glory of God; and the firmament proclaims his handiwork" (Ps. 19:1). God designs the universe to accomplish His purposes in creation and redemption.

The Christian further believes that the universe operates according to natural laws. Nature is not capricious. Its processes are predictable. On that Christians and naturalists concur, but for quite different reasons. In the Christian view, God is faithful to uphold what He has called into existence. Nature, although absolutely dependent upon God for its existence, is also quasi-independent. God allows nature to operate according to the regularities that He has created within nature. As a part of His continuing creation, God is faithful to the very natural processes He has created. Science itself depends upon God's faithful abiding by His own laws of nature in a complex process of natural cause and effect. Otherwise, an ordered life in this world would not be possible.

However, Christians also generally believe that because God transcends nature and is the One who wills the regularities that we call natural laws, He is bound to His own laws only as He *chooses* to be. In His eternal and "supernatural" freedom, God can break into or use the orderly process for His own revelatory purposes as He wills. His divine transcendence in relation to the natural process is partially expressed by the category of miracle in Christian thought. God manifests His power both in upholding the regularities of nature and through the unique manifestations of Himself in miracles.

The Christian can also agree at one level with the naturalist that there is a continuity within the whole process of the universe, from bare energy through life to human mind. The Bible pictures all levels of nature as having been brought out of an initial primeval chaos that Genesis describes as being "without form and void" (Gen. 1:1, RSV). Even humans at one level are continuous with the whole process of creation. The oldest creation story of Genesis pictures man as being made out of the dust of the earth (Gen. 2:7). The Christian can agree with the naturalist that humans are in one way continuous with the rest of nature.

Unlike the naturalist, however, the Christian also recognizes the Bible's assertion that man is discontinuous with the rest of nature, that his emergence represents a break as well as continuity with earlier natural processes. God breathes His own breath or spirit into man (Gen. 2:7). Genesis 1:26 states theologically that God makes humans as male and female in His own image. Although humans are a part of nature, only they of all nature's creatures bear the unique stamp of the image of God. Nonetheless, even as creatures uniquely bearing the image of God, humans remain dust and their bodies return to earth. For that reason, Christians can celebrate the earthiness of the earth and the materiality of human personal existence. Yet in bearing the image of God, humans become the focal point of God's whole creative process. When humans emerge within the natural process, a striking qualitative advance occurs within the universe.

Unlike the naturalist who gazes out upon a valueless universe, the Christian can be more world-affirming than the average naturalist. For the Christian, the universe has value in and of itself as God's good creation. In the Genesis 1 account of creation, at the end of each day and stage of creation, God gazes upon His handiwork and calls it "good." Then when the creative process in its initial phase is completed with the emergence of humans, God calls it "very good." The world has great value, but it is a created value. If the naturalist must view nature as only a brute fact to be accepted, the Christian views nature as a cosmic miracle to be delighted in. If God can take pleasure in the beauty of His own creation, the Christian too can delight in the naturalness of the created world and the humanness of human life. The Christian belief in the supernatural should never draw one away from the world of nature but infuse it with new wonder and meaning. The Christian can give thanks for nature because it is God's created world.

Among naturalists, evolutionary optimists believe that nature is moving toward higher levels of reality. For them, the orientation toward a future higher goal must be explained on purely naturalistic terms. Their explanation in many ways is an act of blind faith. Perhaps the less optimistic naturalists are more consistent when they see the whole process as an accident, as an undirected movement toward a totally unpredictable future. The Christian, however, believes that the whole history of the natural process, which has, in general, moved from simple to complex levels of existence, is being directed forward by the creative activity of God Himself. The future is not indeterminate. There is a future goal of nature and of history that is bound up with the creative purposes of God Himself. The whole system of nature is a stage for the existence and history of personal human life in relation to God.

On that basis, the Christian can properly affirm the value of human life, the importance of social relationships, and the imperative for creative living in the vast complex of nature—all of these being important yet only arbitrary values for many naturalists. The difference is that the Christian has a persuasive basis for affirming these values. In fact, in one Christian understanding of life on this planet, the whole system of nature is viewed as a setting for soul-making or, in modern terms, for the growth of humans toward full authentic personhood.[29] For the Christian, the future personal telos or goal is not an arbitrary human choice but an eternal purpose of God willed before the first elementary energy particle ever came to be.

Because there is a divine Creator of the universe who is immanently present and active in nature and history, the Christian believes that nature is not a closed system. It is impregnated with the presence of God. The God who willed nature into existence chooses to manifest Himself to His human creatures within the limits of the spatiotemporal order. Thus the world and human life are sprinkled with experiences in which the transcendent God discloses Himself to His image-bearing creatures. Most Christians readily admit the earthly dimensions of those divine manifestations. After all, humans are creatures of space and time who live within the spatiotemporal limits of the finite created world. If God is to manifest Himself to creatures within this world, it must be through the medium and stuff of the created world. His revelation occurs in many ways—through mystical encounter, miracle, prayer, changed lives, visions, a sense of divine providence, and other experiences. The very fact that the experience of God comes to people through some natural medium makes the Christian vulnerable to the naturalist's skepticism. Many reflective and self-critical Christians will admit that virtually any alleged religious experience is capable of a naturalistic explanation.

This is particularly true if one insists upon explanatory reductionism. One can always claim that a vision is hallucination, prayer auto-suggestion, the idea of God a wish projection, changed lives the result of psychological alterations, and so on.

The Christian, however, would argue that there is more to the experiences of God than the natural side. The Christian holds that any revelation of God in the natural order is in a sense a two-level revelation. Because God as infinite reality has no alternative but to manifest Himself within finite categories to finite creatures, His revelation is capable of being reduced only to natural events, even though some naturalists might be willing to admit that in well-documented experiences the natural events have a strange twist to them such as a burning bush. Every person can see the natural dimension, but not all are sensitive to the breakthrough of the transcendent. If one's eyes are fixed on the natural category or aspect of the miraculous event, then one will see only nature itself. It may be explained as an unusual event, a psychological projection, a calculated human deception, or something else. In any case, the explanation is purely natural. What the Christian sees and the naturalist does not is that a natural event can be taken up for a higher purpose and that nature can become the vehicle for the self-disclosure of God.

In this sense, then, the Christian affirms the naturalness of even the highest spiritual experiences—because of the belief that God meets us where we are, in the ordinary things of life. Yet the Christian sees "something more" in the ordinary. In and through nature he sees the eternal, the supernatural. Through the veiled stuff of existence he discerns the living God, the absolute Creator upon whom nature itself depends for existence. In so perceiving, the Christian discovers the clue to the divine reality who alone can incorporate the multidimensions of the world of nature and weave the threads into a synoptic pattern that makes sense of the universe, of life, and of oneself. Here alone do I discover why there is something and not nothing and why I am I and not not-I. The whole process of nature is designed to allow me to participate in the divine-human drama of living responsibly before God in this the Father's world.

5

Secular Humanism: Humanity on the Throne

"Glory to Man in the highest! for man is the master of things." Algernon Swinburne's ode to humanity sounds like the motto of secular humanism, a philosophy that has become one of the major contemporary rivals of Christianity.[1] To call it a rival seems strange, because there is so much common ground between the secular humanist's and the Christian's mutual affirmation of the worth and dignity of the human individual. Yet they are in sharp conflict at the point of why human beings have worth. Christians root the peculiar glory of humanity in our status as the highest creatures of God. In a fundamental contrast, the secular humanist affirms the greatness of humanity without reference to God—in effect, placing humanity on the throne of ultimacy that Christianity has reserved for God.

Secular humanism is a lively topic in the news today—because of its advocates and its critics! It is a modern form of one of the two dominating humanist traditions in our Western heritage. With the eroding influence of religion within Europe and the United States, secular humanism has catapulted into prominence as it has rushed into the resulting vacuum and proposed itself as a foundation for values for individuals and society in the twentieth century. Limited numbers of secular humanists have organized into humanist societies in various countries, but secular humanism is primarily a mass mentality that pervades the atmosphere of modern society. Vast numbers of people who might not think of themselves as secular humanists have unconsciously adopted the secular humanist frame as a way of valuing and centering their lives in an age that is increasingly expelling the sacred from history and public life.

Against the background of the nineteenth and twentieth centuries, secular humanism is a predictable phenomenon. If one no longer can believe in a transcendent grounding for the universe, as in the case with many modern secular people, one still must live concretely in this natural world and find some meaning, purpose, and value by which to live. Atheism or naturalism in its various forms cannot provide a coherent set of values for one's brief life on this planet. Of all the available alternative options, humans loom higher in self-evident value than anything else. If one can no longer believe in God, then one can at least believe in the human species. The result is that people who hold conflicting metaphysical views about the ultimate reality of the universe coalesce at the point of affirming the value of human beings. But in secular humanism, it is the value of humans without God.

The prominence and pervasive influence of secular humanism has precipitated a sharp reaction within the Christian church, a reaction that, unfortunately, is often confused and badly informed both about secular humanism and about the wider humanist traditions in Western civilization. Some criticisms are intelligently informed and sharply focused on the secularity of secular humanism. Yet other religious critics, apparently unaware that secular humanism is only one of many forms of humanism which include religious humanism, fire their broadsides at humanism in general. The result is that humanism has become a polemical target for virtually any evil that some people do not like in the contemporary world. In the overstated polemics of some within the church against secular humanism, the church is in danger of losing human values basic to the Christian faith and of destroying a common ground of human values by which all people can live together in a pluralistic society.

Secular humanism is only one of many kinds of humanism. Confessing humanists can be found among atheists, agnostics, rationalists, empiricists, idealists, secularists, Marxists, Jews, Zen Buddhists, Christians, and people who hold other organizing perspectives upon life.[2] One cannot talk indiscriminately about humanism in general. In order to be accurate in evaluating any particular humanism, it is necessary to know what modifier is attached to the term *humanist*. What is common to all humanists is the belief in the value and dignity of human beings and their responsibility for life in the world. Beyond that common affirmation, it makes a great difference whether one is a Christian humanist, a Marxist humanist, or a secular humanist.

Yet whatever the differences among individual humanisms in the foundation for human values, it is likely that humanism, which cuts across other ideological boundaries, has become the most pervasive universal ideology of the twentieth century. It fills the air we breathe and permeates the bone marrow and bloodstream of contemporary Western humanity. It pervades most areas of contemporary life and culture, including literature, art, philosophy, science, education, politics, and even religion. Advocates of humanism include some of the most prominent names in all cultural spheres. Beyond the self-conscious confessing humanists are the vast numbers of people who live by humanist values without much concern for ideology.

Secular humanism is one powerful form of humanism, a form that is in some ways a distinct rival to the Christian faith. From the standpoint of Christian apologetics, it is essential to specify which form of humanism one is concerned with and what within secular humanism creates the problem. Humanisms range all the way from religious to secular, from theistic to atheistic. Some humanisms form a close alliance with historical Christianity, whereas others present a formidable challenge to the Christian faith at some levels. Secular humanism does pose a challenge, but one that can be understood and countered only against an understanding of the history and the larger family of humanism.

Historical Roots and Branches of Humanism

Humanism is not a new creed.[3] It is as old as Socrates' Greece, Buddha's India, and the religion of the ancient Hebrews. The roots of Western humanisms are found in ancient Greece and in some basic theological values of Judaism and Christianity. There are two major streams of humanism in Western civilization—the religious and the naturalistic/secular. The religious is found in the Hebrew view of human life, for example, in the classic expression of the psalmist: "What is man that thou art mindful of him? . . . Yet thou hast made him little less than God, and dost crown him with glory and honor" (Ps. 8:4-5). The roots of both streams are found in ancient Greece. The Greek religious root that parallels the Hebrew is best represented in the figure of Socrates who grounded his affirmation of humanity in a theistic view of God. The naturalistic/secular root is represented by philosophers like Democritus and Protagoras, who both denied the existence of the gods but valued humanity.[4]

From these sources, humanism has woven its way through the whole history of Western civilization. Early in the Christian era, a wedding took place between the basic human values of the Christian faith and many of the Greek philosophical insights about human beings. Humanism surfaced and became increasingly prominent during the Middle Ages in the twelfth-century scholars who studied ancient Greece and Rome and in the thirteenth-century forerunners of modern science like Roger Bacon. The humanism that flowered during the Renaissance was a vital ingredient in the collapse of the hierarchical medieval world and the birth of the modern era. The dazzling list of Renaissance humanists who refocused attention upon human life on this earth includes figures like Leonardo da Vinci, Boccacio, Michelangelo, Erasmus, Montaigne, Francis Bacon, and Thomas More, to say nothing of a series of Renaissance popes. Renaissance humanism remained rooted in theistic religion, but it represented a revolt against the authority of the church, the other-worldliness of religion, and the church's repressive resistance to new knowledge and learning.

Throughout much of Christian history, including the modern era, humanism and Christianity have walked together hand in hand. That alliance began to change with new factors in the post-Renaissance and post-Reformation world, not the least of these being the development of the scientific method. The rapid and widespread application of the scientific method during the sixteenth and seventeenth centuries began to drive a wedge between God and the physical world and, consequently, influenced humanism in the direction of deism and scientific humanism. During the Enlightenment, many eighteenth-century deists and anticlericalists espoused a kind of scientific humanism. By the nineteenth century, as a result, a powerful naturalistic, antireligious form of humanism was advocated by a variety of empiricists, rationalists, and free thinkers, a form that rejected belief in God, in the church, or in any reality transcendent to the closed system of nature within which human beings are destined to live their one earthly life. These nineteenth century thinkers tried to establish the scientific method and reason as the sole basis for understanding and living human life—without any reference to God. In this movement, modern culture gave a rebirth to ancient naturalistic/secular humanism to live alongside traditional Western religious forms of humanism.

The result is that among the varieties of individual humanisms, there are two influential streams of humanism in the twentieth century—naturalistic/secular forms and religious forms. Undoubtedly, an increasingly prominent and influential form of humanism is secular humanism, which is a comprehensive term popularly used to cover a variety of naturalistic forms of humanism, such as scientific, rationalistic, atheistic, and others. Numerous factors have contributed to the growth of naturalistic/secular humanism. Most important have been the vast cultural and religious changes of recent years that have created what many intellectuals now call the post-Christian era. By that they mean that the church no longer dominates the cultural life of the countries of the Western world. We now live in a secular era in which public institutions are no longer governed by the full scope of Christian assumptions. Knowledge, science, and technology have combined to give humanity the power to control and expand the limits and horizons of human destiny. Despite the wars and tragedies of the twentieth century, modern humans have increasing confidence in humanity and have become increasingly preoccupied with the problems and possibilities of this world.

Naturalistic/secular forms of humanism have produced numerous official humanist organizations throughout the world that are dedicated to furthering humanist causes. The International Humanist Union, founded in 1952, now includes thirty-three associations in twenty-three countries.[5] The two most prominent groups in the United States are the American Humanist Association and the American Ethical Union. The American Humanist Association advocates its views through an influential periodical it publishes under the title of *The Humanist*. The American Humanist Association is also the source of two carefully constructed statements of the emerging consensus among leading secular humanists that have had wide distribution in the United States, partly through the efforts of their most severe critics within fundamentalist Protestant churches and ultra conservative political circles. The first statement, published as the "Humanist Manifesto I" in 1933, sets out their position in fifteen straightforward affirmations and was signed by thirty-four sponsors. Then, in 1973, a larger group of sponsors updated, expanded, and revised their position to reflect the changes of the past forty years and published their views in a series of eighteen affirmations known as the "Humanist Manifesto II."[6] The American Humanist Association has struggled to maintain a secularized religious stance, arguing for an intelligent religious basis for a humanism that no longer believes in or needs the support of God. One result is that secular humanism has been officially recognized in a ruling of the United States Supreme Court as a religion.

Although secular humanism is a prominent movement, its critics often credit its organized expression with far more influence than it deserves. The membership of humanist associations throughout the West is relatively small, although the membership lists sometimes read like a selective Who's Who of prominent figures in the natural sciences, the human sciences, the arts, philosophy, and the whole range of human intellectual and cultural life. Among prominent twentieth-century figures who would be identified with the secular humanist outlook, although not necessarily with official organizations, are philosophers like John Dewey, William James, Bertrand Russell, Sidney Hook, Morris Cohen, Jean-Paul Sarte, A. J. Ayer, Karl Popper, and Felix Adler. There are numerous secular humanists within the natural sciences, Albert Einstein, Julian Huxley, and Bronislaw Kasper Malinowski being examples. Humanistic psychology includes such figures as Sigmund Freud, Erik Erickson, Erich Fromm, Abraham Maslow, and Carl Rogers. Among literary giants would be Albert Camus, Samuel Beckett, Archibald MacLeish, and many others. One could list leaders out of every other intellectual discipline and cultural sphere who place a emphasis upon the secular dimension of their humanist outlook even though some may have a religious faith as well. What should be of far greater concern to the Christian is the absorption of *secular* humanist values by masses of ordinary people who are not members of any organization but who represent the greatest impact of secular humanism upon Western life.

It is critically important to be aware that twentieth-century humanism also takes religious forms. There are Jewish, Roman Catholic, and Protestant people who consciously apply a humanist label to themselves, but who make it clear that they are religious or Christian humanists. Christian humanism has a long tradition within the Christian church, dating at least from the late Middle Ages until the twentieth century. In our time, many Christian theologians and church leaders have considered themselves Christian humanists, and that position has been affirmed by major church groups in Roman Catholicism and Protestantism. One could mention mainstream theologians like Dietrich Bonhoeffer, Teilhard de Chardin, and Jacques Maritain from among many others.[7] Not the least of the advocates of Christian humanism is a Roman Catholic Church that has rediscovered its own humanist roots. Challenged by the vision of John XXIII, the Second Vatican Council issued a remarkable reaffirmation of a transcendent humanism. In warning against "a humanism that is merely earth-bound," the Council proceeded to affirm "man's surpassing dignity" and the "supremely human character of the church."[8] Every pope since Vatican II has followed Pope Paul VI in referring to Christianity as a "transcendent humanism," a "true humanism," and a "universal humanism," a humanism that is consciously under God.[9] The World Council of Churches has also produced a number of policies and programs since the early 1960s that reflect strong human commitments.[10]

With such support of humanism within the Christian church and with many Christians referring to themselves as Christian humanists, it is evident that no simplistic negative judgment can be made about all humanisms or even about any particular humanism—such as secular humanism—at every point. All Christians share some important things in common with all humanists, although certain elements within secular humanism are in sharp conflict with the views of most Christians. It is extremely critical that Christians should be informed and discriminating in their reactions to humanism in general and to secular/naturalistic humanism in particular. Only within the framework of a broad understanding of humanism and of the humanist elements within the Christian faith is the Christian prepared to dialogue intelligently with a secular humanist so as to affirm our common ground, selectively criticize the inadequacies of a secular/naturalistic foundation for humanism, and assert the superior basis for humanism in the nonnegotiable transcendent beliefs of the Christian faith. So let us first examine the values that are common to all humanisms before assessing the views that are peculiar to secular humanism.

Common Values Among All Humanisms

Despite their individual differences, all humanisms share a number of important common values. First, the fundamental value of all humanisms is the affirmation of the worth and dignity of human beings. All human beings are morally equal and have equal rights in life. Humanists will allow no other value in nature or history to usurp the value of the human individual.

Second, humanists stress the importance of this present historical world and of persons finding fulfillment in their lives here and now. The humanist, consequently, lives with a sense of urgency about achieving such human values as social justice, equality, freedom, and a fair distribution of the fruits of the good life.

Third, humanists emphasize human freedom and responsibility for our individual lives and for directing the affairs of our world. No humanist is willing to allow the future to be determined by blind fate. All humanists agree that human beings are the chief actors within the historical process. If humans are responsible for life, then humans are free and capable of some degree of self-control and self-direction.

Fourth, humanists generally believe in our human potential for influencing the future toward a better life for the human race. Contrary to the charges made by some of their critics, most contemporary humanists are not naive nineteenth-century optimists about the inevitability of progress in history or the perfectability of the human race. Tempered by the harsh realities of twentieth-century life, most humanists know too well our human limitations and take a realistic view of the radical evils, contending forces, and destructive potential of the modern world. Yet they continue to affirm that the future is open, and they place some faith in human beings as shapers of the future.

Fifth, humanists affirm at some level the capacity of humans through reason and science to solve many problems in society and in relation to nature. All humanists stress the importance of human intelligence and most increasingly advocate the value of science as an important tool for solving many problems in most areas of human experience.

Sixth, the supreme goal of life and society, for most humanists, is usually defined, at least at some level, as the good and happiness of the human family, even though not all humanists will agree what the supreme human good may be.

Seventh, the broad goal of the good and happiness of the human family yields a number of important humanitarian ethical principles.

Humanists are passionately concerned for social justice and for making a decent human life available to all people. Humanists are often prophetic against dehumanizing social evils and advocate community and world responsibility for eliminating such evils as hunger, violence, and war and for improving standards of health, education, housing, welfare, and anything else that affects the human quality of peoples' lives.

Eighth, the humanist emphasis upon the worth, equality, freedom, and responsibility of the human person leads most humanists to a human rights position on many political, social, and economic issues. Humanists generally support political democracy and a fair distribution of economic wealth within a total society. Humanists normally champion cultural pluralism and resist the efforts of any one segment of society to impose their behavioral pattern upon all others within the society beyond those broad universal ethical and moral structures essential to the survival of any society. Humanists usually support religious and nonreligious tolerance within society and advocate a sharp separation of church and state. Humanists usually urge political states to rise above their national loyalties and to find international channels through which to resolve conflict, eliminate war, and alleviate human suffering all over the world.

All of these values are common to every humanism, including secular humanism and Christian humanism. Many Christians would share with secular humanists most of the values suggested here, and some Christians would share them all, although a secular humanist and a Christian would have markedly different reasons for affirming the values. Consequently, any Christian critique of secular humanism must not forget that we do together affirm a number of important human values that are critical to life in a democratic society or a civilized world. And yet as a total world view and at various levels within its overall outlook, secular humanism is a major rival of the Christian faith and of a Christian humanism. That fact raises the question of what it is within the secular humanist outlook that brings it into conflict with the Christian faith.

The Distinctive Views of Secular Humanism

The basic problem with secular humanism, from a Christian perspective, is not its commitment to humanist values that it shares in common with other humanisms but its desire to affirm those values without any reference to God.

First, the distinctive character of secular humanism is shaped by its naturalistic worldview and the implications of that for interpreting human life.[11] Naturalism is the view that nature is everything there is and that human life should be lived autonomously according to natural principles and without reference to anything outside of nature or the natural universe. The authors of the "Humanist Manifesto II" frankly acknowledge their own naturalistic orientation and admit that many of their more universal human values are shared by humanisms of other metaphysical orientations. It is possible that many secular humanists have never thought through the naturalistic assumptions of their humanism but have simply assumed a practical secularized version of a more theoretical naturalism, one that lives life in practical terms without reference to God or transcendent reality.

Secular humanism, when conscious of its own naturalistic assumptions, can take one of two broad forms, either metaphysical or anthropocentric. The metaphysical naturalist sets human life in a cosmic framework and contends that nature is a self-originating and self-explanatory whole that requires no further explanation. On the other hand, anthropocentric naturalists, John Dewey being one example, have little conscious metaphysical concern and prefer to concentrate on actual human life as it is found within the course of nature. I would argue, however, that an anthropocentric naturalism presumes a metaphysical naturalism as its basis and hence that secular humanisms are at least tacit metaphysical naturalisms.[12]

Second, this naturalistic worldview makes secular humanists antisupernatural. They reject a theistic God or any other transcendental basis for life on earth. The universe, they argue, is self-existing and not created. In contending that any account of the origin and processes of nature must pass the test of scientific evidence, they are confident that there is not sufficient evidence for the existence of the supernatural. Yet even if there were, the supernatural would be meaningless or irrelevant to the survival and fulfillment of the human race.

Third, secular humanists regard humans as the fortuitous, chance product of a blind evolutionary process. Humanity is not the result of a special creative divine act or even of some immanental purposive drive within the universe itself. There is no dual human nature in which there is a separate soul or a "ghost in the machine." The total human personality is a function of the biological organism interacting in a material, social, and cultural world. Among modern secular humanists, the old-style humanist anthropocentrism, in which humans are viewed at the center of the universe, is now laid aside. Humans might be the most important value on this earth, but measured against the immensity of the universe humans are relatively inconsequential.

Fourth, this view that humans are a chance emergent out of a purposeless natural process leads the naturalistic humanist to deny that there is any reality in a person that can survive death. Consequently, humans are not immortal. The individual may continue to exist in his progeny or influence but not as an identifiable conscious self. Life in this world is important—simply because it is the only life there is!

Fifth, like all humanists, secular humanists hold that humans are responsible for their lives and destiny; but unlike traditional religious humanists, they hold that humanity is *solely* the master of its own fate. There are no deities or transcendent powers to which people can appeal for help or to which they are accountable. If we are to be saved from our problems, we must save ourselves. Secular humanists advocate the maximum individual autonomy that is consistent with social responsibility. Hence, they reject all ideologies—religious or political —that remove human responsibilities, foster dependencies and escapisms, or inhibit humans from reaching their full potential. Through their own intelligence, goodwill, and cooperative skills, humans can survive on the planet Earth, explore space, and find fulfillment for all human beings.

Sixth, secular humanists place a heavier emphasis than do some other humanists on reason and science as the *only* tools available for solving our problems and shaping the future. Constructive reason must be tempered by humility, compassion, and love and linked with feeling that expresses itself in the arts. But reason and a controlled science can solve problems in the natural world, the nature of the human self, human society (including politics, economics, social structures, and so on), ethics, and even religion. Our proper concern today should be with nature and history and not with the metaphysical preoccupations of the past generations. The use of critical intelligence can break the bondage of old religious mythologies and other illusions about our human situation. Secularists oppose all tyrannical ideologies that limit the use of human intelligence, resist new scientific truth, or impose a particular code of belief upon a whole society.[13]

Seventh, although naturalistic humanists place their own faith in humans, most of them hold that humans are morally neutral, being intrinsically neither good nor bad. Although hopeful about the capacity and potential of human beings, most secular humanists view a human as an organismic phenomenon with all kinds of shaping forces within and without that may be turned to good or evil. Some naturalists are optimistic about our human future because they believe, as does Julian Huxley, that the next stage in evolution is not toward a higher species but toward the psychosocial humanization of the human race.[14] For the most part, however, this naturalistic faith and hope in our human future is tempered by a realism about our present human limitations.

Eighth, secular humanists deny absolute ethics or moralities. Although there are different approaches to ethics among the secularists, they all agree that humans are on their own without any divine guidance. The basic principle in secular ethics is usually some interpretation of the greatest good or happiness for the greatest number of people. As A. J. Ayer has argued, nobody has proved that the greatest happiness is the highest good, but it is so self-evident that it is probably not necessary to do so.[15] It's up to individuals to apply that principle. Humans, however, do not make their ethical choices in a vacuum but can draw upon a common pool of knowledge, experience, and wisdom. Science itself is a key ethical instrument that can discover how a number of basic human goods are not only essential for any organized society but also contribute to human happiness. Secular humanists tend to agree about a group of broad social principles for a human society; but beyond those principles, they advocate tolerant and permissive attitudes about personal patterns of behavior that contribute to the happiness and creative realization of human needs, desires, and personal fulfillment.[16]

Finally, secular humanist attitudes toward religion pose a major challenge to the Christian church. The secular/naturalist is usually indifferent or hostile to traditional religions, particularly to theistic religions, which they take to be an unproved and outmoded view that in its emphasis on salvation diverts people from the real tasks of this world. The naturalists contend that theism's basic assertions about God can no longer be maintained in our scientific world because they cannot pass the test of reason or science. Science now provides the only explanations that are testable, necessary, or relevant to human life in the natural world. The view that the God-hypothesis is indefensible is frequently only assumed and not argued by naturalistic humanists.

Secular humanists contend that theistic religions produce numerous attitudes and life-styles that are undesirable and even destructive to the humanist effort toward the survival and fulfillment of the human race. Theistic religion deprecates human worth and responsibility and creates dependencies that diminish efforts to reach our full human potential. Theists, in their hope for immortality, often reflect an otherworldliness that is unconcerned for the struggle to eradicate the evils of our world and to improve our human situation. Christians are often uncharitable toward non-Christians and view women as inferior to men. Secular humanists maintain that theistic religions, in submission to religious dogmatisms, often resist the truth discovered by science or by other nonreligious approaches to knowledge. The result is that theism produces an irreparable split in the wholeness of the universe and impedes progress in rationality, morality, and even in religion itself.

Secular humanists vary in their prescriptions for traditional religions. Some are indifferent to religion, and some would like to abolish religion altogether. However, other secularists—like some members of the American Humanist Association—value many elements of the religious experience even though they reject the core of theistic religion. Many of these people still regard themselves as religious in attitude and ethics. They would like to replace historic theisms with a new scientific form of naturalistic religion, one without belief in God, that encourages the actions, purposes, and experiences which facilitate the realization of human personality and the cooperative development of the world in the here and now.[17]

These distinctive characteristics of secular humanism present a critical challenge to the Christian faith at a number of points. Part of the Christian's problem in responding to the challenge is that these unacceptable distinctives are wedded to many human commitments that are shared by the vast majority of people within the Christian church, whether or not they should choose to call themselves Christian humanists. The question is, How should the Christian respond to the secular humanist challenge?

A Christian Critique of Secular Humanism

I suggest that the Christian should make, as with all alternative points of view, a well-reasoned response to secular humanism, one that embodies a yes to many of its broad human commitments and a no to the distinctive naturalistic elements that collide with the Christian faith. Few Christians would take issue with the secular humanist's commitment to human worth and dignity, freedom and responsibility, and capacity to influence the course of human history. Nor would Christians, except for some excessively otherworldly types, ignore the importance of life in this historical world and the imperative to achieve maximum happiness and fulfillment for the whole human family. Many Christians are heavily involved in the effort to eradicate most of the same evils that trouble the secular humanist. The Christian in response to the secular humanist should find and affirm as much common ground as is possible between the two views. Those mutual views do provide a common basis on which both can live and often cooperate in efforts to enrich human life in this world. And yet, the Christian must not hesitate to resist the naturalistic worldview of the secularists and to bring a reasoned critique to their radically secular position. In my judgment, there are a number of fundamental points where the secular humanist is philosophically vulnerable to criticism.

First, the secular humanist has difficulty providing a coherent and philosophically defensible interpretative or metaphysical framework for his humanist vision. The naturalist must accept the brute fact of the universe without any sufficient reason for its existence. The naturalist cannot provide a persuasive rational case or a high-probability empirical case that the universe is a self-explanatory whole and that there is no reality transcendent to the system of nature.[18] Secularists who accept the self-evident truth of naturalism as a worldview should be challenged to argue its philosophical credentials.

There are, of course, secular anthropocentric humanists—what might be called soft secular humanists—who work with naturalistic assumptions but who are interested only in historical life and not in metaphysics. If the soft secular humanist claims to be nonmetaphysical, then logical consistency requires that he abandon his metaphysical critique of theistic religion and his arguments for or assumptions of atheism or agnosticism.[19] It is unavoidable, however, for the anthropocentric naturalist to make tacit metaphysical assumptions about the universe as the basis for a naturalistic approach to life. The soft secular humanist should face the imperative to defend philosophically his own tacit metaphysical assumptions. One should not be allowed to protect a tacit metaphysical naturalism by an explicit nonmetaphysical posturing. The secular naturalist has difficulty providing an adequate and defensible interpretative framework for his humanist values.[20]

The secular humanist has a second problem in defending his naturalistic assumptions about human beings. To assume naturalistic explanations is not the same thing as to prove them, even if one grants that the assumptions *might* be true. For example, how does one explain the emergence of human consciousness out of a mindless, material process, a consciousness that then proceeds to understand the process out of which it emerged? Or how does one finally prove that there is no core to the human self that transcends the electrochemical processes of the brain, a fact that is necessary if one is to reject the theistic contention that the self cannot be reduced to the biological organism or to deny that the self may in some way survive the death of the body.

Third, secular humanism is pressed to justify its belief in the worth and dignity of persons on a naturalistic basis. Here again, most secularists simply assume human worth as a given that is so self-evident it does not need to be argued. And then, curiously, although denying that there is any absolute ground or sanction for values, they tenaciously assert that the human person is *the* absolute value in the universe. But the more absolute that one holds to human value to be—as at their prophetic best secular humanists assert without qualification—then the more imperative that one be required rationally to justify that absolute value. I would contend that our human dignity is not at all self-evident within a naturalist worldview in which humans are only one more part of an ecological system that is sustained by life feeding off life, a system that is inherently wasteful of individual organisms, a system within which all individuals—including human individuals—are easily expendable. That is a "brute fact" which runs counter to the high estimate of human beings in secular humanism.[21]

Fourth, secular humanism has difficulty justifying or sustaining its visionary and noble humanitarian program for the world on a naturalistic foundation. Christians affirm the caring, engaged, world-embracing life-style advocated by secular humanists. It is questionable whether the secularist's commitment to an arbitrarily selected set of human values can provide the necessary sustaining impetus for the caring and visionary humanitarian life-style advocated by the secularists. Some years ago, Catholic philosopher Jacques Maritain observed that many of the major secular humanist values are the secularized residue of historic Christian values and that it is "in part Christian impulses gone astray which, in fact, existentially, move the hearts of men and rouse them to action."[22]

Fifth, secular humanists seem in their ethics to be torn between ethical relativism and a passionate advocacy of certain human values that take on, for many of them, the aura of absolute authority. Numerous major philosophical attempts have been made to provide a basis for affirming human values without the props of religious or metaphysical sanctions. It is, however, awkward at best to argue that there are no metaphysical absolutes and yet that some things—like the human person—matter absolutely. The major ethical works by secular humanists give the impression that secularists want to live by many values of the traditional religious conscience but without a metaphysical view adequate to sustain them.[23] It is not consistent to render *prophetic* judgment on inhuman practices on the basis of a mere arbitrary assumption of the value of human life.

Finally, secular humanism has existential limitations. Naturalism cannot provide satisfying answers to many individuals' deepest and most urgent existential questions and longings, particularly for some ultimate meaning to individual life and the cosmic process. Admittedly, there are various immanental answers to those questions. But those answers ignore one of the key factors in human experience— the incurable drive of individuals toward ultimacy, transcendence, or depth. The secularization of the sacred cannot alter the fact that humans remain, even in the twentieth-century secularized world, *homo religiosus.* Any definition of what it means to be a human being that ignores the human drive toward transcendence has not grasped the depths of an existing human being. That existential fact means that many people, in order to become fully human, must express their longings for the eternal and ground their own lives in the transcendent being who alone can actualize our full human potential.

To sum up, I have argued that Christians should affirm their broad common ground of concern for the human person with the secular humanist but at the same time bring pointed criticism to bear upon the naturalistic assumptions that are often not philosophically argued and the naturalistic worldview that, when clearly formulated, cannot provide an adequate rationale or sustaining motivation for the humanist vision to be translated into effective human action. That naturally raises the question of whether the humanist vision may be better founded and motivated from within a Christian worldview.

Christianity as a True Humanism

A true and full humanism requires a transcendent grounding. The Christian can contend that the Christian faith, and theism in general, provides a more coherent philosophical framework for interpreting and grounding humanist values and a more dynamic motivating and sustaining power for a program of action than do secular humanisms. That claim must be set against the secularist's charge that theistic religion often militates against the realization and fulfillment of the human person and the constructive shaping of life within history. In my judgment, their accusation does fit some institutional expressions of Christianity in its history. So one ought to admit that, historically and in the present era, there are some theological postures and practices within the church which do not enhance human values. There are groups that dehumanize persons and, in their eschatological hope, neglect the problems of history. In those and other cases, secular humanism may play a prophetic role in rendering judgment on any theology or institutional structure that does not affirm the worth of human beings and one's responsibility for life in this world during one's lifetime. The secular criticism could help a portion of the church to rediscover its own theological humanist roots and to articulate more precisely and live out more fully the humanist dimensions of the Christian faith. In admitting that some secular criticisms are at least partly accurate about certain institutional expressions of Christianity, a Christian can then go on to argue that the criticisms do not fit historical biblical Christianity at its best.

Biblical Christianity can provide a persuasive rationale for human values and surmount most of the deficiencies I have suggested within the naturalistic point of view. At the foundational level, Christianity provides a metaphysical framework within which to understand human life, one that is coherent and inclusive of all our human experience within the cosmos. Christianity explains why there should be a universe at all. The sufficient reason for the universe is a personal God who creates the universe through an act of will for His own creative and redemptive purposes. The universe is not just a brute fact that humans must accept; it is the setting for the divine-human drama of creation and redemption. Life and mind are not accidental chance emergents out of a blind, purposeless, strictly natural process; rather nature is the expression of the creative design and will of God.

The idea of creation offers a defensible basis for affirming the worth and dignity of human beings. Secular humanists can only make an arbitrary choice for human worth and dignity as the central value of an otherwise meaningless universe. An accidental quirk of a mechanical universe is the meaning and purpose of the universe! Christians, in contrast, affirm human worth because the Bible pictures humans as the focal point of the whole created order. Christians hold that humans are both continuous with and discontinuous from other life on earth. That fact is best captured in the biblical idea that humans are creatures made in the image of God. The idea of the image of God distinguishes humans from the rest of nature in a personal relationship with God. To be fully human is to be rightly related to God and to other people. This essential relation to God explains the unquenchable human drive toward ultimacy, transcendence, or depth. The idea of the image of God also underlines that the actualization of one's authentic humanity can only occur in community, so that when humans are related properly to one another they reflect the very nature of God Himself—a Trinitarian community in one divine Being. In short, the Christian humanist vision is founded in the nature of God. That is what the psalmist means in saying of the human, "Yet thou hast made him little less than God, and dost crown him with glory and honor." No higher assessment of the nature of a human being could be made than that! Humans are the highest value created by God.

Christians have a biblical basis for human *responsibility* for life on *this* earth. Secular humanists can only root human responsibility in the Promethean assumption that man is the master of his own fate in a purposeless and uncaring universe. The Christian holds that humans are responsible for their fate under God, a responsibility that is grounded in our freedom before God to make choices that affect the quality of our lives and our eternal destiny. Because God respects our freedom, He holds us accountable for the choices we make in relation to His purpose for creation and history. We are given choices under God to manage our lives and the planet in ways that enrich life and glorify God, a responsibility that is not an option but a mandate from God. In the creation, God commands that humans are to be His representatives on earth and are to exercise dominion over nature, humanize the historical process, and improve the quality of life on earth—in effect, to share creative responsibilities with God Himself (Gen. 1—2)! Our responsibility is for life in *this* world, a world created and redeemed by God. Hebrew religion has a this-worldly focus on the good life in God's world, a view basic to the Christian belief that God is redeeming the historical process, indeed, even the cosmos itself. The world, even in its fallenness and evil, is still God's good creation in the process of being redeemed. Christians have a responsibility for life in this world!

Christians can further explain why human beings fall so short of their authentic nature and do not reach their full potential and why so much inhumanity toward humans exists within the human family. Humanity is in contradiction between our existence and our essence —between our essential created goodness and our existential fallenness—which explains our potential for good and our compulsion toward evil. We frequently fall short of our highest standards and act in contradiction to our best intentions. The Christian diagnosis is that the very heart of our problem is our desire to live our lives apart from a relationship or responsibility to God—the Promethean pretension that is the foundation of secular humanism. In the Christian view, the idea of the fall describes a human race that has separated itself from the God who alone can provide the ontological ground for an authentic humanity. As creatures made in the image of God, humans can be most fully themselves only in relationship to God. The Christian view of sin explains why we act in ways that contribute to the human problem and also why we have a potential for reaching toward our authentic humanity and of humanizing life on earth.

Christianity offers hope for a new humanity and a new quality of historical life. The key to that possibility is Jesus Christ, who is both the model of and the way to authentic humanity. Christians believe that Jesus Christ embodied authentic humanity and makes it possible for others to become fully human, too. The biblical picture of Jesus is a portrait of the only fully authentic human being who has ever lived—in His relation to God, in His own selfhood, and in His relationships with other people. This historical man who perfectly embodied the image of God makes authentic humanity possible for people who believe in and follow Him. The reason is that in Christ, God was reconciling the world to Himself and estranged human beings to each other. In faith, people find a reconciliation of their own ambiguous, estranged existence with their essential human nature. In living out of the power of God's Holy Spirit, believers then have the power to love and serve human beings, to engage the problems and needs in personal relationships and in the larger social relationships of the world. This new human style of life is so paramount for the Christian that one of the powerful images for the church in the New Testament is that of the new humanity serving God and human beings in a fallen world.

In defining the nature of God and the purpose of human life, Christianity provides the basis for a transcendent humanist ethic. Because God is love and humans are made in the image of God to live in community, love for others is the natural expression of authentic humanity. The moral necessities or absolutes that many Christians believe are built into the universe, which reflect the nature of God and of authentic humanity, are the concrete applications of love to all areas of historical life. The moral imperatives glorify God and enrich the quality of authentic human life. Biblical religion is *for* humanity! But love makes tough demands in a fallen and dehumanizing world. Christians are redeemed in order to love other people and to serve human needs. Christian love affirms the worth and dignity of all other human beings, and therefore it respects the freedom and responsibility of others for their own lives and refuses to coerce them toward religion or even Christian standards of behavior. Christian love also translates into creative action on behalf of the unloved, the poor, the wronged, and all those who live less than a rewarding and fulfilling human life. To ignore the urgent human problems and needs of the world is to violate the new nature of love that is to be reflected in Christian believers for all human beings.

Finally, Christianity offers hope for human life beyond death. The hope is partly personal. Christians believe that the value of the human person is so great that God gave His Son to enter the historical process and to reconcile the new humanity to Himself for eternity. The worth of the essential human person is so great that the self has eternal significance. The human individual who lives an authentic human life in relation to God will live eternally in his or her essential selfhood in a perfect union with God and all other redeemed persons. That hope places eternal importance upon our responsible living within the historical process. God has said "yes" to humanity, history, and creation in His incarnation in Jesus Christ. When God became man in Jesus Christ, He sanctified the value of human life as human for ever! Our daily human lives in this world bear an eternal weight of glory!

For this reason, the Christian hope is also partly historical and social. History and creation will be redeemed. At the end of history, God will set right the balances between good and evil in a judgment in which people will be accountable for how they have used their responsibility to serve God and the human family. Admittedly, the hoped-for glory of the future age could lead people into an other-worldly preoccupation—but only if they misunderstand the nature of the Christian hope. The future kingdom of God has broken into history in Jesus Christ, constantly presses into our present history, and will come in fullness at the end of history. When rightly understood, the coming kingdom becomes a dynamic motivator of human action in our present history. The church is called to help God actualize within history, as far as possible, the values of the future kingdom of God, so that justice, equality, peace, and human fulfillment begin to take root in our present world. The future hope is a redemptive perfecting of God's original intentions for creation and humanity—an eternity in which authentic human beings live creatively in love before the Creator.

In summary, the Christian response to secular humanism ought to involve a complex dialectical yes and a no. Christians share many elements in the secular humanist's commitment to humanity and human values. In a broken and often cruel and dehumanizing era, Christians should reach out to allies who are *for* humanity and can cooperate with us in areas that affect the quality of human life on earth. We can struggle together against poverty, ignorance, malnutrition, racism, war, political tyranny, and numerous other evils of the modern world. We can agree about the worth of each human individual and the importance of each person finding fulfillment in this life—even though we disagree about *how* this can be done. It is likely that the common core of humanist values that are agreed upon by all humanists, religious and secular, are the only adequate basis for living together in a pluralistic world where people do not hold the same ultimate commitments. In those areas, the secular humanist is a companion in the human struggle. The Christian insistence that human value can be fully grounded only in God should not lessen one's straightforward affirmation of humanity. What is not acceptable for the Christian is to react so sharply to the secular humanist's effort to affirm humanity without God that the Christian appears to be for God and against humanity. The world must not be offered the false choice of God without humanity or humanity without God. The Christian and the secular humanist are both for humanity. And we ought to say so!

At the same time, the Christian must insist that the secularist's intentions and convictions transcend the foundation upon which his humanism is based. We should not hesitate to bring a reasoned critique to the weaknesses of the naturalistic basis for humanism or to assert the superior rationale of the Christian faith for human value. If authentic humanity is defined in a relationship with God as well as with other humans, then Christianity provides a cogent and comprehensive basis for most of the human values so important to the secularist. If one interprets the full human dimensions of the Christian faith, one can make a powerful case that Christianity is the true humanism, one that is *for* humanity as the focus of the creative purpose of the eternal God. Humans are the creatures *of* God, made in His own image. Christians must not allow secular humanists to capture for their own a secularized version of the humanist commitment at the heart of the biblical revelation. In the Christian-secular humanist encounter, our motto could well be: For God's sake and humanity's future, let's be human! And then interpret what it means to be an authentic human being in God's world!

6
Marxism:
History as Autonomous

In 1846 young philosopher Karl Marx wrote, "The philosophers have only interpreted the world in various ways; the point is to change it."[1] And change it he did! Marx's ideas have captured millions of minds, impacted the politics and economics of every continent, and altered the shape of twentieth-century societies in more than one third of the earth. Although many people who live in communist states are not themselves Marxists, Marxist ideology dominates most of the public life and education in those states. Offering revolutionary hope to the economically deprived, Marxism holds a magnetic attraction for numerous people within Third World countries and even many technologically advanced Western countries. Within every contemporary society, there are dedicated Marxists who embrace Marx's worldview and revere Marx himself, in the words of French Marxist Roger Garaudy, as "the father of 20th-century man's greatest hope!"[2] Garaudy confidently proclaims, "Marxism is not only *a* philosophy of our time. It is our time's *sense.*"[3]

Oddly enough, the average Westerner, particularly an American, is not well informed about Marxism. Western attitudes are often developed only from hearing anticommunist political rhetoric that sometimes distorts or obscures the Marxist worldview. In fact, as the most radical revolutionary movement of the twentieth century, contemporary forms of communism do not always reflect the views of Marx. Twentieth-century Communism has been shaped also by interpretations and modifications of Marx by thinkers like Marx's own colleague Engels, Lenin, Stalin, Mao, and a range of other twentieth-century Marxists. Consequently, there are sharp divergencies in Marxist thought and political movements today.

Christians must face the challenge of Marxism. The first step is to achieve an accurate understanding of Marxism and of elements within it that attract so many people. That can best be done by focusing primarily on the thought of Karl Marx rather than through an extended study of Soviet or Chinese forms of Communism. Although no modern communist state has yet embodied the pure vision of Marx and all are heavily impacted by later Communist thinkers, Marx remains the most revered authority for those states. Undoubtedly, Marx is the visionary prophet who captures the highest ideals and motivation of social revolutionaries throughout the world. Because of the multifaceted character of Marx's thought, various people learn from Marx even though they may reject the comprehensive Marxist worldview. Even some Christian theologians in recent years, particularly in the Third World, have entered into dialogue with Marxism, and some selectively appropriate certain Marxist economic analyses in order better to understand and contribute to the human quest for social and economic justice. It is in the thought of Karl Marx—and his close ally Engels—that the worldview and inner logic of Communism are best seen.

It is not easy to grasp the thought of Marx himself—for a number of reasons. Marx was a major philosopher, social critic, economist, political theorist, and periodically a revolutionary activist. The internal development of his thought is complex and not always fully consistent. His own thought is often hammered out in interaction with an astounding array of thinkers, primarily found, as Lenin said, in German philosophy, British economics, and French socialism.[4] Major studies focus on Marx's utilization and modification of philosophers like Fichte, Kant, Hegel, and Feuerbach and trace the extension of his ideas in Engels, Lenin, Stalin, Mao, and numerous other Communist theorists. The voluminous critical writings on Marx are evidence that his thought can be studied from many disciplinary interests and angles.

Obviously, the thought of Karl Marx, to say nothing of Communism as a whole, cannot be treated comprehensively in one brief chapter. Our apologetic concern, however, is not primarily with the intricacies of Marx's economic theories or specific political analyses of events in his own nineteenth century. The enduring challenge for the Christian church is the worldview, the belief and value system, of Marxism that grows out of and is linked with Karl Marx's analysis of the historical situation of humanity. In this chapter, we will examine the heart of Marx's worldview, chart the common concerns between Marxism and Christianity, suggest points of vulnerability in the Marxist vision, and indicate how Christianity can better address some of the Marxist concerns.

The Marxist Worldview

What is it about Marxism that attracts so many people? The heart of its appeal is Marxism's concern with our actual, concrete situation in the world and its intention to change the world. Marxism links thought with action and theory with practice. Marx claimed to develop a broadly scientific approach to reality that begins with an objective examination of humanity within the historical process. From that starting point, Marx formulated his laws of historical development, his interpretation of the nature and meaning of life, his vision of the goal of the future, and his view of the working class as the chief actors in taking revolutionary action to achieve that future. Marx then offered a hope of a future when people will live together in peace, economic equality, and brotherhood without the necessity of a coercive state. The result is a worldview that is atheistic, naturalistic, materialistic, and humanistic. We will examine Marxism as praxis, historical materialism, naturalistic humanism, and a critique of religion.

Marxism as Praxis

One obvious appeal of Marxism to many sensitive, idealistic, activistic people is its emphasis on praxis—practical activity. In his youth, Marx studied classical philosophy and critically interacted with many of the major sources of his own thought (for example, Fichte, Hegel, and Feuerbach, among others). As one of the brilliant circle of young Hegelians, Marx expended great energy "thinking out" ideas. At about age twenty-six, Marx realized that most brilliant philosophical ideas have left the world as it had been before. So he developed a revolutionary new approach when he wrote: "The question of whether objective truth can be attributed to human thinking is not a question of theory but is a practical question. Man must prove the truth . . . in practice."[5] He criticized earlier German philosophy for beginning its speculative thought in heaven and only then descending to earth instead of beginning with active, in-the-flesh humans in their real-life process. It is this concrete life that determines human consciousness as expressed in history, religion, morality, and metaphysics. "Where speculation ends," writes Marx, "where real life starts, there consequently begins real, positive science, the expounding of the practical activity, of the practical process of the development of men."[6]

Practice is the starting point and goal of Marxist thought, and science is the instrument for understanding and directing practical activity. Marx engaged in massive historical, political, economic, as well as philosophical study in order to understand what people do and why they do it, not for the sake of knowledge but to understand the world in order to change it. The world cannot be changed by new ideas unless the ideas lead to revolutionary action. Marx's scientific study led him to cooperate knowledgeably with the dialectical forces of history that he thought were inevitably moving the world toward a future communist society.

Historical Materialism

Marx's general philosophy is often described as historical materialism or dialectical materialism, although Marx himself never used those words. Marx provides the clearest compact statement of historical materialism in *The German Ideology*, which he coauthored with Friedrich Engels. Engels defines historical materialism as "that view of the course of history which seeks the ultimate cause and the great moving power of all important historic events in the economic development of society, in the changes of the modes of production and exchange, in the consequent division of society into distinct classes, and in the struggles of those classes against one another."[7]

Dialectical materialism.—In its conviction that the economic development of society is the *ultimate* explanation of history, Marxism is clearly a materialistic form of naturalism. Naturalism is a philosophical view that accepts the brute fact of nature and finds all explanations of nature and history strictly within nature. Within its naturalistic framework, Marxism then holds that the material world, not mind or consciousness, is the key to everything within history. Marx's materialism is not the crude speculative view that matter is the only reality and that everything in nature and history can be reduced to matter and is materially determined. Marxist materialism is practical and concrete. Its premises focus on real living people in their activity within their surrounding material world as the matrix out of which everything in history derives. Marx was indifferent to speculation about the origin of the universe and the nature of matter itself—questions that he thought abstract from real life. Marx was concerned with matter only as we encounter it in the material world of living beings. Marx scientifically explained how humans arise out of the material conditions of the world and in turn influence those conditions through production and social relationships.[8]

Marx's historical materialism is also dialectical, an idea he drew from the idealist Hegel and modified into materialism. Dialectic refers to the conflicting economic forces within history—basically the forces of production and the social relations of production—that produce new levels or syntheses within the process. Based upon his scientific observation of these forces, Marx formulated his laws of the dialectical movement of history. The basic law is that at a certain stage of economic development within each major historical era, the modes or forces of production conflict with existing forms of social relations. The resulting class conflict leads to a revolution in the economic foundation and consequently in the whole superstructure of society. The conflict between economically determined classes is the primary mover of the dialectic. History, says Marx, "is the history of class struggles."[9]

Using these laws, Marx developed a scientific, comprehensive materialistic explanation of history that integrates everything from the material world to the highest levels and creations of human consciousness. Marx traced the dialectic through the broad historical periods, showing how each era grows out of the conflicts of the previous era and obeys the same economic laws as did all preceding eras. Each stage of history possesses new characteristics, but it builds upon all previous history and its possibilities are partly determined by its immediate preceding state. History is a single, nonrepetitive process of continual change. The decisive revolutionary shifts occur rapidly because of the historically determined conflict between economic forces.[10]

Work: the key to history.—Labor plays a central role in the economic process and for Marxism is *the* critical key to human nature, human history, and even nature itself. In linking humans and nature, work is the instrument that humanizes nature and naturalizes humans. Through work humans create themselves and all of human history. Early humans became self-conscious of themselves as humans and distinguished themselves from animals when they first began to produce their means of subsistence instead of merely taking what nature provided. In producing, they began to create themselves. "What they are," writes Marx, "therefore, coincides with their production, both with what they produce and with *how* they produce. Hence what individuals are depends on the material conditions of their production."[11] Their initial satisfaction of subsistence needs produced new needs which they worked further to satisfy. In the process humans modified nature so that nature now bears the fruit of human labor. Work requires that people enter into social relationships, beginning with the family and then extending into all wider social relationships. Work produces human consciousness and all its creative expressions in culture, philosophy, religion, ethics, politics, and so on. All ideology is the product of labor, and its peculiar character in a given era is determined by the era's type of relations between the forces and relationships of production. Work in its highest sense is creative and has dignity.

Work, however, is also the cause of what is fundamentally wrong in history. In early human history, work produced a division of labor in which individual people performed different tasks. The division of labor led to an exchange of goods, which resulted in the accumulation of private property and the alienation of people from the products of their work. It created economic classes and produced class conflict. In each succeeding era, one class controlled the means and reaped the rewards of production, and the other class provided the labor. Each stage in labor determines a corresponding form of property. In every era, there are the exploiters and the exploited. The privileged minority controls private property and accumulates the capital upon which modern production depends, and the working majority provide the labor necessary for the owner's profit. The end result has been an unequal distribution in society, both quantitative and qualitative, of labor and private property or capital throughout history. The division of labor and private property creates a fundamental alienation of human individuals from each other and from their own true humanity.[12]

Marx roughly traced the development of these divisions from tribal property to ancient communal or state property to feudal or estate property on into modern capitalist economies where the class division is increasingly between the proletariat (the workers) and the bourgeoisie (the capitalists). Class structure always determines the consciousness and ideological views of a society. The dominating consciousness of a society—its government, law, ethics, religion, and culture—is always determined by the ruling class. At a given stage of development within each historical era, the forces of production come into conflict with the relations of production. This leads to a revolution in the economic foundation of society that transforms the whole superstructure of society—the family, morality, religion, culture, and the state—and initiates a new historical era.[13]

The modern crisis.—Marx's view of the present modern crisis was rooted in his economic analysis of the nineteenth century. Even his critics often grant that, right or wrong, Marx was the first great scientific socioeconomist, particularly as reflected in his *Capital*. His extensive economic analyses and theories are too technical and vast to be treated in the present discussion, but the implications of those theories for his analysis of the present historical crisis and worldview can be stated briefly.

Productive labor is the key factor in economic life. In early history, the value of a product was equal to the labor that produced it. Products were directly exchanged for other products or through the intermediary of money on the basis of use value, with the producer enjoying the full value of his labor. As economic life developed into the era of class division and private property, workers began to produce a surplus value in the product that made the exchange value of a product worth more than the labor that produced it. The surplus value went to the owners or ruling class. In the modern industrial era, capitalists own the capital and the means of production and workers supply the labor; labor that produces more value than it receives.[14]

In every historical era the possessors of property or wealth have reaped the rewards of the workers' labor. Although Marx was not consistent in his designation of classes in modern society, he broadly typed the two emerging historically dominating classes as the proletariat and the bourgeoisie. He projected that in modern capitalist states both the rate of profit of capitalists and the standard of living of workers would begin to decline. Capitalists could then cope with the problem of declining profits either by increasing labor's productivity through utilizing more machines and less labor or by cheapening the cost of raw materials through colonial expansion. The workers themselves would ensure that wages remain at a subsistence level because of the competition among workers threatened by the unemployed masses. All of this would be a part of the series of crises in the inevitable clash of the proletariat and the bourgeoisie that would produce the proletarian revolution.[15]

Marx was never more eloquent than when writing about the life of economic alienation and dehumanization of the proletariat within the capitalist system—a situation that unquestionably existed in Europe and the United States in the mid-nineteenth century and persists in many countries today. He sketched a picture of workers dominated by owners, made appendages of machines, laboring in inhumane conditions, with their lives defined in terms of working time. Workers are entitled to the rewards of their labor only as long as they produce a surplus value that goes to the capitalists. They must be overproducers in order to be consumers. They are further impoverished as capitalists create demands for unnecessary products that extract the worker's last money. Living under capitalist despotism, workers were being fragmented as human beings.[16] Marx launched a protest on behalf of workers that shook the economic foundation of Western societies.

Marx was convinced that the historical dialectic was inevitably about to compel a proletarian revolution that would move the world from capitalism through socialism to communism. The world conditions were emerging as capitalists were forging multinational corporations and workers were becoming conscious of themselves as a worldwide proletarian class. Revolution is essential to the achievement of a communist future because material power can only be changed through material power. Because history is always built upon the heritage and within the limits of preceding eras, it is only in a class revolution that the proletariat can "succeed in ridding itself of all the muck of the ages and become fitted to found society anew."[17] A new society will require new human beings who have overcome alienation.

Marx was involved much of his own life in the social revolutions that rocked Europe in the mid-nineteenth century. His views changed in relation to various historical situations in Europe. His *Communist Manifesto* of 1848, which was coauthored with Engels, was a call to action to communist and socialist groups in Europe and to workers throughout the world. He viewed the Communist party as the vanguard of the proletarian revolution, as better understanding history and the direction of the revolutionary proletarian movement, and as representing the proletariat in revolutionary struggles. The closing words of the *Manifesto* have remained a rallying cry for Communists ever since: "Let the ruling classes tremble at a Communist revolution. The proletarians have nothing to lose but their chains. They have a world to win. Working men of the world, unite."[18]

Marx sanctioned violent revolution when necessary, including even the brutal excesses of the Paris Commune uprising. There is some ambiguity in his thought about whether the revolution would be necessarily over a longer period of time or short and catastrophic. Toward the end of his life Marx, unlike some of the more militant Communist revolutionaries, thought that varied types of change would occur in the world. Because of social conditions in the United States and England, for example, he thought that in them there would be a gradual evolution toward communism. Yet in many other countries the change would be rapid and violent. His projections were based on what he considered to be observable trends.[19]

Marx was sure that the revolution would lead to a stage of socialism, the dictatorship of the proletariat, before the final Communist society could emerge. During that time the proletariat will replace the bourgeoisie as the ruling class. In order to seize power from the bourgeoisie, the revolution will require despotic measures such as the abolition of private property, the centralization of instruments of production in the hands of the state, compulsory free public education for all children, and similar measures. The Communist party itself will be the primary actor during that transitional time on behalf of the proletariat. Police and armed services would be retained to prevent the bourgeoisie from again seizing power. But in the course of altering the old conditions of production, the proletariat dictators will sweep away the conditions for the existence of classes and class antagonisms, and, in the process, will abolish its own supremacy as a class and lead to a pure communist society.[20]

The future hope.—The final stage of history will be a worldwide communist society. Marx did not think it possible to provide a detailed picture of the character of the ideal society. With the elimination of classes, there will be no need for controlling authority, which means there will be no state, standing army, judiciary, prisons, or industrial bureaucracy. Crime will be eliminated because the environmental conditions that produce criminals will have been humanized. Religions and traditional morality will wither away, and society will be governed in its relationships by mutual responsibility for the other. Marriage will alter, in that wives will no longer be the property of the husband and children will be the responsibility of the whole society. All class divisions will disappear, and there will be no antithesis between mental work and physical work or between town and country.[21]

In the communist economy, production and distribution will be organized to satisfy the needs of everyone in society. This alternation will both require and produce a new type of human, one who is no longer separated from the product of labor, from other people, or from oneself. Machines will enable the elimination of much drudgery and menial work. Labor itself will be flexible, so that the individual may choose his kind of work and change activities as one desires. Working hours will be limited and work once again will be creative and fulfilling. The communist society will go beyond equal pay for equal work to the principle of "from each according to his ability, to each according to his needs."[22] Above all, there will be a maximum attainment of human freedom that interlocks the fulfillment of individuals and society, "an association in which the free development of each is the condition for the free development of all."[23]

As a future hope based upon a scientific analysis of historical patterns and trends, Marxism has a confident optimism that it is freely cooperating with the inevitable economic dialectic that history is compelling. Consequently, the Marxist hope is grounded in a supreme faith in its own reading of reality. Commitment and sacrifice become the mode of a convinced Marxist's life. Its aggressive effort to change the world toward the certain future is undoubtedly one of Marxism's major appeals to people all over the world who care about the massive injustices and economic inequalities of the world. They still say with Marx, "The proletarians have nothing to lose but their chains. They have a world to win."[24]

Naturalistic Humanism

Marxism is a humanism that affirms the value and dignity of human beings, a humanism that is atheistic, naturalistic, materialistic, and social. With its rigid economic focus, it is earthbound and earth oriented as it aims to eliminate the basic problem and achieve the highest fulfillment of humanity. In denying the existence of God, Marxism assigns to humanity the highest value and creative power in the universe, a status that religion has traditionally reserved for God. The young Marx saluted the Greek Prometheus for saying, "In a word, I hate all the Gods," and suggested those words as a motto against all gods that do not admit human consciousness as the supreme divinity.[25] Humans are the chief actors in nature and history.

Marxism insists upon a strict scientific approach to understanding human life and therefore rules out any value in philosophical speculation or theological dogmatics. Human nature can only be understood within its concrete material and historical situation, and science is the only method for such an examination. Although certain characteristics and needs, such as sex and hunger, are common to all humans, human nature and relative needs are modified in each historical epoch. Even science cannot form an abstract theory of the nature of the human species apart from the individual's specific involvement in a particular social class and historical era.[26] There is no universal human nature.

Naturalism and materialism.—Marxist humanism is rooted in naturalism and materialism. Since Marxism holds that there is no creator to define human nature or purpose, it begins with naturalistic assumptions and the material world that precedes and gives rise to humanity. Humans, like other animals, are linked in the chain of naturalistic biological evolution that arises out of inorganic matter. Marx rejected the possibility of any ultimate explanation of the universe. He argued that questions about the origin of the material world and the first humans abstract from the concrete situation of humans in nature, postulate them both as not existing, and then ask a theoretical question about how they come to exist. Such an abstraction from *actual* existence has no meaning since a living human must ask the question.[27]

Marxist humanism is materialistic not in the sense that all dimensions of human life can be reduced to matter but that the material world is the starting point for understanding human life. Humans eat before they think, and it is out of their material needs in the material world that consciousness arises. As natural beings, humans have natural powers and faculties—tendencies, abilities, drives—that are directed toward and limited by material objects outside themselves, objects that they need and that are essential to the exercise and fulfillment of human drives. The human being creates himself as a natural, embodied, sentient, social being through the exercise of free choice in relation to the material world and within the limitations and conditions of nature and the social context.[28] Marx assumed the innate goodness and perfectability of humans and the power of human reason, as modified by his focus on the industrial context and political economics—an assumption essential to his projection for a perfect humanity in the ideal communist society.[29] Freedom is the highest ideal for human life and, although severely limited for the proletariat in the present alienated history, it will be the dominating characteristic of the future communist world.

Social humanism.—Humanism for Marx is social or communal. "In reality," wrote Marx, "the essence of man is the totality of social relations."[30] The individual is always defined in relationships. Marx often said that man is a species-being, which is his way of referring to the individual's self-conscious awareness of himself as belonging to humanity and acting as a member of the community.[31] An individual's peculiar human characteristics are developed in social activities.[32] Marxism is often accused of valuing collective humanity to the exclusion of the individual so that the individual is always expendable for the sake of society or the future communist world. Such an accusation is often warranted when directed toward the history of the Soviet Union, China, or other communist-dominated countries. It is also true that even Marx himself was willing to override the individual's will or interests during the revolutionary socialist period that leads to the future communist society. But in the future communist society, the individual's highest dignity, value, and freedom are best fulfilled when the value of society as a whole is achieved and all coercion is eliminated and free choice is open to all.

Self-creativity and alienation.—Human self-creativity through the instrument of work is a major focus of Marxism. Man is *homo faber*, man the producer. Work is *the* creative force of the world—in human life, nature, and history. Humans first rise to human self-consciousness when they begin to produce the means of their own subsistence, such as food, clothing, and shelter. In working to alter the external world for their own ends, humans create their own nature by distinguishing themselves from animals, exerting inner control, and unleashing the potentialities that lie within them.[33] At the same time, they humanize nature in adapting it to human purposes. Production requires social relations, so first the family and then wider social relations emerge. With social relations come the human creations of culture, law, ethics, political relationships, and religion—the great achievements of human consciousness. Humans are the creators of nature and history, and there is no need for any other creator.[34]

Within the present concrete human situation, humans are far from the ideal human nature that they were at the beginning of history and from what they will be in the future communist age. Marx had two ways of expressing the economic source of what is wrong in humanity. In his early life, Marx called the problem "alienation," and in his later life, private property and class struggle. In Marx's thought, private property and alienation are closely entwined. Alienation produces private property, and private property produces alienation. Marx distinguished at least three ways in which alienation manifests itself in the development of political economy.[35]

First, humans are alienated from the products of their labor as the products become commodities that belong to the owners of the means of production. The worker no longer fulfills himself and enjoys the product of his own labor; instead the laborer himself becomes a *means* for producing commodities and surplus value for others. Because he must produce commodities for others in order to exist at a mere subsistence level himself, the worker becomes a slave to the products he produces.

Second, humans are alienated from the act of labor, which is a form of self-alienation since humans are essentially defined by creative labor. No longer do workers freely exercise their creative powers and find authentic fulfillment, but they are forced to do work determined by others. The owner dictates the purpose, means, and method of a laborer's work, work that is often degrading, boring, depersonalizing, and often dehumanizing. The forced laborer is unhappy and discontented in his work. His only freedom and leisure are in functions he shares with other animals like eating, drinking, and procreating, not in functions distinctive of a human being. "What is animal becomes human," wrote Marx, "and what is human becomes animal."[36] In being separated from creative labor, a human being is alienated from himself.

Third, humans are alienated from species-life. Creative labor is what defines the human species over against other animals. But alienated labor loses its creative quality, and the individual *must* work in order to earn enough to maintain his bare subsistence. When labor, which is the distinctive characteristic of the life of the human species, becomes a *means* to the subsistence of *individual* life, the result is that the individual is alienated from other individuals. There are masters and slaves, owners and workers, exploiters and exploited. In profiting from the labor of others, capitalists are alienated from their own authentic being in creative work and define themselves in terms of having, of the accumulation of property and capital. Private property is the supreme form of having, and it requires that the many work for the benefit of the few. Consequently, all human beings, capitalists and workers, are alienated from the authentic character of the human species.

Marx's analysis of alienation culminated in his analysis of the destructive power of money, which he called "the alienated *ability of mankind.*"[37] In bourgeois society, money takes on the omnipotence of divinity, defines the nature of the human self, and determines the limits of one's power. "That which exists for me through the medium of *money,*" said Marx, "that which I can pay for [that is, which money can buy], that *I am,* the possessor of the money. My own power is as great as the power of money. The properties of money are my own [the possessor's] properties and faculties. What *I am* and *can do* is, therefore, not at all determined by my *individuality.*"[38] Money can transform human qualities into their opposites, and this inversion of qualities can cause incompatible forces in society to embrace for the sake of money.[39] Money no longer aims to satisfy human needs but to create new needs that drive people to sacrifice, to become dependent on the new need, and then to seek gratification in a newer need, all to the profit of the capitalist and the economic ruin of the consumer.[40] Industrial capitalists use fantasy, caprice, and whim to charm a few more pennies out of their neighbors. Marx contended that the more money one has, the less human and more estranged one is.[41] Thus the accumulation of money dehumanizes both the capitalist and the proletarian and is a consummate symbol of alienation.

Critique of Religion

Marxism is atheistic and critical of religion for a number of reasons. As a historical materialism, Marxism denies the existence of God.

Marx himself became an atheist as a young man. He was convinced that God cannot exist within the territory of reason and that proofs for the existence of God are actually proofs for his nonexistence.[42] He further concluded that belief in a dictatorial God eliminates authentic human freedom and responsibility. He rejected belief in God not so much because he was against God as that he was for humanity. In his doctoral dissertation, Marx called Prometheus "the noblest of saints and martyrs in the calendar of philosophy" for asserting that he would rather be chained to a rock than be bound in the service of the god Zeus.[43]

Marx later came to view religion as a fundamental expression of human alienation. His basic principle of criticism is, "Man makes religion, religion does not make man."[44] Religion is a particularly pernicious form of alienation in that it focuses human hope in a world beyond history, sanctions class divisions, and prevents revolutionary activity by drugging the economic pain of the oppressed. Consequently, Marx argues, "The criticism of religion is the presupposition of all criticisms."[45] One reason that Marx envisioned an imminent proletarian revolution was his judgment that the criticism of religion had virtually been completed in Germany as the cumulative thought of intellectuals like Hegel, Feuerbach, and the young Hegelians had exposed the illusion and alienation of religion and redirected human attention to humanity. The true hope of humanity is not heaven but earth.[46]

Marx's critique of religion focused on its beliefs and its institutional expressions. Why do people hold religious beliefs? Marx had a simple answer. Religious beliefs are illusions that project human hope for a more ideal material life into an imaginary heavenly world. Marx was heavily influenced by Ludwig Feuerbach. A materialist and humanist, Feuerbach contended that the idea of God is a psychological projection of the ideal qualities and perfections of the human race into an imaginary being called God, which results in humanity's alienation from its own best qualities. Hence, Feuerbach argued that the proper focus of humanity is humanity. Marx agreed with Feuerbach that religion is an illusion, but he explained it somewhat differently. The reason for the religious projection is economic alienation. The mass of humanity, living in unjust and inhumane economic conditions, inverts the world's prevailing values and projects as a future hope a perfect world of authentic human values—love, freedom, justice, equality, and relief from the pain of economic misery.[47]

Marx's view of religion was complex, and he recognized that religion has played both a constructive and a negative role in history. During earlier history, religion has served a constructive function in one way. Despite being an ideological expression of economic alienation, religion has nevertheless provided consolation to help make life bearable for the oppressed. In a famous statement, Marx wrote, "Religious misery is in one way the expression of real misery. Religion is the sigh of the afflicted creature, the soul of a heartless world, as it is also the spirit of spiritless conditions. It is the *opium* of the people."[48] Marxism's criticism of religious belief is a demand for people to give up illusionary happiness for real happiness, which in turn is a demand to change the economic conditions that require religious illusions. "Hence," wrote Marx, "the criticism of religion is in embryo a *criticism of this vale of tears* whose halo is religion."[49] The criticism of heaven turns out to be a criticism of earth.

Although religion is an ideology that originates in the projected illusionary hopes of the oppressed, the dominating religious ideology of a historical era, like all ideology, basically expresses the values and serves the interests of the ruling class. Religion focuses the hope of the economically oppressed on another world and teaches principles like self-contempt, humility, and submission—all of which drug human impulses toward radical economic change. Since institutional religion and its teachings serve the interests of the ruling class, Marx rejected the efforts of religious reformers who appealed to the social principles of Christianity as the basis for economic reform. He caustically observed that the social principles of Christianity (meaning the institutional church) have justified slavery and medieval serfdom, defended the oppression of the proletariat, preached the necessity of an oppressive ruling class, and resisted radical economic reform.[50] In fact, Marx argued, when early human beings became alienated, priests were their first ideologists.

Marx's critique of religion is a criticism of the economic conditions that produce religion. He insists that the critique of unjust conditions must not be confined to the level of ideas but that it set material force against material force. In Marx's words, "The criticism of religion ends with the doctrine that *man is the highest being for man,* hence with the *categorial imperative to overthrow all conditions* in which man is a degraded, enslaved, abandoned, contemptible being."[51] In modern communist societies, religion has been barred in public life and education because religion is the classic expression of the human alienation that communist revolutionary activity is struggling to overcome. Communist states usually tolerate private religious faith and limited religious gatherings, as long as religious people do not evangelize. At the same time, religious people are barred from the Communist party and from many social opportunities because of the conviction that the dominating ideology of a society must always be that of the ruling class, which, in a communist society, means the atheistic proletariat dictators of the transitional socialist state. Marxists remain confident that once society has passed through the proletariat's dictatorship of the socialist phase into the rulerless communist future state, humanity will then have no need for the narcotic of religion. Religion will disappear in the inevitable outworking of the economic dialectic of history.

The Marxist critique of religion becomes a primary symbol of its naturalistic-humanistic worldview. Atheism and the critique of religion are unarguably not incidental but essential and central to Marxism. Christianity and a *comprehensive* ideological Marxism clash head-on on numerous critical matters. They are incompatible and irreconcilable worldviews.

A Christian Response to Marxism

Contemporary Marxism represents perhaps the most militant, aggressive, visionary, and engaged ideological rival to the Christian faith in the modern era. The Marxist advocates a coherent, tight-knit, and relatively simple worldview that can be easily interpreted to non-Marxists and is particularly appealing to inhabitants of the Third and Fourth Worlds where poverty and injustice exist and people struggle to find a better life. Marxism has great appeal as well to people in the East and West who are sympathetic to the economic suffering of much of the modern world.

How should a Christian apologist defend the Christian faith against the accusations of Marxists or in dialogue with passionate Marxists? In many parts of the world, this is one of the church's greatest challenges. It is simply a fact that a Christian will not accomplish much unless we are willing to accept the legitimate criticisms of Marxists against Christianity and affirm as much common ground and values as possible between Marxism and Christianity. Only then is the Christian in a position to criticize the Marxist worldview, show how Christianity takes into account some legitimate Marxist values, and demonstrate the superiority of Christianity as a worldview.

What Christians and Marxists Have in Common

When Christianity and Marxism are at their ideological best, they share a great deal of common ground—possibly because Marxism may well represent a secularization of a number of Christian ideals and historical hopes. A good starting point for the Christian-Marxist dialogue is to affirm whatever common ground we share.

Praxis and history.—Praxis is a good place to begin. Both Christians and Marxists place first emphasis upon praxis—the fact that we are called not merely to think about the world but to change it. Christians ought to recognize and admit that many contemporary Marxists are more rigorously committed to changing the world through aggressive activity than are many contemporary Christians. That is a severe indictment of the church. Christians can also agree with Marxists that an adequate worldview must apply to the real-life situation of existing human beings, which requires that the starting point and frame of reference for thinking about reality is not some ideological abstraction but the actual concrete situation of human beings in the world.

Here Christians and Marxists hold several ideas in common. One is that human beings are the chief natural actors in history, so that we make history and are not merely the products of history. Christians, of course, insist that history itself, within which humans are primary creaturely actors, is ultimately the story of creation and redemption that involves both divine and human action. But history is important. Christians and Marxists both hope for an ideal future upon this earth, although we disagree about the nature of that hope and future. In many ways, Marx's vision of the Communist utopia is arguably a secularization of important elements of the Christian hope that can be perfectly realized only in a future that embraces while transcending history.

But Christian faith, while focused on transcendent reality, is also, like Marxism, firmly rooted in history. Contrary to Marx's accusation about the otherworldliness of Christianity, most Christians have held that an element of our eschatological hope is for an ideal future *upon* the earth or a brief manifestation *within* history of that ideal transcendent future. Because the hope is historical as well as transcendent, Christians are called upon by God to attempt to make actual within present history those ideals of the future coming kingdom of God, while knowing that they can be perfectly realized only in a future that transcends the earth. For that reason, Christians and Marxists share a commitment to praxis, the need for revolutionary activity to change radically the world's prevailing structures of evil, although we strongly disagree about the causes of evil and what is acceptable revolutionary activity. The Communist fervency in responding to Marx's call, "Working men of all countries, unite!" based upon his conviction that workers have a world to win, ought to stand in judgment over many Christians who respond indifferently to the call of Jesus to His followers to help eradicate the oppressive evils of the world.

Values within the world.—Despite the contrasting worldviews, Christianity and Marxism share some common values, although Christians will modify or qualify those values. The largest area of common ground is many of the human values espoused by Marx—such as the central value of humanity, the worth of all people, the need to humanize nature and the economy, and human responsibility to shape history and nature—values that have sometimes been denied by twentieth-century communism as its worst. No less than Marxists, Christians affirm the value of *this* world and of people living productive, happy, and fulfilled lives within it, although Christians subordinate the world's values to those of the kingdom of God.

Christians and Marxists both affirm the importance of work to human history. Work is vital to making humans human, although Marxists view it as the crucial distinction between humans and animals, and Christians view it as a primary mandate to exercising our uniqueness as creatures made in the image of God. Both agree about the alienating dimension of such labor, the contradiction between the ideal creative nature of labor and the actual drudgery of much labor, although Marxists view economic processes as the cause of alienation, and Christians hold that it results from human sin (Gen. 3). Yet however different the two analyses about why work is central and alienation a fact, both agree about the powerful role of economic life—the forms and relations of production—in the formation of society, ideology, and historical change. Although Marx overstated case, modern Christians grant that one can formulate descriptive laws of historical change that make possible a high level of predictability about how society functions within historical processes.

Christians can concur with much of Marx's critique of economic and social injustice and alienation in society and affirm his prophetic passion for the poor and exploited laborers in the modern economy. If Christians had embodied the teachings of the prophets or of Jesus Himself about the poor, the oppressed, and the exploited (Luke 4:18-19), Marx's criticism of religion should have been radically altered. Similarly, Christians ought to affirm many of Marx's observations about the power of money over people and its dehumanizing exploitative role in modern economies. Jesus repeatedly condemned those who accumulate riches and oppress the poor. He pictured money as a god that can control peoples' lives and admonished: "No one can serve two masters. . . . You cannot serve God and mammon" (Matt. 6:24). James warns the rich that "the wages of the laborers who mowed your fields, which you kept back by fraud, cry out" (Jas. 5:4). Or Paul wrote, "For the love of money is the root of all evils" (1 Tim. 6:10).

Human nature and alienation.—Despite Marx's naturalism and materialism, certain aspects of his view of human nature are broadly compatible with Christianity. For one thing, both views hold that humans have continuity with animals and nature, although they conflict about why there is also discontinuity. Marx contends that humans become human through work, whereas Christians see the uniqueness in God's creation of humans in the image of God, which introduces a transcendence missing in the Marxian view. Christians concur with Marxists that humans are social beings, but for the reason that God creates humanity as male and female, so that it is as social creatures that we together bear the image of God. Both Marxism and Christianity affirm the value of the individual within society, but with some sharp distinctions. Although Marxism brings the individual and society into balance in its projected future age, it frequently minimizes the value of the individual in *present* history, where the individual has instrumental value to the good of the whole society. In contrast, Christianity places value upon the individual in present history as well as in the eschatological future, contending that the human is truly human only in relationship and that relationships are truly human only when the integrity and worth of each individual is genuinely preserved.

Christians and Marxists also share much common ground about the importance of work to authentic human existence. Marx holds that work is *the* essential mark of humanity, so that he defines the human being as homo faber—man the worker. For Christians, homo faber is not the distinguishing feature of human beings, but it is an essential part of living out our human responsibility under God to exercise dominion over the earth, as Genesis 1:23 states it. Work is important for Christians because it is a reflection within human image-bearers of our mandate to be cocreators with God in the earth that He has created and placed under human responsibility. Work is vital to our humanity, but it does not define our essential humanity.

Christians and Marxists alike view alienation as the fundamental human problem, although the two analyses of alienation are sharply different, primarily because there is a transcendent depth and comprehensiveness in the Christian analysis that is absent in the Marxist. Marx interprets alienation as rooted in economic realities in which workers are separated from the products of their work, from themselves, and from other people. Marx traces the impact of alienation in the division of labor and class struggles throughout the historical process. Christians certainly recognize that alienation touches all these dimensions of the individual's life and the historical process as a whole, but they argue that economic alienation is only one expression of alienation, not the root of all alienation. Marx is right that alienation is a primal state of humanity, but it is triggered by the very thing Marx prizes so highly—our human Promethean rebellion against God. That rebellion causes humans to abandon their authentic creaturely role and to suffer alienation from God, their true selves, and other people. Christians reject Marx's contention that economics is the root and cause of all alienation. Yet both concur that present humanity is fallen from its ideal nature and requires corrective action. For the Marxist, the cure is to change the economic structures that produce alienation. For the Christian, the only solution is the reconciliation of human beings to God, which is the only ground for attaining authentic humanity and of eliminating our alienation from other human beings.

Critique of religion.—Christians should listen to much of the Marxist critique of religion. Marx criticizes the church's failure to embody the gospel it proclaims. Christians ought to admit that certain historical expressions of Christianity have likely been illusionary projections of historical wishes into a heavenly world, with the result that such otherworldly religion has had a drugging effect upon the poor and oppressed who have resigned themselves to monstrous injustice in society's economic and social structures. Indisputably, some forms of Christianity have been among the most conservative forces in society, frequently defending injustice in the face of prophetic critics. Although Marx generalized about Christianity and ignored many of its social revolutionary expressions, much of his criticism is drawn from specific historical examples. Institutional religion, as he pointed out, has often served the interests and values of the ruling class, so that the church has been rendered impotent to bring prophetic judgment to the exploiters of society. Marx also spoke perceptively about the destructive effects of any alliance between the throne and altar, such as existed in his own native Germany, a warning that ought to be heard by theocrats in any society.

Christians have no greater taste for religion as ideology than does Marx. The heart of Christianity cannot be reduced to ideology, and Christian dogmatic formulations and their accompanying institutional structures can easily do some of the things of which Marx accuses Christianity. Christians, however, would sharply reject Marx's assumption that Christianity is nothing more than an ideology produced by economic conflict and alienation, an ideology that will disappear when the economic structures that produced it have been changed. The heart of Christianity is a transcendent gift to historical creatures who are to live creatively and redemptively within God's own history of creation and redemption—a gift and way of life that cannot be reduced to any ideology. Yet when heard prophetically, Marxism does challenge the Christian church to focus upon concrete problems of people within the actual historical process, to recognize that people eat before they think and that salvation must concern the whole person within society in the concrete flow of history!

A Christian Critique of Marxist Views

Although interpreting them differently, Christianity and Marxism do share some common concerns and commitments. Yet at a more comprehensive level, they represent sharply conflicting worldviews.

Consequently, Christians take strong issue with Marxism at numerous decisive points. It is important for Christians to know where Marxism is vulnerable to a Christian challenge of its adequacy as a worldview. Let me suggest several key issues.

The path to knowledge.—Marx holds that all knowledge must be based on a scientific approach. Consequently, he rejects all speculative thought or revealed theology. The Christian certainly utilizes knowledge gained through the scientific observation of nature, history, human individuals, and society but contends that science alone cannot arrive at all possible knowledge or even sufficiently explain the essential nature and mystery of empirical reality. Philosophy and theology are also important avenues of knowledge that must be integrated with scientific knowledge. Similarly, Christians reject Marx's contention that questions about the origin of nature are abstract and improper. If there is a dimension of transcendence in human life and nature that points beyond itself, then it is entirely appropriate to ask what this "something more" is. If Marxists choose to explain humanity strictly as a product of nature and matter, then it is natural for one to inquire why there should be a world of nature at all.

The nature of human life.—Marxism's view of the nature of human life is vulnerable to challenge at a number of points. First, the Marxist view that humans are essentially homo faber, man the worker, vastly oversimplifies human nature. In fact, Marx cannot sustain his own best ideals about human life without some transcendent dimension in human nature that makes those ideals possible.

Second, Marx's vision of an ideal communist future is based upon his assumption that humans are naturally good and that their alienation and misdeeds are the result of economic forces outside themselves. So Marx can naively assume that when evil economic structures are changed, people will naturally live by the highest human ideals. Christians regard that as a superficial diagnosis of a profound alienation far deeper and more tragic than the conflict between economic forces. The problem underlying all human problems, including economic alienation, is the rebellion and apostasy of human beings against their creator. The human problem is rooted in the will. Consequently, Christians contend that a shift toward a more humane economic life may be desirable, but it cannot alter the deep spiritual source of alienation in human beings or in history.

Third, Christians also reject Marx's contention that human freedom and an omnipotent God are mutually exclusive realities. Unfortunately, Marx misunderstood the nature of the biblical God, who is not, as Marx conceived him to be, a tyrannical, all-determining dictator. Marx also had a selective view of freedom. For the Christian, the highest kind of freedom is the freedom to be what we essentially are—namely, creatures made to be in relation to God and to one another as we exercise responsibility under God over the earth.

The nature of history.—Christians disagree with many of Marx's ideas about human history. Christians reject the view that nature and history can be explained exclusively by natural principles relating to the activity of human beings. Difficult as it is to observe, Christians envision nature and history as expressions of the creative and redeeming activity of God as well as of the creative activity of humans. History is far too complex to be reduced to the strict economic principles of Marx. One force in the historical dialectic is the revealing, judging, redeeming activity of the God who is the author of the drama of creation and redemption in which humans are the chief created actors.

In contrast to Marx, Christians further argue that the ideal future age can never be achieved fully *within* human history by human effort alone. The ideal future can be initiated only by God. Christians can agree with a number of broad Marxist hopes for the character of that future age—a classless society where each according to his ability cares for each according to his need, a society in which there is no coercion and there is maximum human freedom, a society in which true humanity will be attained for all people. In conflict with Marx, Christians know that our highest achievements within history will always fall short of our highest ideals, so that our final hope must be rooted in the saving activity of God who alone will actualize the kingdom of God.

Because of the Christians' more tragic understanding of human alienation, they disagree with Marx's naive assumptions about the relative innocence of leaders of the Communist party during the dictatorship of the proletariat in the socialist transitional phase toward a final Communist utopia. Twentieth-century history itself has refuted Marx's assumption. Communist parties in many different countries have often not acted on behalf of the workers. In fact, workers are routinely the greatest force of resistance to the communist state, particularly among Russian satellites. Within communist states, party leaders in many instances become oppressive counterparts to capitalists in capitalist countries. Marx's critique of the evils of capitalists can as easily be turned on the bureaucrats of communist states. There is a similar naiveté in the Marxist assumption that party leaders will ever willingly relinquish their power, abolish the state, and usher in the pure communist stateless future in which all people are free, equal, and respect each individual within the society. The problem is that all human beings are infected with original sin, which includes all ruling classes, communist as well as capitalist.

Sin also impacts eschatological possibilities. Because of original sin, whether analyzed from a Christian or a Marxist perspective, there is no reason to assume that the dialectic of history will cease when the communist era is ushered in. Marx has no basis for assuming that the first conflict between the forces and relations of production will not repeat itself in the ideal future and on into an endless cycle of future ages. Marx's problem is that he is left with the same kind of people in the new age that inhabited the fleeting paradise before the first economic fall. The new era requires new people, for the Christian or for Marx. The Marxist alteration of the economy and education of the populace cannot alone produce Marx's hoped-for new quality of life. Jesus penetrates beneath the film of the Marxian surface diagnosis to point out that sin comes from within the human heart and that the only cure for such a deep problem is a radical change of life within human beings that only God can provide. Consequently, Christians reject Marx's view that revolutionary violence is the only way to usher in the new era of the dictatorship of the proletariat as a transition to the ideal communist state. Christians are called to be spiritual revolutionaries, but they know that the perfect new era will be birthed and made permanent only through the saving activity of God.

Religion.—Christians ought to accept certain of Marx's prophetic judgments on religion and yet reject his fundamental assumptions about the nature of Christianity. One is his assumption that *all* religion is an illusion that drugs the pain of people. Admittedly, people have at times projected their ideal selves into the picture of God or their historical aspirations into another world, but neither Judaism nor Christianity at their best have done that. From a logical standpoint, one can easily counter the projectionist arguments. It is more difficult to refute the historical evidence for his observations that religion is used to dull the pain and resistance of exploited people to unjust social structures and is used by exploiters to subjugate workers. That has frequently happened. Yet it is also a fact that religion has at times been revolutionary and prophetic on the side of the oppressed. Marx and Engels both knew that, but they interpreted such instances—as in the case of the Anabaptists—as themselves being expressions of economic, not religious, factors. Above all, the Christian must contend that whatever the failings of the church, such Marxian accusations are not true of Jesus or of the Christians who have best caught the vision of Jesus.

Christians would further dispute the Marxist view that religion will disappear when the economic conditions that produce it have been overcome. History itself has refuted that view. Religion has not vanished in any communist country in the transitional socialist phase before the communist era begins—in Russia, China, or any other country under the domination or influence of those two major powers. The reason is that humans are homo religious, religious beings, who strive for transcendence, for ultimate explanations, for grounding their lives in the ontological reality that underlies and permeates the universe. Humans, who are made in the image of God, will strive toward the God in whom they live and move and have their being. Humans are existentially gripped by ultimate concern.

Morality.—Marxism's understanding of morality was vulnerable to critique. Marx himself was ambivalent about morality. In his formal analysis, he contended that morality is one of the ideologies produced by economic conflict and that it basically reflects the values of the ruling class. Yet, like an Old Testament prophet, Marx rendered shattering judgment on numerous evils in society, from the oppression of the working class to bourgeois marriage that regards women as property. His projection of ideals for the future communist world is clearly a secularization of many Judaeo-Christian values such as justice, equality, love, peace, and freedom. There is a transparent inner contradiction between Marx's view of religion and morality as ideology and the humanistic values so prominent in his thought. Marx treated these as absolute values and yet relativized revolutionary ethics, so that right is defined as what furthers the revolution of the proletariat. From the Christian perspective, Marx's eschatological moral vision is far more defensible and compatible with the Christian faith than is his revolutionary ethic.

Economics.—Christianity provides no basis for a particular economic system. However, certain Christian insights do provide a critique of Marxism at some points. Christians would generally hold that private property is not necessarily evil, certainly not from a biblical perspective. At the same time, biblical Christianity teaches that the individual has no *absolute* ownership of property and that God is the ultimate owner of all the world's property. Therefore the individual is always responsible to God, to other people, and to posterity in the management of property. The Christian faith speaks strongly about the excessive accumulation of property to the detriment of the human family.

Strictly from the standpoint of economic theory, many economists criticize some of Marx's ideas as being too simplistic. Although many of his ideas (for example, the forces and relations of production, use value, surplus value, class struggle, the nature of ideology, historical dialectic, and so on) may provide useful economic insight, they are too reductionistic and simplistic in terms of how the modern economy works. Marx could not foresee the major modifications that would take place within many capitalist systems of the world during the twentieth century, many of which have corrected some of the evils that concerned Marx. Only strict ideological Marxists today can accept the full Marxist analysis without major modifications of his economic views. The recent revisionism that has reintroduced capitalist incentives and private property into the Chinese economy are a historical monument to the economic failure of strict Marxism. What is unmistakable is that history and human life are far too complex to be reduced primarily to economics.

What Christians Can Add to the Marxist Vision

One cannot be *fully* committed to the Marxist worldview and be a Christian. However much we might learn from Marxism or common ground we selectively affirm, there is a fundamental difference between the two worldviews that makes them rivals for the ultimate allegiance of human beings. In fact, in terms of doctrine, corporate identity, ethical vision, historical hope, and public ritual, Marxism has many elements of traditional religion. Christians can shape a more adequate vision of human life, human history, nature, and reality as a whole than can Marxists. Many responses Christians make to atheists, naturalists, and humanists apply equally to Marxists. In final summary, let me note some fundamental Christian values that ought to be argued specifically in relation to Marxism.

First, the Christian doctrines of creation and redemption provide a more adequate basis for understanding the nature and purpose of the universe, history, and human life. Christianity gives substantial but not ultimate value to the universe and the place of humans within it. All reality is the drama of creation and redemption in which, under God, humans are the chief actors in helping God achieve His purposes within the universe. That vision provides an understanding of the origin and goal of nature and history and the purpose of human life.

Second, Christians better understand the true nature of human beings. A human person is really material (here Marx is partly right) but also something more—an embodied spirit, a whole person, body and spirit. As a person of spirit and flesh, humans have both material and spiritual needs, neither of which may properly be neglected.

Third, Christians more profoundly understand the depths of the human dilemma, the problem within the individual and in society. There has been a fall, as Marx discerned, but the cause was not economic, as Marx thought. The fall results from a fundamental rebellion of humans in their relationship to God, a rebellion from which all other historical evils flow. Alienation is rooted in the human will—our Promethean aspirations to be our own Gods.

Fourth, Christians have a more defensible view of the nature of the new humanity. The new humanity will not be achieved by the elimination of economic conflict. The human family will be changed only through the activity of God as he creates a fellowship of the Spirit through the saving mediation of Jesus Christ in redeeming people into a right relationship with God. Within that redeemed fellowship, a new reality will occur. The ontological stuff of the universe—divine love—will be the glue and creative power that holds together the new humanity and brings it to fulfillment.

Finally, Christianity provides a better basis for praxis by grounding human activity in the power of God. As Christians face Marxists throughout the world, the struggle will not be won simply through the exchange of ideas. Christians must meet the Marxist challenge to change the world and not merely to interpret it. A militant, engaged, risking Marxist movement can be successfully countered as a world-view only by a militant and thoroughly committed Christian church that in interpreting the gospel also embraces the world, particularly the disenfranchised and oppressed people, in a struggle to bring about a more just world order as we also minister to the spiritual needs of individual people. Marxism is one challenge that the church dare not ignore!

7
Nihilism:
Affirmation of Nothingness

A few years ago, the Beatles captured the sentiments of a large number of twentieth-century people in their song "Strawberry Fields Forever." Reflecting the wave of despair, the sense of futility, the vacuum of values, and the storm of meaninglessness that have engulfed many modern human beings, they sang that nothing is real; there is nothing to get hung up about. Such feelings unconsciously reflect what we formally call "nihilism." The nihilist concludes that nothing within our experience of life has any meaning or value. Life must be lived, if it is to be lived, in light of the nothingness in which we are trapped. The nihilist theme has been spoken, sung, written about, and meditated on by diverse groups from unsophisticated and bewildered high-school kids to hippies to artists to middle-class business people to philosophers. Their message may vary in application, depth of understanding, and seriousness of reflection. Still a singular sound comes through: Nothing is real!

Western civilization has, in its dominant expression throughout the Christian era, defined the meaning of life and the values of society in relation to a theistic understanding of God and His purposes in the world. Since the modern era began in about the seventeenth century, the theistic shaping of human perspectives has steadily eroded. Atheism and naturalism have seized many people's minds. Since naturalistic atheists must live in this world, most of them find it essential to develop some way to define meaning and value in a world without God. Many opt for a naturalistic humanism. Others conclude that the world has no discernible meaning or value and that we are faced by an ultimate void of nothingness—a judgment that provides the foundation for nihilism. "Nihilism," as Mi-

146

chael Novak suggests, "is an ideological interpretation imposed on the experience of nothingness."[1] Not all nihilists stamp their experience of nothingness with a philosophically rigorous nihilistic interpretation of life. Nihilism reaches far beyond its self-conscious and formal ideological advocates to those who are thematically attracted to nihilism judgments about existence.

The wave of nihilism that erupted in the nineteenth century has reached tidal heights in the twentieth century. The term *nihilism* came into increasing scholarly use in the early nineteenth century and was popularized in the last half of that century. From its origins in language until today, the term has been used in various ways.[2] The great impetus toward the modern understanding of nihilism came from a number of towering prophetic literary figures of the nineteenth century who, however diverse their overall thought, foresaw the coming nihilism that would threaten the very cultural foundations of the West. Some wrestled with nihilistic elements in their own lives and managed to overcome them. Soren Kierkegaard, Fyodor Dostoevsky, Leo Tolstoy, and others—above all, Friedrich Nietzsche—formulated definitive insights into the nihilist phenomenon. Of all those prophetic figures, Dostoevsky most brilliantly shaped the implications of the coming nihilism in his epigram, "If God does not exist, everything is permitted."[3] It was Nietzsche, however, who provided the most extended analysis of nihilism and remains until today the single most influential force in unleashing the nihilist theme into modern culture.

In his classic study of the development of nihilism, Johan Goudsblom argues that nihilism is rooted in the Socratic imperative to know the truth with absolute certainty.[4] The struggle with the truth imperative initially occurs among intellectuals of various types who face their own contemporary challenges to absolute truth and then press on to a nihilism that radically questions all certainties. A few great nineteenth-century thinkers first engaged the problem and introduced the nihilistic rationale into European culture. Ever since, the nihilistic theme has coursed through Western culture. Once the nihilist dilemma is set loose in culture, contends Goudsblom, it is often unattached to its original truth imperative and becomes democratically available to a wider society as a thematic sense of meaninglessness. Even though its influence is often indirect and difficult to trace, it impacts both culture and individuals. It reverberates in the theater, film, books, and pop culture. Its implications are expressed in numerous popular slogans. "All truth is relative." "Anything is moral as long as it doesn't hurt anybody." "Life is pointless." "Existence is absurd." Slogans like these are widely disseminated in modern culture and reflect the popular outworking of a nihilist analysis of existence.

Nihilism needs to be examined at two levels: first, in its technical rationale; and, second, in terms of its less technical forms in the wider culture. We can more perceptively understand the popularized expressions of nihilism by first examining Nietzsche's development of the classic rationale for nihilism.

Nietzsche: The Classic Nihilistic Rationale

Friedrich Nietzsche was the first great thinker to develop in detail the threat of nihilism. He diagnosed it as a phenomenon at work in European culture and within himself and predicted that in the following two centuries nihilism would unfold with all its implications in the societies in the modern world. Nietzsche's analysis of nihilism is so thorough that many scholars consider most modern literary treatments of nihilism to be mainly commentaries on Nietzsche's thought. Nietzsche's identification with nihilism is a curious turn, given the fact that Nietzsche was the son and grandson of pious Lutheran pastors and was himself a first-year university theology student destined for the pastorate. At about the time he turned to philology in his second university year, he became an atheist. After a brief career as a philologist at the University of Basel, Nietzsche pursued his great love of philosophy and produced the brilliant work that has permanently imprinted the history of the West. He became the self-designated prophet who proclaimed the death of God and the inevitable approach of nihilism.[5]

In a life spanning from 1844 to 1900, Nietzsche lived through what he considered to be a major cultural crisis in the history of Europe, a crisis that had been building for several centuries and that would have a long-term shaping effect on the future. On the surface, the nineteenth century was optimistic, assertive, surging forward in knowledge, technology, and culture, and convinced of the inevitability of progress. In Nietzsche's diagnosis, however, the very foundations of Western culture were crumbling under the pressure of the imperative to know the truth, an imperative that has been a driving force out of the Greek and Christian heritage. All Western culture had been built upon the assumption that there is absolute truth and value in the universe. Nietzsche's own search for truth led him to see the failure of every expression of truth and value in culture—in metaphysics, morality, religion, and science.

Various factors had led to an increasing loss of the absolute in society. Hegel had emphasized that life is a process of becoming. In the mid-nineteenth century, Darwin produced persuasive biological evidence that everything is in process, change, and becoming, and that nothing is final or absolute. Nietzsche rejected certain aspects of Darwin's theory, yet he was convinced that science has now established the natural process of change, which fatally eliminates any possibility of absolute states. He concluded that what humans call truth also evolves and is tied to the perspectives of individuals and particular cultures. Consequently, truth can never be viewed as absolute. In distinction from many nineteenth-century thinkers who held that science is now replacing the old truths at the heart of Western culture with the empirical facts of science, Nietzsche contended that science does not deal with a real world or more accurate truth any more than did older approaches to knowledge. Science offers only human theories, arrangements, and judgments about a basically irrational and structureless physical world. Science itself can provide only causal explanations of individual phenomena but never meaning and value for existence as a whole. Even in an age of science, life cannot be explained, and the world and humanity no longer have any meaning or value.

At the heart of the European crisis, in Nietzsche's analysis, was the collapse of Christianity as a believable faith—a situation that was precipitated by Christianity's own values. A truth imperative lies at the center of Christianity. Humans are commanded to know the truth. Christianity then becomes its own judge, for when the truth imperative is turned upon Christianity itself, the Christian faith proves not to be the truth. Nietzsche reached his conclusion from a variety of perspectives. He was convinced that numerous leading nineteenth-century thinkers—such as David F. Strauss, Ludwig Feuerbach, and Arthur Schopenhauer—had demonstrated the untenability of Christianity. When the theological attack on Christianity was placed alongside Darwin's evolutionary thought—at least as Nietzsche understood him and his theory—God was no longer a necessary hypothesis. Darwinism provided from within nature itself all that is necessary to explain the life process. In Nietzsche's translation, Darwin's rejection of teleology and purpose for chance and mechanism eliminated the idea of a purposeful, ordered, and hierarchical creation built around humanity.[6] In fact, Nietzsche fulminated against the antinatural moral teachings of Christianity as the most pernicious influence in Western life, primarily because it resists the will to power that Nietzsche concluded is the identifiable basic force within the universe.[7]

This historic development was cataclysmic for the whole of European society. Christianity had provided the foundation for every aspect of European culture, for all expressions of beauty, truth, and goodness in areas of morality, art, social relationships, and politics. Now God as a cultural phenomenon had died, a fact that masses had not yet realized. Society was going on just as before, observing the same historic institutions, structures, values, and belief in the centrality of human life in the universe and in the purpose of history—but now without an adequate metaphysical ground to sustain their beliefs and practices.

In dramatic fashion, Nietzsche highlighted this fact by trumpeting of the death of God. In his *Gay Science,* he wrote: "The greatest recent event—that 'God is dead,' that the belief in the Christian God has become unbelievable—is already beginning to cast its first shadows over Europe."[8] The loss of God had already occurred, yet few people were aware of it—a situation Nietzsche portrayed in his famous parable of the madman who on a bright morning lit a lantern, ran into the marketplace, and cried, "I seek God! I seek God!" Many in the crowd were superficial atheists who began to laugh and ask, "Has he got lost!" "Did he lose his way like a child?" "Is he hiding?" "Has he gone on a voyage?" Jumping into their midst, the madman cried, "Whither is God? I will tell you! *We have killed him*—you and I! All of us are his murderers! But how did we do this? . . . God is dead! God remains dead! And we have killed him! . . . What was holiest and mightiest of all that the world has yet owned has bled to death under our knives: who will wipe this blood off us? . . ." The listeners did not understand. "I have come too early," said the madman. "My time is not yet. This tremendous event is still on its way . . .—it has not yet reached the ears of men."[9] Nietzsche is saying that atheists must face the full implications of the nonexistence of God—which most had not yet done. Once the death of God is realized, nihilism is the only course to follow, for the reason that everything that had previously defined life, purpose, structure, and goal is irretrievably lost. Hence a metaphysical judgment must be rendered: There is no meaning or value!

In Nietzsche's view, integrity demands that we face the implications of the death of God and the consequent nihilism. "Let us think this thought in its most terrible form: existence as it is, without meaning or aim, yet recurring inevitably without any finale of nothingness: *the eternal recurrence.*' "[10] He asks, "What does nihilism mean? *That the highest values devaluate themselves.* The aim is lacking; 'why?' finds no answer."[11] The implications of this shift are ominous. Given its long cultural history, the West has been led to believe that life *must* have a purpose anchored in a transcendent heavenly world. When belief in that absolute order vanishes, Western values collapse in that they no longer have a foundation. And that is nihilism—a phenomenon destined to sweep the West!

Nietzsche analyzed three stages in nihilism's development as a psychological state that makes a cosmological judgment about reality. First, the individual seeks a meaning or aim in events that is not there. The search could settle on different goals, in that any goal at all will constitute some meaning. The first stage of nihilism occurs when one realizes that the world of becoming and process aims at nothing and achieves nothing. There is no discernible goal. With that, one discovers how much self-deception, waste of strength, and insecurity have previously characterized one's life. In the second stage, one discovers that existing things have no unity or pattern and that what one has regarded as a totality, a system, an underlying organization of reality has only been arbitrarily imposed by humans upon nature and history. In the third stage, one comes to view the world as a deception and then proceeds to project an ideal or true world out beyond the natural world. But one discovers that it, too, is a psychological fabrication in which one projects values from the natural world that are designed to maintain and increase human domination of the earth. These values also finally devalue themselves. At the end of the three stages, aim, unity, and truth are all lost, and the world is seen to be valueless. Since the God who has been at the heart of those values is now dead, there is no viable basis for values or meaning in the world.[12]

As a result, belief is crumbling everywhere. Metaphysics is now seen to be illusory—a search after what cannot be known. There is no world beyond or thing-in-itself beyond appearance. Science deals with a sham world that deceives us and is not what it appears to be. Physics has shown that matter is an illusion. Art focuses on a world of nature that is indifferent, cynical, and ugly. Politics is no longer governed by eternal structures but by mass opinion, herd morality, and vulgar values. The traditional distinction between the concrete world of life and the world of higher spiritual values is now untenable. The higher realm is a psychologically projected dream world. Morality is a peculiar expression of error. Moralities are now seen to be human constructions, and there is no moral order by which to judge individual moralities.[13] In fact, Western morality interferes with natural instincts and drives and requires humans to submit to certain standards and structures that are tied essentially to Christian assumptions about a just and omnipotent God, good and evil, the purpose of life, life after death, and the higher eternal good world in contrast to this fallen illusory world. The Western moral tradition has now disintegrated because of the disappearance of the higher world and science's exposure of the physical world as mere appearance.[14]

Nietzsche contended that all the so-called truths, meanings, and values of Western culture are only human constructs. "The deeper one looks," wrote Nietzsche, "the more our valuations disappear—meaninglessness approaches. We have *created* the world that possesses value."[15] All human creations of value—science, religion, morality, art—are expressions of the will to power, the fundamental impulse by which humans attempt to impose order and structure upon a chaotic and irrational world. The whole range of the cultured world is a fabrication created to serve certain human needs. Once that is seen, the ordered meaning and values—as understood in Western civilization—collapse.

Nietzsche analyzed several types of nihilism. The most radical form of nihilism is "the conviction of an absolute untenability of existence when it comes to the highest values one recognizes; plus the realization that we lack the least right to posit a beyond or an in-itself of things that might be 'divine' or morality incarnate."[16] There are also various expressions of preliminary types of nihilism like pessimism, suffering, or pleasure. When either suffering or pleasure dominates the other in one's experience, it is a signpost on the way to nihilism—because neither absolute suffering nor pleasure allows an ultimate meaning to existence. Nihilism may take an active form, expressing itself as "a sign of increased power of the spirit"[17] that at its most radical is a violent force of destruction.[18] It may also take a passive form, representing a "decline and recession of the power of the spirit"[19] that at its weakest is weary and no longer attacks life. Buddhism is the most extreme example of passive nihilism. Nietzsche considered nihilism in some form to be the normal condition of humanity.

In earlier Western history, Christianity had been an antidote against nihilism until its collapse as a basis for value. There are many different attempts to avoid the emptiness that nihilism demands, with the result that people in Nietzsche's time represented an incomplete nihilism. Most attempt to escape nihilism without revaluating their values (which, for Nietzsche, means the creation of another basis for values), but that only produces an opposite effect and makes the problem more acute.[20] Nietzsche analyzes the numerous ways people attempt to narcoticize themselves to avoid facing the full implications of nihilism. They may become intoxicated by music, destroy noble things, adopt uncritical enthusiasm for single human beings or historic eras, or work blindly as instruments of science. The narcotic may take the form of opening oneself to small enjoyments, generalizing in pathos about oneself, mystical enjoyment of eternal happiness, the pursuit of art for its own sake, self-disgust, continual work, fanaticism, or sickness due to immoderation.[21]

Most prevailing forms of nihilism remain incomplete. People go on trying to preserve values posited by the Christian faith—but now without faith. These ways include this-worldly solutions that aim at the ultimate triumph of truth, love, or justice, or hold nonegoistic negating moral ideals, or believe in a "beyond" in order to secure some metaphysical comfort. One may try to discover a governance of things that rewards, punishes, educates, or improves. One may still believe in good and evil, so that one envisions being called to a task on the side of good. Or one may develop contempt for the "natural" or desire or the ego. Of course, some may continue to allow the church to obtrude into life's pivotal events.[22] From Nietzsche's analysis, it is obvious that many incomplete nihilists would not be aware that they are nihilists and struggle to avoid having to face the implications of their lost basis for values. If that is the case, the nihilistic temper may also escape detection by the superficial observer of people in modern society.

As the nineteenth-century herald of nihilism, Nietzsche provided a prophetic oracle for unaware and incomplete nihilists. Convinced that nihilism is inevitable for the West, Nietzsche attempted to speed its arrival so that it can then be overcome. So he philosophized "with a hammer," as he described his work, aggressively attempting to destroy the old values rotting at the heart of European civilization. He was convinced that the only solution for nihilism is to face it head-on, embrace it, and attempt to transcend it—a course he called the "revaluation of values." The major themes of Nietzsche's later thought—will to power, *amor fati* (love of fate), eternal recurrence, and the superman—are all part of his effort to revaluate values, to go beyond good and evil, truth and untruth, as they had been historically understood. The fact that the world is absent of form and meaning, has no goal and purpose, and is indifferent to human life and attitudes should not lead people to negate the world but to embrace it, to give a "Dionysian affirmation of the world as it is, without substraction, exception, or selection."[23] This requires one to abandon all previous hopes and expectations, to accept one's fate, and to live joyfully in a world of nature and people that is cosmically insignificant—what Nietzsche called *amor fati*, the love of fate.

At the heart of fate is the fact of eternal recurrence. Nietzsche thought that this insignificant and meaningless world is destined to repeat itself interminably, so that the same things happen time and time again in an endless cycle of meaninglessness. "This," he wrote, "is the most extreme form of nihilism: the nothing (the 'meaningless'), eternally!"[24] The driving force within this eternally recurrent process of nothingness is the will to power, which underlies all other human drives and cultural expressions. Taking issue with Darwin's view that the life process is a struggle for survival, Nietzsche argued in contrast that the evolutionary force at every level is the will to power—a critical idea that Nietzsche never clearly explained. At the level of human mental or spiritual life in science, philosophy, art, and religion, the will to power is expressed in the interpretations people give of life, which reflect the will of the stronger to dominate and overcome others. Nihilism, in recognizing the meaninglessness of existence, clears the way for a creative will to power that consciously imposes its form and meaning upon the process. The new form and values will be vital naturalistic values that serve the life of the individual, values that for the emerging superman, at least, go beyond traditional ideas of good and evil. The new type of human will be the superman who will rise above the herd morality of the masses and lead the way in the revaluation of values in light of nihilism. The superman affirms and accepts life in its totality, including its suffering and meaninglessness, and imposes his own arbitrary meaning upon it.[25]

In attempting to transcend nihilism in his own life and to sketch the path for its cultural overcoming, Nietzsche never successfully resolved the tension of affirming and yet attempting to transcend nihilism. "The philosophical nihilist," he wrote, "is convinced that all that happens is meaningless and in vain; and that there ought not to be anything meaningless and in vain. But whence this: there ought not to be? From where does one get *this* 'meaning,' *this* standard?"[26] Lapsing into a mental breakdown in 1889, Nietzsche never overcame the tension. He did, however, analyze the historical process that had produced the emerging nihilistic phenomenon and the varied expressions of it in individual human life—sometimes conscious and sometimes unconscious and incomplete. Not the least, he remains the most influential source of a powerful idea that is set loose in the modern world, an idea that floats in the cultural atmosphere, one breathed in like an infecting virus by masses of people who have never systematically worked through the technical dimensions of the nihilistic problem and yet *feel* deep-rooted intimations of nothingness.

Twentieth-Century Nihilism

Nietzsche's nihilism, and that of other nineteenth-century nihilists, developed in an optimistic age when European culture was triumphant, knowledge was increasing and society improving, and evolutionary mythology was dominating the socioeconomic-political outlook. But they saw the decay, the rot, the vacuum at the heart of it all. What if they had lived in the twentieth century, which in many ways has been a tale of lofty dreams and noble aspirations shattered on the anvil of our actions. Throughout much of the world humans dehumanize humans. Individuals are lost in the swirl of mass humanity. Political tyranny, totaliterianism, and fanaticism ravage large segments of the human family. After two world wars and a dizzying number of local wars, the planet lives under the threat of nuclear extinction. The newsreel of discordant inhumane images fleets across the mind-the cacophony of bombs exploding, sirens wailing, women shrieking; the vignettes of wives widowed, old people homeless, racist slurs, Orwellian doublethink. There are the haunting images—the skeleton of Hiroshima jutting into the sky; the stacked corpses of Buchenwald; the sunken eyes, distended bellies, drooping skin, and pallid color of the world's starving children. Riots, revolutions, counterrevolutions, terrorism, ravaged cities, scorched earth, fouled waters, raped land, poisoned vegetation, polluted air, bulging prisons—they are all there! Put them all together and it is easy to say, "Life is a cosmic accident without meaning or purpose."

Given the nature of the opening chapters of the twentieth century, it is not surprising that a wave of nihilism erupted after World War II, so that many of the greatest literary figures of the twentieth century at least passed through a nihilistic phase, and their work represented a committed effort to transcend nihilism. Among the well-known writers who have struggled with the threat of nothingness or nihilism in their writings, often reflecting a stage in their own lives, are Miguel Unamuno, Paul Valéry, Henry de Montherlant, André Malraux, Franz Kafka, Albert Camus, Jean-Paul Sartre, Eugéne Ionesco, Samuel Beckett, Jean Genet, Bertolt Brecht, Nikos Kzantsakis, and many others.[27] Few of these writers could be characterized as nihilists in their overall work. Nevertheless, all make the nihilist phenomenon a prominent feature in many of their writings, and most of them have struggled to surmount the meaninglessness they have perceived in the modern world. The nihilist posture is represented in numerous classic characters within many of their works. Even the titles of some classic modern literary works underline the nihilist threat. Who can forget the haunting images of Eliot's *The Waste Land* and *The Hollow Men,* Faulkner's *The Sound and the Fury,* Sartre's *No Exit* and *Nausea,* Kafka's *The Trial,* Camus's *The Plague,* and O'Neill's *Long Days Journey into the Night?*

The post-World War II theater has also echoed at times with cries of meaninglessness. Despairing elements throb in the works of such great dramatists as Ionesco, Brecht, Genet, Beckett, Osborne, and Pinter. Recurrent themes are life without sanctions, lords without God, death without reason, and questions without answers. In plays like Genet's *The Blacks* and Ionesco's *The Bald Soprano,* the first and last scenes are identical and almost nothing happens in between. That is life: materialized absurdity flung into momentary space between prenatal and posthumous nothingness!

The threat of nihilism has been formally treated in one way or another by most existentialist thinkers, many of whom assume that nihilism is, at a minimum, a stage through which most modern people must pass on the way toward some constructive pattern of living. In fact, many of the most instructive accounts of the problem of nihilism have been autobiographical, as authors represent a dimension of themselves or a stage of their life in one of their fictional characters— Kierkegaard in the figure of Johannes Climacus, Dostoevsky's *Memoirs from the Underground,* Chekhov's *A Dreary Story,* Sartre's *Nausea*—in which their writing is integral to their own effort to overcome nihilism. Heidegger observes, "No one with any insight will still deny today that nihilism is in the most varied and most hidden forms 'the normal state' of man."[28] The human individual is engaged in a struggle to surmount the threat of nothingness or, as Paul Tillich put it, the threat of nonbeing.[29]

The nihilist threat is subtle and is found in diverse expressions that do not always give the impression of the nihilistic posture—for the simple reason that the nihilism may not be wholly conscious or may be repressed deep within the psyche and disguised by opposite appearing masks. Early in the century, philosopher Karl Jaspers, while still a young psychoanalyst, analyzed a number of nihilistic typologies.[30] Combining his typologies with several others that have been proposed, one may point toward various broad expressions of disguised forms of nihilism. Some are clearly escapisms, others represent a resignation to life, others are oriented to the future, others are preoccupied with the present moment, while others are consumed with self-interest.

What might be called forms of resignation include such attitudes as helplessness, boredom, emptiness, or a sense of betrayal—attitudes widely distributed through the populations of the Western world, particularly among young people. A second expression of nihilism, and one way to transcend resignation, is through escapisms of various kinds—intoxication and drugs, hedonism, free sexuality, the repression of moral inhibitions, a flight to pietistic religion, or an otherworldly religious faith that denies the reality of the earth. A third broad category of incomplete nihilism is built around a preoccupation with the self, either positively or negatively. This may express itself through a life-style of self-interest. One may assert the self's values through attachment to any variety of contemporary fanaticisms that attempt to force one's personal values upon all other people. In an opposite reaction, one may attempt to lose the self through self-effacement in the service of some ideal or through submission to various heteronomous systems that dominate the individual in politics, issue-oriented causes, ethical systems, or religious movements, all of which absolve the individual of responsibility and arbitrarily impose a value system upon the meaninglessness that one feels. A fourth broad response is to focus upon the future, either in hope or despair, so that the individual may either lose himself in utopian illusions about the imminent possibilities of the world's future or become mired in despair about the hopelessness of the world. Finally, one may lose oneself in the moment and become possessed by immediacy, which can occur in several ways. One may celebrate the here and now, with no thought for tomorrow. Or one can stoically accept the nothingness of the world and live in spite of it. Or one can take action to destroy and annihilate in order to precipitate the arrival of nihilism. Or one can achieve a form of existence that incorporates and becomes one with the nihilism one espouses.

Even if one adopts a nihilist creed, one must still go on living—unless one chooses suicide. For the nihilist rationale, suicide is not usually an option, for the simple reason that if nothing is real, then one cannot logically justify suicide. Therefore, there are few complete and consistent nihilists. Most find some way to resolve the nihilist dilemma and to survive its threat. Numerous writers illustrate the varied paths by which one can attempt to surmount a nihilist interpretation of the lack of ultimate meaning of life and the universe. Among the creative responses that one can make to the nihilist threat are resignation, heroic defiance, a celebration of nihilism for the sake of humanity, a radical revaluation of values, or a sublimation of the nihilist threat in various incomplete forms of nihilism.

Resignation may best be seen in the work of Franz Kafka who may be the greatest example of consistent modern nihilism. His nihilism is sketched in his parabolic writings through memorable characters who capture his own atheistic questioning throughout his life of the ways of a God he does not believe exists. He portrays the irrational and inexplicable character of a finite life against the backdrop of an infinity that cannot be explained. Kafka remained a seeker for a faith he could not attain. Among his most gripping portrayals of the enigma of his own life was his novel *The Trial*, in which the central character is pronounced guilty and punished by an unknown court for a crime he never committed, representing a parable both of Kafka's own life and of the metaphysical terror of the human race. In the face of the absurdity of the process, the character finds it useless to resist, so he submits to death in a world absent of justice. Man's only crime, concludes Kafka, is that of having been born. His nihilism centers in his view of the total absence of God and the futility of seeking ultimate meaning. To all such questions there is only silence.[31]

Nihilistic resignation is graphically depicted in the works of various artists. Chekhov in *A Dreary Story*, for example, describes a man facing old age after a long and successful life. He is now overcome by a sense of not-knowing and uncertainty about everything, leading him to conclude, "I am vanquished. If it is so, it is useless to think, it is useless to talk. I will sit and wait in silence for what is to come."[32] Such resigned helplessness may be transformed into a life of resigned humdrum survival, as represented, for example, in Roquentin in Sartre's *Nausea*. Roquentin comes to the point where he says, "Now . . . I am going to survive. Eat, sleep. Sleep, eat. Exist slowly, softly, like the trees, like a pool of water, like the red seat of a tram . . .I know very well that I wish to do nothing; to do something is to create existence—and there is more than enough existence as it is."[33]

Albert Camus is a good representative of a heroic response to the nihilistic threat. Nihilism itself is powerfully portrayed in the early works of Camus like *The Stranger, The Myth of Sisyphus, Caligula,* and *The Misunderstanding.* Camus is possessed by the tragedy of the absurd. In *Caligula,* for example, Caligula concludes that death makes life meaningless and humanity unimportant. He then attempts to deprive people of their illusions so that they are forced to face the nothingness of existence. He hates people's weak submission to life's outrageous conditions. Camus's own life was an effort to surmount those implications. Despite his judgment that there is no God or ultimate meaning to life, Camus found some things within life to be infinitely valuable—for example, being alive, love, and the power to protest death. So he attempted to ground those values in a natural context. Revolting against nihilism and attempting to impose his own order upon the chaos of the universe, Camus affirmed what he called the "sanctity of negation,"[34] by which he meant the heroism of a life without God. He thought that the human must struggle to transcend despair.

In *The Rebel,* Camus advocates a humanistic philosophy of revolt by which one transcends the absurd. He traces the course of nihilism to its production of an inhuman logic. If the universe is absurd, everything is permitted and nothing is sacred or forbidden. Nihilism, he wrote, is "nothing but a prolonged endeavor to give order, by human forces alone and simply by force, to a history no longer endowed with order."[35] He rejected the type of nihilism that seeks absolute power, because it inevitably results in inhumanity toward human beings. Rather the rebel must set a limited goal beyond the confines of nihilism, a goal centered on the value of the human person, justice, and happiness, representing a positive morality grounded in justice.

Jean-Paul Sartre represents what might be termed a celebrative solution to nihilism. Sartre denied every being a nihilist. However, the nihilist elements of life obtrude repeatedly in the early works of Sartre. One can argue that the nihilist problem is the background for the whole Sartrean existential approach to life. As a young man, Sartre became convinced that there is no God and no a priori definition of the human being or life. One begins with the fact that man simply is. Man exists before he is defined. "Man is nothing else," wrote Sartre, "but that which he makes of himself."[36] In his decisions, a human being is responsible for himself and for all humans. This existential situation involves anguish, because one must choose responsibly from among a plurality of possibilities without any rules or guidelines. In this situation, one must act in abandonment, facing right to the end the consequences of God not existing. One must not surrender the existence of God with the least possible expense, so that one attempts to retain a priori value, truth, morality, and so on—but now without the existence of God. For Sartre, if there is no God, there is no a priori good. In that sense, Dostoevsky was right. If God does not exist, everything is permitted, and an individual cannot depend on anything within or outside himself for guidance. Man is free—as Sartre said, condemned to be free—so that the individual must act responsibly. Because one can choose only those possibilities available to one's own will, one acts in despair. This does, nonetheless, allow creativity in the evolving human process of deciding what one shall become. The fundamental truth, for Sartre, is "I think, therefore I am," which represents the absolute truth of human consciousness, a truth that gives a human dignity and makes him the creator of a kingdom of values within the universal limitations that define our fundamental situation in the universe. Sartre does not take the human individual as the end, for human essence is still to be determined. As self-surpassing about what he will be, the individual is an aim beyond himself. For Sartre, nihilism is a discovery, much like Nietzsche's, that there are no absolute truths and values. But unlike Nietzsche, who could never resolve the tension within himself even with his posturing about revaluation, Sartre celebrates the creative role of the self in establishing values through existential choice. The individual fills the role of God for himself.

We have already examined the solution by which Nietzsche attempted to resolve the nihilist dilemma by a revaluation of values. For Nietzsche, the haunting specter of his vanished God remained, and his ambivalence about the loss of God was an incurable malady. His revaluation was more cosmic than Sartre's, in the sense that it involved forces in the world of nature itself such as the will to power and eternal recurrence. Moralistic spirits will often attempt to provide another basis for values, as did Nietzsche. We have suggested that another way to handle the threat of nihilism is to sublimate the threat so that it is acted out in disguised and incomplete forms. In these and other ways, nihilists attempt to go on living in the face of their nihilistic reading of the universe and life.

Nihilism represents no visible movement, no cult of adherents, no singular solution. It is thematic, existential, atmospheric. The nihilist dilemma and theme make contact with the emptiness and meaninglessness that many modern people feel. Nihilism then becomes a dominating feature of the mental landscape of moderns for whom life does not add up, wheels do not mesh together, and nothing makes sense, who are caught in the grip of a paralyzing sense of emptiness and meaninglessness and are threatened at the very core of their selfhood. Many people who would not formally think of themselves as nihilists are nevertheless at some point on the way toward complete nihilism or have passed through a nihilistic phase on the path to establishing an acceptable pattern of life. The nihilistic threat is often embedded at the heart of suicidal impulses that are experienced virtually universally in certain phases of human experience. Not uncommonly, when one can cut through the bluster and bluff, ideological compulsions, delusions, and fanaticisms of people, there is underneath a profound *dis*-ease, a fundamental uncertainty, an engulfing threat of nonbeing, a deep-rooted fear that life has no meaning. Undoubtedly, this modern dilemma is grounded in the loss of a foundation for truth and values through the disintegration of religious faith over the past two centuries. When one personally experiences the loss, one must either resign or find some immanental way to structure life and to impose order and values upon it. But whatever the solution, the nihilistic threat is still there.

A Christian Response to Nihilism

Nihilism is among the most difficult of modern ideologies for the Christian to respond to. Representing no formal movement, no tightly defined credo, and no broadly uniform profile, it is widely diffused in modern culture, most frequently in forms that are disguised and not easily recognizable. The Christian needs to be prepared to deal with the phenomenon from the formal ideological versions of a Nietzsche to the popularized appropriations of the nihilistic theme out of the cultural milieu. It is important for the Christian to understand the nihilistic worldview, to know what areas of authentic insight may be found in the nihilistic diagnosis, to be aware of where nihilism is critically vulnerable, to accept the legitimate elements embedded in the nihilist critique of Christianity, and to offer a constructive response to the nihilist challenge.

Affirming Elements of Nihilism

In one way Christians are indebted to nihilists. Atheism and naturalism have attracted increasing numbers of advocates over the past several centuries of Western life, people who have assumed that not much is lost when belief in God is laid aside. Nihilism challenges such an easy abandonment of religious belief and ruthlessly draws out the logical, ontological, and metaphysical implications of the loss of an absolute grounding for the universe and for human life. It forces atheism and naturalism no longer to live out of the residue of their vanished Christian heritage and to face the stark terror and emptiness of living in a universe without God. The foundations of culture in all its phases are shaken. Even if the nihilist surmounts his own nihilism in a positive way, the nihilist critique remains valuable as a stark look, without glossing or minimizing, at what it means to live in a universe without God.

At this point, the Christian would thoroughly agree with the nihilist analysis—*if* there is no God! If there is no God, then the threat of meaninglessness is overpowering. In fact, that is a familiar biblical theme, one expressed in several ways. The Old Testament pictures God in His creative activity bringing light out of darkness and an ordered creation out of a chaotic earth that is without form and void (Gen. 1:1; Isa. 45:18). God upholds the world's order and forces back the chaos that threatens to crash in and destroy the created order (Job 26:7). In powerful images set in its ancient nomadic environment, the poetic imagination of the Old Testament writers pictures the terror of the night, the deprivation of the desert wastes, the threatening afflictions, and the potential destruction that lurks in the world and against which God alone offers sufficient protection. In a similar way, biblical thought agrees with nihilists that the reality of God is the only tenable basis for traditional forms of morality, because a holy God builds moral structures into the fabric of the universe that reflect his own nature. Finally, Christians would agree with nihilists that death is the ultimate threat. Its sudden cancellation of one's possibilities makes life a final absurdity—if there is no God to anchor life in some transcending purpose that can incorporate the stark fact of the death of every person. If there is not some way to set right the balances in the total cosmic sweep of existence, to redress the wrongs suffered by substantial portions of the human family, then life may trigger the nausea Sartre spotlighted so brilliantly in his play by that title.

But, of course, Christians reject the fundamental assumption upon which that diagnosis is built, namely that God is dead and that there is no a priori grounding for truth and value. Therefore Christians reject any kind of immanental solutions of atheistic nihilists. On the other hand, Christians can be grateful in a sense for the nihilists' stark diagnosis, a dogged analysis that is in a powerful way a negative preparation for the good news of the gospel. Only when one has looked nothingness in the face without minimizing its threat is one prepared in impotence to listen to a transcendent solution to the nihilist dilemma.

It may be that Christians can profit by listening to elements of the nihilist criticism of religion. At least some nihilists are not unacquainted with the Christian faith, and yet they have not been per-suaded. Nietzsche, the son of a Lutheran pastor and a short-term theology student, is a good example. His understanding of the Chris-tian faith was notably defective, even at times perverse in his inter-pretation. Nevertheless, in the midst of all his distortions, Nietzsche brought criticisms to which the church should remain sensitive. He criticized the assimilation of Christianity to cultural values. The brunt of his criticism was directed toward what he considered an-tihuman tendencies in the church. One may discount Nietzsche's twisted view of the natural inclinations of the human being—the will to power that leads to the production of the superman—and still ask what core truth there may be in the grotesque antihuman caricature he etched of Christianity. There are, in honesty, expressions of Chris-tianity that militate against some of the finer human values like the healthy affirmation of this life, the natural appetites, the experience of joy, the sampling of the good life in society, culture, the arts, and the enjoyment of beauty in this present real world. Certain interpre-tations of Christianity reject the humanness of human life. Similarly, Christians might listen to Nietzsche's criticisms of ecclesiastical figures, again granting that he spoke in wildly excessive language. He railed at priests as poisoners of life; as parasites who live off people's sins, fears, and guilts; as people who resist sensuality and science and suppress liberty and life. Nietzsche must have experienced enough of those attitudes among clerics to serve as his own basic justification for his massive onslaughts against the church and what he viewed it as doing to human life.

A Critique of Nihilism

Nihilism is perhaps the most ephemeral of all contemporary ideologies. A critique of it cannot be directed toward those disguised and incomplete forms of nihilism that are its most common expres-sion—because in those the nihilist problem is largely unrecognized, and what there is of it is likely buried in the subconscious where it remains the driving force behind its expressions as disparate as a hedonistic life-style and the destructive, annihilating frenzy of a Naziism. Consequently, a critique must be directed primarily toward the formal expressions of Nihilism in thinkers like Nietzsche. Let me suggest a number of points where nihilism can be countered by a Christian thinker.

The fulcrum of the nihilist rationale is atheism. Interestingly, the nihilist's atheism is most often assumed and rarely argued, even by Nietzsche himself or other prominent thinkers of the twentieth century. How did Nietzsche become so convinced that there is no God? He seems to have adopted a form of the projection theory introduced by Feuerbach and made prominent by Freud. In perhaps his most direct statement, Nietzsche wrote: "In former times, one sought to prove that there is no God—today one indicates how the belief that there is a God could *arise* and how this belief acquired its weight and importance: a counter-proof that there is no God thereby becomes superfluous.—When in former times one had refuted the 'proofs of the existence of God' put forward, there always remained the doubt whether better proofs might not be adduced than those just refuted: in those days atheists did not know how to make a clean sweep."[37]

Such a clean sweep is convenient for the nihilist, of course, because it relieves him of the far more difficult path of building a persuasive case that God does not exist. However, this sweeping and unargued assumption also commits one of the more fatal logical fallacies—the psychogenetic fallacy—and is therefore particularly unimpressive in any philosophical discussion. Even if atheism proved to be the case, it cannot be established by such psychological sleight-of-hand tricks as Nietzsche employed. Much more formidable are the arguments against God based upon the inordinate amount of suffering in the world. But even here most nihilists move from the fact of suffering to the conclusion that the existence of God is incompatible with such suffering, and normally the case is not argued in any formal terms at all. So at this point, the Christian has every right to ask for the case that the nihilist is making against the existence of God. Without such a case, the nihilist view cannot finally be sustained.

A second point of vulnerability concerns how the nihilist arrives at his own solution to the nihilist problem. Frequently, the solution is *intuited*—a fact perhaps best illustrated by Nietzsche. When Nietzsche developed his scheme of revaluation, his key ideas were largely intuited. He appropriated the idea of will from Schopenhauer and intuitively transformed it into his idea of the will to power. Drawing upon the inspiration of both Eastern and Western sources, Nietzsche intuited his idea of eternal recurrence. He was convinced that it would receive scientific corroboration, but it remained a dominating intuition. Based upon his assumption that the universe is meaningless and his intuitions such as will to power and eternal recurrence, he, in effect, proposed a recast metaphysic, after having argued against the possibility of metaphysics. The contradiction is obvious. There is nothing wrong in principle with arriving at knowledge through a brilliant intuition. But any intuition needs to receive some argumentative elaboration as it correlates with other forms of knowledge. Why exactly should one be convinced of Nietzsche's view of the will to power, or eternal recurrence, or love of fate—ideas that swirl with Nietzsche's literary brilliance like an explosive and unpredictable fire storm? Like Nietzsche, other nihilists often do not justify their own solutions to the nihilistic dilemma.

A third point of vulnerability is that nihilists tend to make an absolute judgment that nothing is real or meaningful, an absolute judgment that there are no absolutes! The contradiction is found at various levels within the nihilistic outlook. One may say, being *is* nonbeing. Or I *am* nothing! Or there *is* no self! Even in asserting nothingness, one establishes that nothingness *is.* In measuring the sweep of life and concluding that there is no meaning, one still measures the lack of meaning by some standard of meaning. So the question arises, where do we get this idea of meaning by which we assert that nothing is real? A far more modest way of assessing existence is to say that there is no meaning to the universe that I can *personally* discern. It is quite another thing to say that there is no meaning at all. It may be that the problem is in my perception or understanding, not in the lack of meaning within the universe.

This may mean, fourth, that the nihilist critique does not probe deeply enough. Why are there ruptures and disharmonies within the universe? If life is a tragic dilemma, one might ask how it got that way. Then there is the question of whether that is the whole story. How can one explain so much creativity and beauty in the world and love, caring, tenderness, goodness, and joy in the human family? The problem with the nihilist is that he only skims the surface of the deep and makes a selective critique on a flat plane with only two-dimensional glasses that lack height and depth perception.

A fifth criticism is that the nihilist affirmation runs counter to the deepest human characteristics that cry out for ultimate meaning, for beauty, truth, and goodness, and for the lasting value of love and the eternal worth of human personality. One cannot guarantee that such drives, instincts, and appetites can find satisfaction. But just as thirst occurs because we are creatures who require water for life, and hunger because we require food, so the aspirations for the eternal may have their corresponding objects as they develop within human personality. All that is part of our unique humanity. One may assume that amoebas or flat worms or fish or insects or primates, with all their struggle to survive, do not find themselves locked into an existential quest, urgently asking questions of meaning, pressing mystery to disclose itself to them. While at one level, any sensitive human will look squarely at some point in life into the yawning abyss of possible nothingness, it is a rare human who is willing to snuggle lightly into that vacuum as a final solution for the human situation.

A sixth criticism is that the loss of a moral foundation can produce disastrous results in society. When Nietzsche called for a radical revaluation of values, he understood that it is not possible to sustain traditional Western human values apart from a transcendental basis. Consequently, he assumed that a new basis for values would have to reflect the fundamental creative processes of nature, which he took to be the will to power. Thus in the new era beyond nihilism, morality would have to be beyond traditional ideas of good and evil. The superman would embody that supramoral life and transcend the herd morality of the masses of people. In fact, many of Nietzsche's proposed new moral ideas remained reflective of a fairly conventional morality. Yet the theme of beyond good and evil that Nietzsche introduced, when wrongly appropriated, as in the case of Naziism, can wreak havoc in society. Nietzsche would have rejected the blond beast that ravaged Europe, but his ideas were construed as the basis for that phenomenon. In the twentieth century, the "anything is permissible" theme has produced staggering inhumanity as people have brutalized and terrorized with little conscience in the name of some special cause. There is no guarantee that the moral restructuring, as in the case of a Nietzsche, a Camus, or a Sartre, will contribute to the good of the human family.

Finally, the nihilistic solutions normally require too much of average people, either in the degree of resignation or in the herculean capacities for tragic heroism. Most people find it impossible to live at that level in the face of the nihilistic diagnosis of life, which may partly explain the large amount of incomplete nihilism, the inability to face the nihilist dilemma head-on, resulting in the sublimation of the threat at the popular level.

Nihilism or Christianity: Which Faith?

Nihilism and Christianity embody the two most profoundly opposite readings of the universe and human life. Nihilism contends that nothing is ultimately real or meaningful; that there is no absolute truth or value; that human life is an unsolvable enigma; that there is no ultimate explanation for the universe, either its origin or goal; that life has no purpose; that if there is any order or pattern of meaning in life, we must impose it ourselves. Nihilism contends that there is no being, but only becoming—blind, irrational, accidental becoming. Christianity, in contrast, asserts that there is being behind the process of becoming, a Being who provides an absolute ground for truth and value, a Being who explains the existence of anything at all and the purpose and goal of the universe and individual human life, a Being who transcends and yet is radically within the process, creatively moving it toward His own future goal. Two faiths! And there are no absolute guidelines as to which position is right. Each viewpoint weighs whatever evidence it takes to be relevant and then makes a leap of faith in affirming its particular reading of the way things are. What are the factors that may tip the balance one way or another?

For one thing, Christians agree that the threat of nonbeing is there in our experience. It is *logically* possible that everything is chaos and that there is no explanation for existence and no absolute ground for truth and values. It is possible that everything is becoming, transitory, ephemeral, perishing, accidentally and blindly plunging on into an unknown future. It is possible, as Theodore Dreiser has said, that humans are parasites, inhabiting the epidermis of a midge among the planets—and nothing more! It is possible that life itself is *the* theater of the absurd and we are unwilling actors in the cosmic tragedy. Beyond the logical possibility, most Christians do not minimize the *actual* threat of nonbeing. In interpreting the universe as an ordered creation that God willed out of an absolute formless void and continues to uphold against a threatening chaos, the biblical writers speak eloquently of the flashes of nothingness there to be seen and experienced in the created order. It is both logically possible and on the basis of selective evidence empirically arguable—if one ignores the evidence for creative order and the personal experiences of God—that the nothingness which we observe punctuating the creative process may actually dominate our patterned order of existence and be life's final word. So Christians will admit the possibility that nihilists may be right, even when we believe they are wrong.

It is also the case that most nonnihilists, including Christians, on occasion, existentially feel the threat of meaninglessness and dread the ominous pressure of nonbeing. In all honesty, there may be some of that experience in the classic dark nights of the soul or the more transitory doubts that Christian believers almost universally have at one time or another. Perhaps the nihilist threat is there in the doubt that always remains the underside of faith. From the laments of the psalmists who vividly describe the aloneness, the darkness, and the loss of a fixed point in their experiences of the absence of God to their modern counterparts facing the terrifying complexities of the twentieth century, the dread of nothingness is no stranger to the religious pilgrim. The Christian ought to admit that a dialectical interplay does occur within the life of faith as faith finds a way to transcend the paralyzing menace of nothingness.

On the other hand, the nihilist can appeal to no strictly rational argument for accepting nihilism. For if there is no truth, then it cannot follow that nihilism is true. Even granted the possibility that there may be a certain type of limited rationality in the nihilist view, one still cannot prove the nonexistence of God or the lack of teleology in the evolutionary process or the absence of an absolute ground for values—even though one may make a persuasive case against them all. In the final analysis, nihilism represents a grand intuition, a cosmic bias, a personal preference or fear, a Gestalt that rings with final authority to some people. Once seen, the Gestalt appears to be utterly convincing. It may arise for various reasons—rational, emotive, relational, or spiritual—but at root it may reflect a perplexed metaphysical bias, possibly a projection of the psychic Angst upon the universe. In this sense, Nietzsche's only substantial argument for atheism cuts both ways. The only question is which, if either, is right?

In confronting life, there are reasons to reach a nihilist conclusion. But that is only half the picture. The fact is that many experiences resist a nihilist reading. Some things are of value and have meaning, however compelling one's nihilist urges may be. Truth, beauty, goodness, and love remain the bedrock of human existence through the shifting phases of cultural time. The resurgent power of those human attachments says some things are true and of value. Even when one attempts to lay aside belief in God, those values still surge through the human spirit and will not be consigned to oblivion. From the brooding contemplation of all the nihilistic elements of life, one looks outside and sees daffodils poking yellow plumes through the ground. A rose exudes its scent into the air. A bird sings—happy, content, taking what nature serves up, with not the slightest hint of despair. A brilliant sun summons nature to life after the dormancy and death of winter. The cycle of life and creativity goes on. Plants bloom, animals birth their young, snows melt and the streams gurgle, fish sport, birds fly—all predictably, beautifully, and seemingly purposeful. Everything recurs—the beauty and the pain, the light and the dark—and its very dependability triggers the intuition that life happens out of an ultimate ground that transcends and orders the process. A child's laughter, the twinkle in an old man's eye, a lover's caress, the embrace of a friend, the caring touch of a Mother Teresa—it is all a collage that is the counterpoint to the images of nothingness that render a negative judgment on reality. At a minimum, these experiences make one *want* to pass beyond nihilism to affirm something. Nihilism runs counter to the deepest instincts and drives of the human person—the faith and hope that there is meaning, despite all the negative intrusions into human experience. At best it may still be that these experiences, even in a nihilistic era, remain signposts for the way to God!

Nihilist and Christian hold rival faiths. The tragedy of nihilism is that the nihilist has not gone far enough. The nihilist analysis sounds strangely like the starting point for the Christian faith. What is left after the nihilist analysis? The emptiness of life without God, the guilt for complicity in the human dilemma, the sense of being carried on the tides of fate, the disruption of death and the question mark it places over life! If that is the final word from life, then we too should conclude, like Sartre's character, that there is no exist from life. But in the Christian perspective, it is only when we are brought low and understand at the core of the self the threat of nonbeing that we are prepared to receive the grace of God. Recurrently through the Bible, the stark look into the abyss of nothingness is the transitional step to finding God and ultimate meaning. That is something of what Paul had in mind in writing that Christ "has delivered us from the dominion of darkness and transferred us to the kingdom of his beloved Son" (Col. 1:13).

Philosopher Karl Jaspers has defended nihilism as a necessary philosophical phase on the way to philosophical faith. Nihilism strips away self-deception. It destroys the illusion that life is a rational, ordered, harmonious process. When meaning must be found only within the structures of this world, we rapidly discover those structures are incapable of bearing absolute meaning. Nihilism can propel one into a search for a new transcendent dimension to life, one which illuminates, gives new value to, and transforms our encompassed natural world.[38]

The Christian faith offers exactly that—an inbreak from beyond, eternity entering time, God becoming a human being, a revelatory light dispelling the world's darkness, a center point of meaning in the midst of ambiguous human history. Still the heart of the Christian faith itself is a paradox, a historical contingency that does not manifest itself with forceful persuasiveness to every observer, a cross that sets a scandal before autonomous human life and intellect. If the center of the Christian faith, the Christ event, is the key to meaning and value, then it cannot be approached like a simple arithmetical problem to be solved. It is the ultimate mystery that must be confronted, a mystery that will disclose itself to those who approach it in humility and risk the commitment of their lives to it.

There is another way to transcend the nihilist threat than those we have examined, and that is through the act of faith that in the midst of the storms of meaninglessness that roar through human experience, there is a key that opens a door to meaning and lasting value. That approach is highlighted in Soren Kierkegaard's figure of the knight of faith,[39] the individual who faces the nihilist threat and is not willing to resign either to meaninglessness or to a safe intellectual faith. Rather the knight of faith dares, risks, and commits to the paradoxical—even absurd to the rational intellect—assertions of the Christian faith that at one point in human history eternity enters time, God becomes man, and that this one contingent event becomes absolute truth for every person in every generation. But the truth can be found only in a personal encounter with the contemporary Christ, an encounter that requires a leap of faith into the darkness, a leap that trusts we will be caught in the loving arms of an eternal God. Only in that radical leap can meaning finally be found and the ever-present nihilist threat continuously thwarted. The relationship with God provides the ontological grounding for truth, value, purpose, beauty, and other realities that matter most in human life—all of which are threatened and become groundless in the nihilistic dilemma.

In some ways, the Christian can sympathize with the nihilist. Many Christians have stood on the brink of the abyss of nothingness and have been saved from plunging over only by a trusting personal relationship with God through Jesus Christ who is the way, the truth, and the life. That personal confirmation through the leap of faith is a factor in resolving the conflict between the two faiths that nihilism can never claim. The nihilist must always wrestle with the possibility that there may be a key to meaning *if* he could only find it. The Christian, although threatened at times by the possibility of nothingness, knows personally that there is a key to meaning because he has found it in faith in Jesus Christ.

8
World Religions:
The Search for Ultimacy

Imagine a visitor from outer space making a rapid tour of the various continents and cultures of the planet Earth with the assignment to describe the characteristics of the highest intelligent species of life called Homo sapiens. No matter where the visitor observes human culture, from aboriginal peoples to those in advanced technological societies, the landscape is punctuated with religious temples, holy shrines, and groups of people engaged in religious rituals. Such a neutral interpreter of humanity would undoubtedly describe humans in one way as religious creatures—as homo religiosus. However diverse its expressions, religion is a universal characteristic of the human race.

Although secular ideologies are rapidly expanding their influence in the modern world, the vast majority of humans are still adherents of some form of religion. Of the four and one-half billion people alive in the early 1980s, about three billion claim allegiance to some form of religion. Of the three billion religious people, one billion nominally claim to be Christians and the other two billion are distributed through the variety of other world religions and religious cults and sects. Although the one billion people who hold some secular ideology increasingly dominate many centers of culture and power that most decisively shape the structures of the future world, the Christian apologetic task from a simple quantitative measurement is most critical at the point of the encounter with the great world religions. The encounter raises difficult theological and missiological problems for the Christian church that require both knowledge of world religions themselves and a theological understanding from within Christianity.

The Phenomenon of World Religions

The religions of the human race encompass the great world religions, which have large numbers of devotees and centuries of heritage, as well as vast numbers of religions, cults, and eclectic sects that are usually geographically and numerically limited. Of the eleven living world religions in today's world, there are approximately one billion Christians, six hundred million Hindus, seven hundred million Muslims, two hundred and fifty million Buddhists, fifteen million Jews, plus varying numbers of Confucianists, Taoists, Shintoists, Jainists, Sikhs, and Parsis. In addition, there are the countless traditional religions of tribal peoples in Africa and several other areas of the world. Within many cultures of the world, there are also small religious sects that claim the allegiance of limited numbers of people.

The great world religions originated in three general areas of the world. The Middle East was the birthplace of Zoroastrianism (modern Parsiism), Judaism, Christianity, and Islam. Hebrew religion produced Christianity and was one source of Islam, which also drew upon some Christian and pagan elements. India was the second geographical seedbed of religion, producing in its long history the numerous expressions of Hinduism, Jainism, Sikhism, and Buddhism. China was the source of Taoism and Confucianism. Shintoism originated in and has been confined to Japan. The traditional religions originating in Africa are still a prominent force on that continent.

In the modern religious setting, Hinduism is the main religion of the subcontinent of India, an area within which Jainism and Sikhism are largely confined. Theravada Buddhism dominates Southeast Asia, and Mahayana Buddhism is prominently found in parts of Northern Asia and has some influence in Japan. Islam is virtually identical with the culture of the Arab world and has many adherents in Northern India and Africa. Christianity is the prevailing religion in Europe, the Americas, and Australasia, and has numerous adherents in all other parts of the world with the exception of the Arab nations, where there are still few Christians. Christianity, Islam, and certain Buddhist and Hindu sects are all to some extent missionary religions. That fact, combined with the phenomenon of massive emigration out of Third World countries into Europe and the Americas, means that the Christian encounter with world religions now occurs over much of the world, including within European and American societies.

Increasingly, American and European Christians are involved in the apologetic task with adherents of other world religions.

The Nature of Religion

Given the wide diversity of the phenomenon of religion, one must ask the question of what exactly religion is. What is there in common among these religious responses of human beings that groups them under the single term "religion"? The nature of religion can be addressed from a more abstract philosophical level or from the concrete level of examining what most people recognize are world religions. Philosophers have no universal agreement about the more abstract category of "religion." The philosophical definitions of religion vary from broad to narrow. Some definitions of religion are so broad as to include every person who lives out of any ultimate concern or centers life upon any supreme value, which encompasses far more people than are in formal religious movements. On the other hand, religion can be defined so narrowly that movements normally regarded as religions are excluded—for example, religions that do not include a specific belief in God or that may not involve religious ritual.[1]

Our present purpose is not to resolve the philosophical debate about the nature of religion. It is reasonably simple to define phenomenologically the nature and characteristics of identifiable world religions that command the allegiance of large numbers of people. John Hick proposes a good definition of religion in this sense as "an understanding of the universe, together with an appropriate way of living within it, which involves reference beyond the natural world to God or gods or to the Absolute or to a transcendent order or process."[2] Although religions may disagree about the nature of the ultimate reality that transcends the natural world, all religions seek after or respond to, and then proceed to organize and structure life around, what they consider to be ultimate in the universe. Given the great geographical, cultural, and racial diversities of the human family in its universal religious quest, it is not surprising that wide variety, along with some identifiable common ground, exists among the world religions.[3]

World religions embody certain common structures that are normally found in varying levels of prominence, although one or another of the structures may be quite minimal or even absent in particular religions. Each religion holds a body of beliefs—doctrines, myths, historical memories—that interpret life for its adherents. Ritual practices such as worship, prayer, sacrifice, meditation, pilgrimages, and recognition of holy places or shrines are almost universal. Most religions set out an ethical pattern of life or a behavioral way of life that shapes the character of the individual and often of a society dominated by the religion. Religions also usually produce institutional structures such as a religious order or priesthood that preserves and conducts cultic practices around temples, shrines, and holy places. Finally, religions create a wealth of symbolism in architecture, literature, art, and music that profoundly impacts the cultures in which the religion is found. Individual religions place more or less emphasis upon any one of these particular structures.

The formal structures of religions are ways of focusing the basic human concerns about one's life and place in the universe that are expressed in common themes and patterns among the religions. One common characteristic is that devotees of each world religion hold deep convictions about their religious faith or experience. In each religion, serious adherents exhibit devotion and commitment to what they consider ultimate—a personal God or gods, an impersonal God, cosmic order, some absolute ground of all that there is, or even a future void into which one may enter. Most religions also describe or mythologize how the universe came to be, what its basic structure is, and what its ultimate future will be. Every religion proposes an explanation of the nature and structures of human life and a definition of its purpose. Religions, consequently, analyze and offer a solution to the human problem. Almost universally, the human problem is diagnosed by some variation of the theme of alienation. Humans seem universally aware that they are separated in some way from their essential or true selves and are not what ideally they should or yet will be. Religions then prescribe some way of salvation, a path by which alienated humans can be liberated, enlightened, unified, or redeemed. Usually, rituals are evolved that help the religious person overcome alienation and express worship of whatever is ultimate within his religion.

Comparative Teachings of World Religions

Although world religions have common structures and thematic concerns, they do not all teach basically the same things, as some people allege. There are striking differences in what religions teach about what is ultimate, the nature of the world, human life, the human problem and its solution, and the future of human life and of the universe.[4] The greatest divergencies are found between the theistic religions of Christianity, Judaism, and Islam and the great religions of the East. The theistic religions tend toward an exclusivism which asserts that theirs is the true way to God, and Eastern religions generally are inclusivistic and hold that there are many equally valid ways to God or to ultimate reality. Hinduism and some forms of Buddhism are capable of embracing any form of religion as a valid way to God. Christianity and Judaism have much in common, the chief difference relating to their respective views about Jesus. Islam, in its radical monotheism, shares some ideas with Judaism and Christianity. And here and there within other world religions are striking parallels to Christian ideas, such as the personal monotheism of Bhakti Hinduism. But on the large scale of world religions, there are sharp differences in the answers that religions give to basic human concerns. A full understanding of these similarities and differences requires a phenomenological study of each religion within itself. For purposes of illustration, we can selectively note representative answers to common human concerns from individual religions.

The concept of the ultimate.—The most crucial element in religion is the view of what is ultimate within or beyond the universe. The concept of the nature of the ultimate reality varies from ideas of a personal theistic God to an impersonal God to numerous gods to an indescribable absolute to a virtual agnosticism. Judaism and Islam share with Christianity a belief in a personal theistic God, although Islam emphasizes more strongly His sovereignty and transcendence, and Judaism and Islam both reject the Christian doctrine of the Trinity and the belief that God became incarnate in Jesus Christ. Bhakti Hinduism holds a theistic view of God that pictures God (Brahman) as personal, as the creator of the world who is differentiated from the world and humans, and as a God of redeeming love and grace. African traditional religion also worships a high God among the many lesser divinities. Mahayana Buddhism attributes intelligence, love, will, and reflection to Dharmakaya (the absolute truth-body of Buddha). In its view that Dharmakaya differentiates itself in all sentient beings in order to become aware of itself, Mahayana may be close to a panentheistic view of God.

Yet there are views of God that are far from theism. Within Hinduism alone, views of God range from a practical atheism through popular polytheism to monistic pantheism to dualism to theism. In Vedic Hinduism, the oldest strain of Hinduism, there are many gods, a polytheistic view that still prevails in popular village Hinduism all over India. In underdeveloped countries in the South Pacific and in Africa, popular religion still focuses upon various divinities, even though in Africa a high God is also worshiped. At the opposite pole are monistic or pantheistic views of God or ultimate reality found so frequently in Eastern religions. Advaitic Hinduism defines Brahman as the sole ultimate reality, as the Great Self which embraces and is identical with all human selves and which makes the illusion of the world and the individuality of the human self. Brahman is indescribable and nonpersonal, although it is manifest in a wide variety of deities within human experience, deities which are the practical focus of Hindu worship. In classical Hinduism, the chief manifestations of Brahman among the many deities are the chief divine triad of Brahma, the creator God; Vishnu, the preserver; and Shiva, who represents the creative and destructive powers of God. Both Confusianism and Taoism hold an impersonal concept of the ultimate reality. Despite its primary interest in human life in this world and its disinterest in metaphysical questions, Confusianism nevertheless refers to "Heaven" as the overarching source of order and life, indicating some transcendent point of reference. Taoism recognizes the Tao, the Way, as the ultimate ground of existence and as the norm and rhythm of the universe by which people should order their lives. Jainism teaches a dualism between innumerable human souls and matter and pictures the absolute as composed of the collective union of perfected souls who have escaped the wheel of reincarnation. Finally, Theravada Buddhism at one level is agnostic and refuses to speculate about ultimate reality, and yet in another way its focus on Nirvana as the ultimate void that cannot be characterized as either being or nonbeing takes on a transcendent dimension in the life of the devotee.

   The world.—Every view of God has a corresponding view of the world. The great religions, consequently, view the world in different ways. For Christians and Jews, the world is God's good creation, differentiated from and yet dependent on God. It is a real and substantial world in which God is working out His creative and redemptive purposes, so that both nature and history are moving toward God's future redemptive goal. Muslims view the world in similar terms, although making God more transcendent to the world and events more determined by the inexorable will of Allah. Monistic Hinduism generally regards the world as illustory and as only one of a series of both higher and lower worlds that are a part of the endless cycle of reincarnation from which people need to escape. The world itself is created not by the purposive act of God but as the product of the sportive play or cosmic dance of Brahman, the impersonal God. As an illusion to be transcended, the world has no eternal purpose. Buddhism views the world as a realm of suffering caused by the desire for the permanency of a substantial individualized self. It is a world of impermanence and illusion from which one needs to cross over into the void of Nirvana. At the opposite pole, dualistic Hinduism and Jainism view the world of matter as eternal alongside innumerable individual souls and as a barrier to the liberation of the soul from the cycle of reincarnation into the collective union of the absolute. In contrast, both Confucianism and Taoism take the world as a given along with human life, refuse to speculate about its origin or future, and teach people how to live effectively within it.

Human beings.—Christianity and Judaism view humans as creatures made in the image of God and, therefore, differentiated from God. As persons created good for the purpose of being related personally to God and to other persons and of exercising dominion under God over the earth, individual human beings are of infinite worth. Islam shares many of those ideas although it minimizes the personal aspect of the human relationship to a more transcendent God. Eastern religions have varied views of humans, but for the most part they are far from the theistic religious views, either identifying the soul with God or denying the substantiality of the human self. In monistic Hinduism, everything real is one with Brahman, and what appear to be individual selves are but differentiations of the one Great Self—Brahman-Atman. The uniqueness of the I and the individual personal destiny of the human self are nothing but an illusion. In the pluralism of Samkhya Hinduism, countless numbers of individual selves exist from all eternity and are born into matter in order to become conscious of themselves and in eventual perfection to enter into the collective union of the absolute. Theravada Buddhism, in its anatta doctrine, denies the substantial reality of the self and holds that what is called the self is simply the momentary coalescence of the five aspects that make up human life—bodily form, feeling, sense perception, mental formations, and consciousness. Yet in a contrasting view that parallels some important Judeo-Christian insights, Bhakti Hinduism teaches that the human self is created as personal, related to but differentiated from God, and, although imperfect because of its deeds, capable of a personal relationship with God.

The human problem.—Analyses of the human problem parallel the different concepts of the human self and God. Sin is the basic problem in theistic religions that worship a holy God, whereas in the monistic or pantheistic religions of the Far East, the problem is ignorance or desire. Rebellion against God is at the center of Judeo-Christian views of sin, whereas Islam pictures sin more as a breaking of the laws of God than as a rupture of a personal relationship with God. In Hinduism and Buddhism, the varied analyses of the human problem revolve around the law of karma, the law of the deed that determines one's next reincarnation, and the law of samsara, the law that individual souls are reincarnated many times before finally being absorbed again into the oneness of Brahman or entering into the void of Nirvana. Within those laws, Advaitic Hinduism teaches that the human problem is ignorance, one's mistaking the illusion of the permanence of the world of matter and the distinctive individuality of the self for the ultimate reality of the soul's identity with Brahman. This illusion keeps one trapped in a series of reincarnations in other bodies, which may be higher human selves or even animals, depending upon how one observes karma, the law of the deed. In contrast, dualistic Samkhya Hinduism teaches that the eternally real world of matter, particularly in the obstruction of the body over the soul, prevents the soul from transcending matter and entering into the final collective absolute reality. Buddhism places the individual's plight on the entrapment in a world of suffering brought about by the desire to maintain either the individuality of the self or the illusion that there is a self. Mahayana Buddhism denies the individuality of the self, and Theravada the reality of the self. As long as humans desire to be differentiated as individual selves, one can never escape the cycle of rebirth into a world of suffering and enter into Nirvana.

The solution to the human problem.—Not surprisingly, world religions do not prescribe the same solution for the human problem, although each advocates some type of salvation. Jews place salvation in the gracious and righteous initiative of God in establishing a covenantal relationship with His people. Christians hold that salvation from sin to a reconciled and righteous life in God is made possible by faith in God's gracious act of salvation in Jesus Christ, who is the Mediator between God and human beings. For Muslims, the solution and the chief duty of humans is to obey God's laws, as found in the Koran and later Islamic traditions, and to observe the Five Pillars of creed, prayer, charity, the holy month of Ramadan, and at least one pilgrimage to Mecca. Theravada Buddhism prescribes an eightfold path of rightness that can be properly followed only by a monk who becomes an ascetic in order to transcend desire, attain enlightenment, and enter into Nirvana. Thus only the arhat, the monk, can attain salvation through his own self-reliance.

Salvation for the Hindu can come in any one of four major ways—through knowledge, work or discipline, love or devotion, or psychological exercises like yoga. These paths help one to overcome ignorance and to realize the soul's oneness with Brahman. There is no urgency in salvation because each soul is destined to live through many lifetimes. Only the Brahmin caste and the second highest caste can theoretically escape reincarnation and be absorbed into Brahman, the impersonal ultimate reality. Confucianism and Taoism stress self-reliance. In Confucianism, one obeys the good moral law within himself. Taoism teaches the observance of the Tao, the way that governs the universe and orders life. At the opposite pole from the emphasis on self-reliance are Mahayana Buddhism and Bhakti Hinduism. Mahayana offers salvation to many more people than monks. There is a Mahayana version of grace in which ordinary people are assisted by people who have incarnated the Buddha spirit and by the boddisatvas, people who have attained a degree of enlightenment that places them on the brink of Nirvana but who out of compassion for others farther behind, refuse to enter and return to help others toward Nirvana. Bhakti Hinduism, based upon its theistic view of God, teaches salvation by a gracious God who redeems the devotee into a personal relationship to himself. Meditation is the road to enlightenment in Zen Buddhism, an enlightenment that cannot be described in words but which brings transformed wonder to the enlightened one's experience of ordinary life.

The good life.—One's view of salvation implies some idea of what constitutes the good life. For the Christian, the purpose of life is to glorify God through a life of *agape*, the divine kind of love that reaches out to all people in service, a love that is the key principle to be applied in all the concrete ethical situations of life. The good life for Jews centers upon living righteously before God. Muslims achieve the good life by obeying the detailed laws of Islam, which govern every aspect of life in an Islamic society. The chief virture for a Theravada Buddhist is wisdom and for a Mahayana Buddhist compassion as each respectively follows the eightfold path. For Hinduism in general, the good life consists in obeying the dharma, that is, the duties that one's position and circumstances in life impose, including religion, custom, morals, and caste in society. Shintoism closely identifies the good life with Japanese nationalist values.

The final goal of life.—Religions also differ in what they consider to be the final goal of life. For Christians, the goal of life is union with God and the redeemed in heaven, a final union that preserves the identity of the individual in a universal relationship with the people of God, a future that is the purpose and goal of the created order and human history, and into which they will also be transformed. Similarly, Islam anticipates a dual future of a heaven for the righteous, which in its delights is a qualitative extension of a joyful earthly life, and a hell for the damned. Monistic Hinduism teaches that the final goal for humans is the absorption of the self into Brahman-Atman, the Great Self, the impersonal reality. Buddhists picture the ultimate future as the enlightenment that allows the human to escape the craving for individualized selfhood and to enter Nirvana, which Theravadists interpret as an indescribable void and Mahayanists as bliss, in which the individualized self vanishes. Taoism and Confucianism, in their concern for the present life, refuse to engage in such metaphysical speculations about the final goal of human life.

At the encompassing level of a total world view, theistic religions are teleological, emphasizing the reality of the created order and history and engaging in action to change the world toward its future goal of redemption into the eternal life of God, which places an urgency upon how the individual lives his own life. In sharp contrast, Eastern religions generally view history and nature as timeless, as caught in an endless cycle of repetition, which leads to a quietist attitude that accepts and does not attempt to change the world. This life has little urgency because the majority of people have many more lives to live before attaining the perfection that allows them to enter into absorption with Brahman or the void or bliss of Nirvana and thus to escape the illusion of the world.

These examples illustrate the common structures and thematic concerns and the wide divergencies in the way the world religions respond to those universal human concerns. Each religion, however, offers a coherent interpretation of human existence within its own frame of reference, a frame that depends upon and grows out of its basic idea of what is ultimate in human experience. The concept of God or the ultimate is *the* critical element in religion, all other beliefs and practices growing out of that. When religions tend toward a Christian view of God, there are other similarities as well; and when the view of God is different, the divergencies of other beliefs from Christianity are more pronounced in the degree that God is viewed as one or many, as personal or impersonal, as transcendent or immanent, as creator or as an indescribable but nonpurposeful absolute.

The concept of God is even more crucial for the Christian encounter with world religions because the Christian understanding of God is unique among the world religions. The Christian view of God reshapes its inherited Jewish monotheism by God's revelation of Himself and redemption of the world in Jesus Christ. Consequently, Christians affirm belief in a Triune God, one God in three persons, who has incarnated Himself in the man Jesus Christ within human history and who is present throughout history in the person of the Holy Spirit. The focal point of the Christian encounter with world religions is Jesus Christ and what belief in Him says about God.

A Christian Understanding of World Religions

The Christian apologist needs to understand world religions at two levels. First, any Christian who is serious about the apologetic task with devotees of other world religions should study in some depth the teachings and practices of the individual great world religions as well as the similarities and differences between world religions. As important as the knowledge of world religions is in informing the apologetic task, the Christian's theological understanding of world religions is not determined primarily by phenomenological, historical, or comparative study of world religions. The Christian assessment of the value of other religions in relating people to God is determined for most Christians by theological perspectives derived from the core of the Christian faith itself. So the second and most critical level of understanding is what the Christian faith itself teaches about the value of other religions.

How then should the Christian theologically understand world religions? There is no absolute concensus on that question within either the ancient or modern church. Many factors, not the least the biblical and theological, influence the varied positions. Both the Bible and historical theologies reflect diverse attitudes that range from disdain and rejection of other religions as expressions of idolatry to respect and affirmation of the worship of God in other religions as tentative and preparatory responses to the biblical God. Attitudes toward non-Christian religions vary even more within the modern church from the extremes of relativistic and pluralistic views that affirm the value of all religions to exclusivistic views that totally reject all religious responses outside Judeo-Christian religion. Within the middle of those extremes are various views that affirm the positive element in other religions but hold to the finality of revelation and redemption in Jesus Christ.

Christology and World Religions

The crucial factor in the Christian understanding of world religions is how the church views revelation and redemption in relation to Jesus Christ. Christology largely determines a theology of world religions and a parallel theology of mission. If one asks the question, How and where is God best and finally revealed and where is salvation achieved? the almost universal Christian answer has been: In Jesus Christ! Christianity is historically centered upon its belief in the New Testament witness that Jesus Christ is the final revelation and redemption of God. John focuses both of those dimensions in saying, "Grace [salvation] and truth [revelation] came through Jesus Christ" (John 1:17).

The New Testament teaches that the final and most perfect revelation or self-disclosure of God has come in Jesus Christ. Jesus reveals what God is like, the true nature of humanity, and how life should be lived. John interprets Jesus as saying, "He who has seen me has seen the Father" (John 14:9). Paul asserts that we have "the light of the knowledge of the glory of God in the face of Christ" (2 Cor. 4:6). Both John and Paul teach that the very Word by which God created the universe became incarnate in Jesus (John 1:14; Col. 1:19-20). Jesus is also depicted as the embodiment of the perfect human image of

God in His living perfectly as an authentic human being before God (Heb. 4:14-15). In His sacrificial love and service of humanity, Jesus also demonstrates God's purposes for human life (Mark 10:35-45).

The New Testament further portrays Jesus as Redeemer. It consistently teaches that the full and final redemption of humanity, indeed of the cosmos itself, is achieved through God's reconciliation of the world to Himself in the life, death, and resurrection of Jesus Christ. In Paul's classic words, "In Christ God was reconciling the world to himself" (2 Cor. 5:19). The New Testament repeatedly claims that this was a once-for-all act of redemption at a particular point in history in a specific human individual (Heb. 10:10; 7:27) for the sins of all human beings (John 4:42; 1 John 2:2; 4:14; Rom. 8:32; 5:19; and others). This exalted estimate of Jesus leads to the assertion, "And there is salvation in no one else, for there is no other name under heaven given among men by which we must be saved" (Acts 4:12).

Much of the divergence in the church's estimate of world religions lies in the different ways individual theological traditions interpret the revelation and redemption in Jesus Christ. The varied Christologies within the church result from different understandings of biblical authority, interpretations of the New Testament, and ways of relating the Bible and theological traditions. Is Jesus unique and essential or not? Depending upon the answer, one may be a religious pluralist or a particularist. Is Jesus Christ's redemptive work only in His revelation, or is He both Revealer and Redeemer? Is there a general revelation, as the theologians refer to it, outside the special revelation in Judeo-Christian salvation history? If there is such a general revelation, how does it relate to world religions? Is there any saving value in the general revelation? If so, how does the saving value relate to God's act of revelation and redemption in Jesus Christ? For the Christian particularist, there is the question of how Jesus can be the only redeemer if there is some saving value in general revelation and possibly in other religions. The answers to these questions will largely determine one's theological understanding of and approach to other world religions.

Alternative Views of World Religions

With a risk of overgeneralization, let me suggest that at the broadest level there are three major understandings of world religions within the church, with a number of variations possible in each broad view: a relativistic and pluralistic view; a radical exclusivistic view; and a particularist view of continuity and discontinuity. Each option holds a rather different combination of views concerning Christ and His work, general revelation, and how Christians should relate to other religions.

A relativistic and pluralist view.—First, there is the relativistic and pluralistic view that revelation and redemption are found in all religions, just as in Christianity. This view rejects the claims of the New Testament about the uniqueness and indispensability of Jesus Christ. The work of Christ is usually interpreted strictly as revelation, so that any redemptive value in the life of Jesus resides in His new disclosure of truth—for example, that God is love or that human life has great potential. Based upon this Christology, one can then regard Jesus as only one revealer among many revealers like Gautama, Lao-tzu, Muhammad, and others. One might grant that the revelation of Jesus is a higher or even a final form of revelation in comparison to other revealers or other religions—but the difference is only one of degree and not of a kind. Jesus may be important for Christians but He is not essential for everyone.[5]

It follows, on this view, that revelation and redemption are universal in all world religions. Often relativists will argue that God continually presses in upon the human family with a disclosure of Himself in various revelations. The varied concepts of God in the world religions are the result of limited and broken human conceptualizations of the same God, the one God who transcends all our finite understandings of Him. Consequently, the concepts of God in world religions unavoidably reflect each religion's peculiar cultural characteristics and limitations. Salvation is equally available in all religions. Christianity is one of numerous paths to God. Advocates of this view would agree with the Hindu teaching about salvation: Whichever path men choose is mine![6]

In relating to world religions, relativists can take one of several approaches based upon openness, mutual respect, and affirmation. One can urge a dialogue with adherents of other religions that is designed to enrich each partner's experience of God in his own religion as the world religions peacefully coexist in a pluralistic world. Or one can engage in a dialogue, based upon a radical openness to each other's religion, that is prepared to combine the best elements of each religion into a new syncretistic religion that transcends all existing religions. In this approach, there may be dialogue, but there is no apologetic task or world mission with the intention of converting people to faith in Jesus Christ.[7] The relativistic view of Christianity and world religions has had few advocates in the history of the church.

A view of radical exclusivism.—There is a second widely held Christian view of world religions that is radically exclusivistic and rejects the value of other world religions. In this view, Jesus is understood as both Revealer and Redeemer, the one individual through whom God has reconciled the world to Himself. This view is not only particularistic in asserting that all salvation is in Christ, but it takes quite literally the New Testament assertion that there is no other *name* by which we may be saved. Thus the only way that the salvation in Christ may be appropriated is by hearing and responding in faith to the gospel of the historic Jesus.

In practical terms, this view contends that salvation requires a formal identification with Christianity. Two major positions within the church represent variations of this basic conviction. Traditional Roman Catholicism taught a dogma for many centuries that emerged during the patristic period and became of central importance during the Middle Ages. The formula was: Outside the church, there is no salvation. The formula was applied not only to adherents of other religions but to heretics and schismatics within the Christian church, including Protestants, until the church changed its dogma in the mid-twentieth century, most dramatically in Vatican II.[8] The Protestant variation on this general exclusivistic position is that there is no salvation outside Christianity, by which is usually meant a formal hearing of the gospel and a specific faith response to God through the name of Jesus. There is no possibility of being saved through God's redemptive act in Jesus Christ without hearing the gospel of the historic Jesus.[9] Both exclusivist versions affirm the absolute uniqueness of Christianity, and traditional Roman Catholicism confined that to the Roman Catholic Church.

Christian exclusivists usually hold one of two views about general revelation and its relation to world religions—although both agree that there is no saving general revelation. The most extreme position —for example, that of Karl Barth—argues that all revelation is saving but that there is no general revelation outside the Judeo-Christian revelation that centers in Jesus Christ, a revelation that is basically witnessed to in the Bible and in Christian preaching. All religions are expressions of the idolatrous human search for God and not of revelation. All religion, including the human side of the Christian religion, is an expression of sin and falls short of the revelation of God in Christ. Revelation and redemption come only in the Judeo-Christian Word and not through religion.[10]

There are several ways that this view may interpret how salvation is appropriated. In Barth's view, salvation is exclusively in Christ but the whole human race is elected to salvation in Him. The task of the church is to announce to people that they are elect in Christ and call upon them to live out their salvation in faith.[11] It is likely that most Christians who share Barth's view that there is no general revelation think, in contrast to Barth, that the only possibility of being redeemed is in hearing and responding in faith to the preaching of the Christian gospel.

A second view is that there is a general revelation of God which is corrupted by human sin, a revelation sufficient to make people accountable for their sin but not to save them. This view of general revelation draws heavily upon the kind of rationale reflected in the first chapter of Romans about the revelation of God in nature that leaves people without excuse but which because of sin was rejected for the sake of idols representing created life instead of the creator. Thus some revelation may be found in other religions, but not in enough clarity to make salvation possible in any way apart from hearing the gospel of Jesus Christ.

These exclusivist approaches adopt a militant missionary style that rejects any possible positive value in world religions and regards their structures and beliefs as the products of our idolatrous human striving after God. The one view of general revelation assumes no point of contact within other religions for the gospel. The other view might assume a minimal point of contact in that there is enough light to place people under the judgment of God. In a dialogue with the adherent of another religion, the Christian apologist or preacher might assume a dim awareness of God and a sense of sin that could prepare one for hearing the good news of Jesus Christ—but nothing more.

A view of continuity and discontinuity.—A third view of world religions contends that there is both a continuity and a discontinuity between Christianity and world religions and that Jesus Christ is the source of both. Quite as much as the exclusivist view just discussed, this approach is also a Christian particularism and is convinced that wherever there is salvation, it is always through Jesus Christ. The difference is that in this view some people who have never heard the name of Jesus may appropriate the saving efficacy of God's historic redemption in Jesus through a tentative but genuine faith response to the presence of the cosmic Christ in general revelation. In making the salvation in Christ contingent upon a faith made possible by grace alone, this position is far from universalism.

This general view, which has deep roots in the early church, is widely held in the modern church, both Protestant and Catholic. Vatican II followed the lead of some Catholic theologians in broadening salvation to include their separated brethren in Protestantism and also those of genuine faith in other world religions—although they still feel the theological necessity to include all the saved in some way within the framework of the Catholic Church. The Catholic Church now speaks of baptism by desire or of anonymous Christians or of ordinary and extraordinary salvation or of implicit faith—all of these being ways of including within the Church those of authentic faith outside the institutional Roman Church.[12] Similar ideas, including additional ideas like the latent church, are used within Protestantism to describe people who have not heard the gospel but who have responded to Jesus Christ through His light in general revelation.[13]

Advocates of this third view usually affirm some form of the following principles as a basis for their position on the continuity and discontinuity between Christianity and world religions. First, all human beings are sinners who have rebelled against God and are alienated from God. Each person is therefore responsible for his or her own sin, stands personally under the judgment of God, and needs salvation. Because we are in bondage to sin, we cannot save ourselves.

Second, all redemption occurs through God's historic act of reconciling the world to Himself in the person and work of Jesus Christ, a once-for-all redemptive act for the whole human race. Within this general view there are various theories about how we are redeemed through the work of Christ, yet there is a strong common conviction that John's interpretation of Jesus was correct in Jesus' words, "No one comes to the Father, but by me" (John 14:6). The critical question here is how the salvation in Christ may be appropriated by faith. The normal and preferred way, the way that provides the fullest conscious experience of God and an informed understanding of the Christian way of life, is in hearing the gospel and responding in faith to Jesus Christ as Savior and Lord. However, a conscious response is not possible for one who has never had an opportunity to hear the gospel. In this view, there is a possibility that people might be saved who follow in faith what limited light they have in general revelation —which implies several important things about how general revelation relates to Christ and salvation.

Third, God reveals Himself from many directions to all human beings in all historical eras. The Bible repeatedly asserts that God does not leave Himself without witness and that the divine light enlightens the mind of every person (see John 1:9; Rom. 1:19-20; Acts 14:16-17; 17:22-34 and other passages for examples). This general revelation comes in the beauty and regularity of nature, an awareness of the moral law, human conscience, and reason. It is possible that broken and inadequate responses to these forms of revelation may be found within the world religions.

Fourth, all revelation, as the New Testament teaches, is through the eternal Son of God, the Word through whom God created the universe. John expresses this by saying of Jesus, "The true light that enlightens every man was coming into the world" (John 1:9). The cosmic Christ is present even where the gospel has not been preached.

Fifth, this general Christological revealtion is capable of saving people *if* they respond to it in what corresponds to faith. If one makes a tentative faith response to general revelation, it is an implicit initial response to the eternal Son of God, the Word who became incarnate in Jesus of Nazareth, as He is universally present in the light of general revelation. The response of people to the light of the Son of God in general revelation might be viewed as an implicit faith in the historic act of God in reconciling the world to Himself in Jesus of Nazareth—a parallel to the saving faith of the Old Testament redeemed. Perhaps this is what John interprets in the mind of Jesus when He speaks of the previous experience of the first hearers of the gospel: "But he who does what is true comes to the light, that it may be clearly seen that his deeds have been wrought in God" (John 3:21).

Sixth, in this view there are several ways of building a rationale for how exactly people are saved through responding to Christ in general revelation. One approach places salvation mainly in the revelatory work of Christ, in which case the special revelation in Jesus Christ is the fulfillment and final criterion of all general revelation. The continuity is that all revelation is through the eternal Word; the discontinuity is that the difference in degree between historical special revelation and general revelation is so great that it becomes a difference in kind. A second approach inseparably ties the saving power of general revelation to God's objective redemption of the world to Himself in the life, death, and resurrection of Jesus Christ. Then the saving efficacy of a faith response to revelation—general or special—is centered upon the objective change in the world's relationship to God through the atoning work of Jesus Christ.

Seventh, it is important that human beings have a conscious personal relationship to God through faith in Jesus Christ as Savior and Lord. There is a strong missionary imperative to share the gospel because there is a name for the light of general revelation and a historic act of redemption to be consciously appropriated into one's life. Those who hold this theological position are willing to leave the eternal destiny of devout people in other world religions to God. But this perspective is committed to helping people enter into the fullness of the abundant life here on earth as they learn of Jesus Christ, His teachings, and His saving work and consciously commit themselves to Him as Savior and Lord.

Adherents of this third view believe that Jesus Christ provides the continuity and discontinuity between Christianity and world religions. The continuity is not in the religions themselves but in the revelation that may be present in them in broken and distorted forms. To the extent that any religion captures an authentic element of the general revelation of the cosmic Christ, there is a continuity with the special revelation that comes through Hebrew and Christian history. The discontinuity is in the *historical* character of special revelation, a discontinuity that becomes radical in the incarnation of God in Jesus Christ. In this sense, Christianity may be viewed as the fulfillment of all that is authentic in other revelations or other religions but as radically transcending other religions because of Jesus of Nazareth.

Based upon this theological understanding, one can approach other religions in openness, appreciation, and affirmation of the preparatory light of God that may be within them, and yet advocate the uniqueness and universality of Jesus Christ and His historical presence in the church, with the assumption that the eternal Word may already be at work in the lives of some devout people in other religions. Then the key is to interpret Jesus Christ who is the source and final criterion of all revelation and the *sole source of salvation.*

Historic Theological Parameters

How then, in light of the various views, are we to understand world religions in terms of revelation and redemption, and what does that imply about the Christian encounter with world religions? My purpose in writing this book is to contribute to the apologetic ministry of the Christian in today's world and not necessarily to argue for my own theological view at every point. On this question, however, one must make at least some broad judgment about what falls within the parameters of the majority of church traditions within historic Christianity.

Consequently, in my view, one level of the Christian apologetic task is to resist the advocates of religious relativism and pluralism within the Christian church. Although this has historically been a distinctive minority view in the church, there are still contemporary advocates of some version of this idea. If one is a universalist, there is no apologetic task or world mission of the church beyond a dialogue for mutual enrichment or, in some cases, for syncretistic purposes. There are at least two major problems with this position. One is that relativists or syncretists who contend that all religions teach basically the same thing are guilty of either a lack of information about world religions or a strained interpretation of their teachings. The argument that all religious roads lead to the same goal certainly does not hold at the level of actual teachings within the religions. What is the goal? God? Nirvana? Brahman? Or something else? The second problem relates to the particularist claims of the Christian faith. Relativists often assume that what is of value among religions is what they have in common. But that assumption ignores the historic claim of Christianity that what is central to its beliefs is what is historically unique to Christianity—Jesus Christ.

The vast majority of Christians and Christian churches have held that Jesus Christ is in some way essential for the salvation of anyone who lives in eternity with God—although they do not always agree on how that is possible or on what categories of people may be redeemed. Substantial biblical and theological cases can be made for either a strict exclusivist or a more open particularist approach. Both views hold that salvation is only through Jesus Christ. In either view, Christians have reason for an aggressive missionary approach to the great religions of the world. There is a difference in attitude in that the exclusivist makes a negative judgment about other world religions that provides little point of contact for the gospel; in contrast, the open particularist is more accepting, affirming, and open toward a possible point of contact in the religious devotion of the adherent of a non-Christian religion and in any revelatory light within the other religion. In the exclusivist view, the gospel is shared in order for a person to be saved, however rich the quality of his previous religious experience. In the more open particularist view, the gospel is presented in order to introduce many people for the first time to a life of faith and salvation and possibly to bring the preliminary or implicit faith of certain devout religious people to a conscious focus and fulfillment in the historic Jesus. Thus the key point of contact in the dialogue with world religions is Jesus Christ.

The Christian Encounter with World Religions

World religions are a perennial challenge to the Christian church. The Christian encounter with adherents of other world religions differs in many ways from its encounter with other rivals. In every apologetic encounter where alternative ideas are discussed, the Christian should respect the personhood, the honest search for truth, and the caring dimensions of people who are committed to other viewpoints. If the world religions are rivals to Christianity, they are rivals with a difference. Within the world religions themselves, as well as in the religious quest of their adherents, there is a transcendent dimension, however differently it may be defined. As people affirm the rich inclusive nature of their particular religion, they are responding consciously to a transcendent ultimacy that lays claim upon their lives, either a universal order or some kind of God. World religions are monuments to homo religiosus, to the unquenchable religious thirst of human beings.

Consequently, many devotees in other world religions do not have to be converted to a belief in God or, in many cases, to a love of God. In the lives of many of these people, there are awe and wonder, fear and attraction, adoration and unworthiness, openness and radical commitment to the holy dimension encountered within their religion. Many of them enter into the discipline of religious liturgy as a way of bringing themselves into harmony with God or what they consider to be ultimate in the universe. Their religious experience issues in a pattern of life that often produces noble human spirits who live by the highest ethical standards. What they do not know is the full revelation of God in Jesus Christ or God's historic act of redemption of the world in Him.

Adherents of other religions hold views of God or ultimate reality that may be close or far from the Christian view of God. Their ultimate concern clearly takes a religious form that deserves the highest respect from Christians even when the religion, measured by a Christian view, may be filled with error and inadequacy. The common ground of a religious response to the transcendent is always holy ground where we stand together as fellow seekers after God. Other world religions may be rivals to Christianity, but the devotees within them are fellow pilgrims seeking after God, even when they call Him by another name or by no name at all.

Paul in his sermon at Athens provides one of the best paradigms for the Christian encounter with devotees of other world religions. Paul's attitude toward other religions is complex. When speaking within the church, Paul could condemn religion as an idolatrous product of human sin. Yet here is the apologist Paul who, observing among the many Greek statues to the gods the Athenian statue to the unknown God, says to the Athenians: "What therefore you *worship* as unknown, this I proclaim to you. The God who made the world and everything in it . . . made one from every nation of men to live on all the face of the earth . . . that they should seek God, in the hope that they might feel after him and find him. Yet he is not far from each one of us, for 'In him we live and move and have our being.' . . . The times of ignorance God overlooked, but now he commands all men everywhere to repent" (Acts 17:23-30). Here Paul is sensitive to persons and affirms their limited worship of God. After commenting that God will overlook their previous ignorance, he proceeds to name the unknown God who has redeemed and will judge the world in Jesus Christ. Then in light of the full gospel, he calls upon them to repent. Here, as always, Paul preaches Christ Jesus and Him crucified (1 Cor. 2:2).

If the crucial element in religion is the concept of God, then the focal point of the Christian encounter with world religions is Jesus

Christ—for the reason that the Christian concept of God centers in Him. The Christian encounter with world religions does not begin with, nor is it primarily concerned with, the similarities or differences in detailed doctrines, liturgical practices, or ethical principles—except as these may illuminate or grow out of the truth in Jesus Christ. The apologetic task is not primarily a comparative study of world religions so that at every point one may show the consistent superiority of Christianity. What is most important to the Christian is not what is shared between Christianity and other religions but what is unique to Christianity—Jesus Christ. The Christian's interpretation of Christianity to an adherent of another religion should begin with a presentation of the uniqueness of Jesus Christ, who He is and why He is Savior and Lord.

In interpreting Jesus Christ, one is led into a discussion of the Christian concept of God. Jesus can be understood, in fact, only in light of the Hebrew view of God, a view that He assumed and then enriched and extended. For this reason, Jews and Christians share many ideas about God and His purposes in the world. These ideas provide numerous points for dialogue in interpreting the total worldview that centers upon Christ and comparing it to those of other religions. Among the most fertile Hebrew ideas is that God the Lord is one personal God who alone is eternal. Out of grace and love, God created a good world and individual substantial persons who are differentiated from Himself and yet dependent upon Himself. God is transcendent to the world and yet immanent to the world, so that the world is both quasiindependent and yet absolutely dependent on God. The God of holy love is omnipotent, omniscient, and omnipresent. He is the God of creation and history who, out of grace, redeems people to Himself within the historical process. Other distinctive Judeo-Christian ideas grow out of these basic ideas: the reality and created value of the world, the distinctive and substantial self of humans, and the worth of human beings, the creatureliness of humans, the seriousness of sin, the need for redemption, the redeeming activity of God, and the basic purpose of life in glorifying God by loving and serving human beings.

In Christianity, the Hebrew conception is redefined by Jesus Christ, in particular at the points of the incarnation and the Trinitarian nature of God. Jesus was called Emmanuel, God-with-us, by the early church. He was God incarnate. In light of the experience of God in a human person, the church insists that God must be viewed as at least personal, however far beyond human personhood He may be. The incarnation underlines the infinite worth of a human being and the importance of the natural and historical processes. The incarnation spotlights the desperate character of human sinfulness, the need of the human for help from beyond himself, and the radical nature of the divine love that takes human sin upon Himself. The incarnation ties the church to historical particularity, to the belief that the solution to the human dilemma is found in God's act in Jesus Christ on behalf of the whole human family and the cosmos itself.

The incarnation of God in Christ also redefines the nature of Jewish monotheism. The one God is experienced as Father and Son. Growing out of the Christ event was the ministry of the Holy Spirit in the life of the early church, a Spirit closely identified with Jesus Christ and the Father and yet differentiated from them. This threefold experience of the one God led to Trinitarian monotheism, the view that there is only one God who is in three persons. The belief in the incarnation of God in a human person and the belief in the Trinity form the unique elements in the Christian view of God.

This understanding of God creates a scandal of particularity in relation to all other religions. The idea of the incarnation that God has become a concrete human being is a scandal to the Jews who still look for the coming Messiah. The incarnation is offensive to the transcendent monotheism of Muslims who could not conceive of the sovereign holy God becoming human, although they recognize Jesus as one of the greatest of the prophets. At the opposite pole, Hindus and Buddhists can easily accept the idea of God becoming incarnate in humans but think that this happens many times. Hindus believe that God has incarnated Himself repeatedly in avatars, deities who personally embody the impersonal godhead on earth. Buddhists believe the Buddha spirit is incarnate in numerous Buddhas and to some extent in the boddisatvas, the savior figures who help others toward Nirvana. So at the very heart of the Christian faith, the Christian apologist must find ways to interpret the Christian confession that Jesus alone is the incarnation of God and therefore Savior and Lord.

The idea of the Trinity also is a problem in opposite ways, depending upon the partner in an apologetic dialogue. Jews tend to regard the idea of the Triune God as an encroachment on the radical monotheism of Hebrew religion, and Muslims consider Trinitarianism to be polytheistic or close to it. On the other hand, some Hindus and some Buddhists have no difficulty conceptualizing one God experienced as many—although their ideas are far from Christian Trinitarianism. Brahman is beyond our conceptual experience for Hindus, and yet the impersonal God is experienced in many deities, not the least in the Hindu triad of Brahma, Vishnu, and Shiva. Some Buddhists hold something like a Trinitarian view in their three-body concept of the Buddha. The Christian apologist must explain, on the one hand, how the one being of God can be experienced as three persons and, on the other hand, why the three persons cannot be many more.

In focusing upon Jesus Christ, and through Him upon the concept of God, the Christian apologist's intention is not to engage in an extended academic discussion of Christology in which the adherent of another religion may be led to affirm a new system of thought. The goal is to demonstrate enough of how God has come to us in Christ that the adherent of the other religion is able to encounter God in a fresh way through faith in Christ. The person's new way of thinking or system of thought will naturally grow out of the encounter. Then whatever may be true in other religions, much as in the case of the Old Testament religion, can be taken up and transformed in the understanding of Jesus Christ, and what is not consistent with Him will be laid aside. Based upon the criterion of Christ, what is true in other religions may be viewed as preparatory for the encounter with God through Jesus Christ. What is false will be viewed as an expression of a limited response to revelation or as a construction of our broken human ways of seeking after God. Jesus Christ is *the* key issue!

The commitment to the centrality of Jesus Christ both binds and liberates the Christian in the encounter with world religions. It is binding in that Jesus is the universal Revealer and Redeemer. At the center of Christianity is the belief in the universality of Jesus Christ. Christianity is not a Jewish or Greek or Roman or Western religion. At the heart of Christian theology is a particularism of salvation that requires a universal proclamation. God's particular reconciliation of the world to Himself through Jesus Christ is the source of salvation for the whole human race. Consequently, the church has a universal missionary impetus. For the church to coexist with other religions, with a relativistic assumption that all are equally valuable ways to

God, would be to betray its own essential nature. Such coexistence would be natural for a Hindu whose faith is built around a relativistic conviction: Whichever path men choose is mine! But relativism is *unnatural* for the Christian who is convinced that Jesus Christ is the way, the truth, and the life. Whatever the Christian's theological position about whether there may be some saving element in general revelation, biblical Christianity ties finality in revelation and redemption to Jesus Christ. Because of this conviction, the Christian will bear witness to Jesus Christ without hesitation or embarrassment.

At the same time, the Christian can be open to the faith of people in other religions, and possibly even learn some things from them, because of the conviction that all truth about God is a gift of God through the eternal Logos or Son of God and that it therefore can be correlated with the final truth in Jesus the Christ. One is then free to view any tentative response people in other religions have made to the truth as they understand it as an implicit and preparatory response to the full revelation and redemption of God in Jesus Christ. The combination of a conviction that the salvation in Christ is for the whole human family and of an openness to the preparatory character of the revelation through the cosmic Christ allows the Christian to approach the adherent of another religion with openness, affirmation, and expectancy that many will respond to the fullness of the revelation and redemption that is God's gift in Jesus Christ.

9
Christianity's Apologetic Task with Its Contemporary Rivals

Christian apologetics is a perennial task of the church. From the apostolic era into our present generation, Christians have been admonished by 1 Peter 3:15: "Always be prepared to make a defense [*apologian*] to any one who calls you to account for the hope that is in you." Apologetics has been variously understood within the church. Its particular definition and expression are often shaped by the individual historical context within which apologetics takes place. Basically, Christian apologetics is the conscious, and often systematic, effort to make a persuasive case for the truth of Christianity, deal with the numerous specific questions that arise within our common human existence and our search for answers to ultimate questions, justify its overall interpretation of reality in relation to other worldviews, and defend it against attacks by its ideological rivals and opponents. Apologetics may speak either to the doubt and questioning of believers within the church or to people outside the church who are not religious believers and who may be committed to an alternative worldview, religious or secular.

Christian Apologetics Among Pluralistic Worldviews

The need for intelligent, caring apologetics is heightened in the pluralistic, global community of the contemporary world. In a marketplace of dizzying choices of values, basic commitments, ultimate concerns, and worldviews, Christians, perhaps more than at any time in the history of the church, should be prepared to give a reason for the faith that is in them. The practical apologetic task is a vital and essential element in the overall evangelistic ministry and world mission of the Christian church.

In this book, I have chosen to deal with major representative alternative rivals to the Christian faith, most of which reflect a comprehensive worldview. The fact, however, is that much of the apologetic activity of the church does not occur on such a wide intellectual horizon. Many pressing apologetic problems grow out of the immediacy of a life situation, and they are expressed in the most straightforward way about a limited problem or area of concern. "Why did my baby die?" "Why doesn't God intervene to stop the holocaust or the Cambodian slaughter?" "How do you know there is a God?" "What happens at death?" "Are miracles possible?" "Isn't it really the case that all religious are basically alike?" "I have concluded that God is really a psychological projection of human wishes." "How did the universe come to be?" "Is God a necessary hypothesis in a scientific world?" And so the everyday apologetic questions go!

The truth is that most popular apologetic dialogue and a good deal of apologetic reflection take place on a much more limited scale than we have been concerned about in this book. But a critical engagement with rival worldviews is important for would-be apologists because very often the more limited apologetic questions and problems within the everyday arena reflect a larger worldview, a view that may not be consciously in the mind of the person struggling with a particular problem or advocating a certain intellectual position. As a result, intelligent responses to smaller-scale concerns often are enhanced by some grasp of the larger worldviews that we have engaged in this book. One can better understand and probe certain attitudes or problems when they are positioned within the assumptions and contours of an identifiable worldview. Many of the principles I have developed may be easily utilized in the more limited apologetic encounters that take place in the lives of Christians today.

It is also the case that worldviews are in a sense an abstraction. Worldviews may be elaborated in books and dealt with at a purely philosophical, intellectual, reflective level. In ordinary real life, worldviews are never abstract ideologies. They are always held by persons—often with great passion and tenacity. In any apologetic encounter between persons who hold alternative worldviews, profound personal dimensions always enter into any apologetic conversation. The personal elements of everyday apologetic encounters are of critical importance, but that is the subject of another book.

I have been concerned with the Christian encounter with rival worldviews and with the objective, critical evaluation of alternative views that occurs in philosophical or theological discussion. Within that frame of reference, a number of important evaluative and dialogical principles are useful to the large scale intellectual dimensions of the practical Christian apologetic task, both in critically engaging rival views and in advocating Christianity. I have utilized many of these principles in my apologetic treatment of Christianity's modern rivals.

Engaging Alternative Worldviews

How does one proceed to engage alternative worldviews? A Christian apologist must begin by attempting to understand a particular rival to the Christian faith. It is not possible to dialogue and interact with a worldview that one has not taken the trouble to understand. I have attempted in this book to provide basic insight into the views of selective major rivals to the Christian faith. One ought to struggle to get inside the alternative worldview and to grasp its inner logic and holistic perspective. That requires effort, openness, and some degree of objectivity.

If one intends to defend or advocate Christianity in relation to any rival, then one ought to engage the strongest case that can be made for the alternative point of view. It is relatively easy for one to live with the illusion that one has successfully engaged and countered an alternative worldview—if one deals only in simplistic formulations, caricatures, distortions, or satirizations of the other view. A simple test for whether we are dealing with a strong case for another worldview is to state our understanding of that worldview in such a way that a serious adherent of that worldview will concur that our statement is what he things or what that worldview represents.

The Christian ought to grant as much truth as possible, with integrity, to any alternative worldview, but without conceding either too little or too much when measured from a Christian perspective. In any encounter between rival worldviews, there will be common ground and substantive differences. If a serious intellectual engagement is to occur, both elements must be explicitly and candidly recognized.

Different types of Christians resist recognizing either the common ground or the differences between worldviews. Some Christians hold that all the truth of Christianity is found only in Christianity and that, consequently, there is no common ground among worldviews or any ultimate truth to be found outside of the Christian revelation. In my judgment, that is an indefensible position, even when measured from within the Christian revelation itself. The Bible indicates that the light of the creator God and the universal Christ breaks into the awareness of people at some level—even if only dimly—throughout the human family. Much truth can be found in all human experience. That also may be true in human religious experience, even though the truth may be limited in scope or insight and mingled with misunderstanding or error. Where there are elements of truth in alternative worldviews that are compatible with a Christian perspective, Christians would best affirm those elements and then attempt to relate them to Jesus Christ and to the larger Christian worldview.

At the opposite pole, some Christians tend to obscure or minimize the differences between Christianity and alternative worldviews, as though the differences do not matter. Biblical Christianity rejects any relativizing of truth, for the fundamental reason that it is grounded in the particularity of God's revelatory and redemptive act in Jesus Christ. Whatever ultimate truth may be found in general human experience or in formal worldviews, it will be completed and fully illuminated only when it is integrated with the final revelation and key to all truth that we have in Jesus Christ. Consequently, in the encounter between rival worldviews, the distinctive differences, as well as the common ground between worldviews, should remain in focus.

A Christian apologetic encounter with any modern rival will normally involve a probing of the alternative worldview. Certain principles can be helpful in critically engaging or challenging another worldview. In general, one ought to focus on the heart of a worldview and, in raising questions about its defensibility, concentrate on its strengths and not its weaknesses. One ought to probe the underlying presuppositions, which are often hidden, of a particular worldview. Are they justified? How were they arrived at? How has the adherent of an alternative worldview come to be committed to this particular position? Has one seriously worked through the rationale for the worldview, appropriated it out of a cultural context, or acknowledged it on the basis of some respected authority?

I have suggested in chapter 1 that there are several formal tests for a worldview—for the Christian worldview or any of its contemporary rivals. First, is the worldview coherent? Do its major ideas integrate into a consistent and persuasive holistic interpretation of reality? Second, does the worldwide correspond with known facts of our universe or human life as we now understand them? Third, does the worldview comprehensively embrace all dimensions of human experience in such a way that it illuminates the totality of human life in society and in the world? Fourth, does the worldview translate into practical application to everyday existence in such a way that it makes sense of daily life and integrates one's ordinary activities into one's understanding of the purpose of the universe and of existence itself? Finally, is the worldview universal, one that in principle can transcend all parochialisms—the peculiarities of historical eras, geographical limitation, and cultural identification? Ultimate truth ought to be true for all people in all times and places.

Advocating a Christian Worldview

The Christian apologetic encounter with alternative worldviews also involves an advocacy and defense of the Christian faith that inevitably demands certain basic knowledge and skills. If the Christian apologetic encounter with alternative worldviews requires that a Christian apologist understand other worldviews, it is equally imperative that one must be at least a modest student of Christian theology. One does not have to be a professional theologian. But certainly a Christian apologist must have a reasonable understanding of basic Christianity, including its foundational theological ideas and a broad sense of how those integrate into a more comprehensive worldview. Only in this way can one be intelligently aware of any common ground and of the distinctive differences between Christianity and a particular modern rival. Many Christian laypersons, fortunately, have a sufficient grasp of Christian theology for this purpose.

One should not only know but also be capable of stating and interpreting in simplicity and clarity the core of the Christian faith. Otherwise, it would be easy for the essentials of Christianity to be obscured as one travels the contours of a larger worldview. A Christian should develop some capacity to state the essential core of the faith in a variety of ways in order to communicate within the distinctive frame of reference of individual persons who adhere to different alternative worldviews. At the same time, the Christian apologist should have a broader understanding of Christian theology and how it can be extended into a comprehensive worldview.

The defense of Christianity will occur at different levels. In any specific dialogue, adherents of other worldviews will normally raise critical questions about some aspects of a Christian worldview. Christian apologists must be prepared to hear those critical questions or challenges, without being defensive, and then to respond intelligently to them. The only sufficient preparation for dealing with criticisms of or attacks upon Christianity is to have become acquainted with them in study and dialogue. Serious challenges or objections to Christianity should be seriously engaged by a Christian apologist.

A defender of Christianity should be prepared to demonstrate how Christianity can successfully meet the tests that Christians insist on applying to alternative worldviews—internal coherence, correspondence with all known facts of the universe, a comprehensive embracing of all areas of experience and reality, applicability to everyday life, and a universal claim for the whole human family. I am convinced that Christianity, when compared with all the major alternative worldviews, can best meet these tests of truth for life and provide the most persuasive answers to the varied longings and questions of modern human beings.

Finally, the advocacy and defense of Christianity always requires an invitation. No matter how extensively humans engage ultimate questions at the level of ideas, a faith element is always involved in one's commitment to a particular worldview. That faith element—for an atheist, a naturalist, or a religious believer—represents a risk, a leap, that goes beyond the firm logical grounds of a particular worldview. In the case of Christianity, the commitment is not to various intellectual components of a worldview but to a person who is the ultimate embodiment of truth and the key to integrate all truth. The very heart of the truth of Christianity is personal. Jesus said, "I am the way, and the truth, and the life; no one comes to the Father, but by me" (John 14:6).

After a Christian apologist has made the best possible case for Christianity, one must invite the adherent of another worldview to commit himself or herself to Jesus Christ. Only in a personal encounter with the living Christ can one come, in the fullest sense of the word, to know the truth of Christianity in such a way that the intellect, affections, and will converge in a personal appropriation of the truth that embraces but also transcends our ordinary logic. In that leap of faith, the best logic of a Christian worldview is rooted in the logic of the personal relationship of a human being with the living God. Out of the inner core of a personal relationship with God, the Christian then can develop an intelligent understanding of Christianity and integrate it with the comprehensive knowledge we have of the universe into a satisfying and defensible worldview that will prove to be persuasive to many modern people in a pluralistic world.

Endnotes

Chapter 1—Christian Apologetics in the Contemporary World
1. Martin Heidegger, *Being and Time*, trans. John Macquarrie and Edward Robinson (New York: Harper and Row, 1962), pp. 172-174.
2. Michael Polanyi, *Personal Knowledge: Towards a Post-Critical Philosophy* (Chicago: University of Chicago Press, 1958), pp. 69-245; *Knowing and Being* (Chicago: University of Chicago Press, 1969), pp. 123-210.
3. William Shakespeare, *Hamlet*, Act I, Scene V, Line 166.

Chapter 3—Atheism: Life Without God
1. Friedrich Nietzsche, *The Gay Science*, trans. Walter Kaufmann (New York: Vintage Books, 1974), III, 125, pp. 181-182.
2. See Antony Flew, *The Presumption of Atheism and Other Philosophical Essays on God, Freedom and Immortality* (London: Elek/Pemberton, 1976), pp. 13-30.
3. See as examples J. L. Mackie, *The Miracle of Theism* (Oxford: Clarendon Press, 1982); Bertrand Russell, *Why I Am Not a Christian* (New York: Simon and Schuster, 1957); George H. Smith, *Atheism: The Case Against God* (Buffalo, N. Y.: Prometheus Books, 1979); Stein, Gordon, ed., *An Anthology of Atheism and Rationalism* (Buffalo, N. Y.: Prometheus Books, 1980).
4. Antony Flew, *The Presumption of Atheism*, pp. 31-34.
5. Thomas H. Huxley, *Collected Essays* (London: Macmillan, 1904), Vol. V, p. 239.
6. An excellent treatment of similar categories of atheism is in S. Paul Schilling, *God in an Age of Atheism* (Nashville: Abingdon Press, 1969), pp. 115-134.
7. See Kai Nielsen, *Contemporary Critiques of Religion* (New York: Macmillan, 1971), pp. 135-136; J. L. Mackie, "Evil and Omnipotence," *The Philosophy of Religion*, ed. Basil Mitchell (New York: Oxford University Press, 1971), pp. 92-104; Antony Flew, "Divine Omnipotence and Human Freedom," *New Essays in Philosophical Theology*, ed. Antony Flew and Alasdair MacIntyre (London: SCM Press, 1955), pp. 144-169; Walter Kaufmann, *Critique of Religion and Philosophy* (New York: Harper & Brothers, 1958), pp. 129ff.
8. Antony Flew, *The Presumption of Atheism*, pp. 16-20.
9. Auguste Comte, *Introduction to Positive Philosophy*, ed. and trans. Frederick Ferré (Indianapolis: Bobbs-Merrill, 1970).
10. A. J. Ayer, *Language, Truth, and Logic* (New York: Dover Publications, Inc. 1946), pp. 114-120.
11. Friedrich Nietzsche, *The Anti-Christ*, 48, in *Twilight of the Idols/Anti-Christ*, trans. R. J. Hollingdale (Baltimore: Penguin Books, 1968), pp. 163-164.

12. J. L. Mackie, *The Miracle of Theism*, p. 164; also in "Evil and Omnipotence," pp. 92-104.

13. Albert Camus, *The Plague*, trans. Stuart Gilbert (New York: Modern Library, 1948), pp. 117f., 147ff.

14. Richard L. Rubenstein, *After Auschwitz: Radical Theology and Contemporary Judaism*, (Indianapolis: Bobbs-Merrill, 1966), pp. 152-153.

15. Ludwig Feuerbach, *The Essence of Christianity*, trans. G. Eliot (New York: Harper & Brothers, Torchbook, 1957).

16. Jean-Paul Sartre, *Existentialism and Humanism*, trans. Philip Mairet (London: Methuen and Co., 1946).

17. Friedrich Nietzsche, *The Gay Science*, III, 151, p. 196; *The Anti-Christ*, 15-18, pp. 124-128; *Beyond Good and Evil* in *Basic Writings of Nietzsche*, trans. and ed. Walter Kaufmann (New York: Modern Library, 1968), II, 1, pp. 135-136.

18. Sigmund Freud, *Totem and Taboo*, trans. A. A. Brill (New York: New Republic, 1927), pp. 268-269.

19. Sigmund Freud, *The Future of an Illusion*, trans. and ed. James Strachey (New York: W. W. Norton & Co., 1965), pp. 17-19, 21-24, 30, 42, 49.

20. Karl Marx, *On Religion*, ed. Saul K. Padover, Vol. V of The Karl Marx Library (New York: McGraw-Hill Book Co., 1974), p. 35.

21. Walter Kaufmann, *The Faith of a Heretic* (Garden City, N. Y.: Doubleday, 1961), p. 415.

22. Ernst Bloch, *The Principle of Hope*, 3 vols., trans. Neville Plaice et al. (Boston: Massachusetts Institute of Technology Press, 1987).

23. Friedrich Nietzsche, *Beyond Good and Evil*, III, 53, p. 256.

24. See as examples of current critics of the coherence of theism J. L. Mackie, *The Miracle of Theism;* Anthony Kenny, *The God of the Philosophers* (Oxford: Clarendon Press, 1979); and Kai Nielsen, *Contemporary Critiques of Religion*. Examples of the defense of theism's coherence are Richard Swinburne, *The Coherence of Theism* (Oxford: Clarendon Press, 1977); Alvin Plantinga, *God and Other Minds* (Ithaca, N. Y.: Cornell University Press, 1967); Keith Ward, *The Concept of God* (Oxford: Basil Blackwell, 1974); and H. P. Owen, *The Christian Knowledge of God* (London: Athlone Press, 1969).

25. See Basil Mitchell, "Theology and Falsification," *New Essays in Philosophical Theology*, ed. Antony Flew and Alasdair MacIntyre (London: SCM Press, 1955), pp. 103-105.

26. See major treatments of evil in John Hick, *Evil and the God of Love* (New York: Harper & Row, 1966); C. S. Lewis, *The Problem of Pain* (New York: Macmillan, 1943); Austin Farrer, *Love Almighty and Ills Unlimited* (Garden City, N. Y.: Doubleday, 1961); and Stephen T. Davis, ed., *Encountering Evil* (Atlanta: John Knox Press, 1981).

27. C. S. Lewis, *They Asked for a Paper* (London: Geoffrey Bles, 1962), p. 188.

28. As examples of traditional formulations of the arguments that their advocates think provide certainty, see Thomas Aquinas, *Summa Theologica*, I, Questions 2-26; René Descartes, *Discourse on Method*, 4 and *The Meditations Concerning First Philosophy*, 3 and 5; Charles Hartshorne, *The Logic of Perfection* (La Salle, Ill.: Open Court Press, 1967); and Eric L. Mascall, *He Who Is: A Study in Traditional Theism* (New York: Longmans, Green and Co., 1948), pp. 30-82. For reformulations of the arguments in terms of probability, see Richard Swinburne, *The Existence of God* (Oxford: Clarendon Press, 1979); F. R. Tennant, *Philosophical Theology* (Cambridge: Cambridge University Press, 1930), Vol. I, Chap. 11; Vol. II, Chap. 4; and Richard Taylor, *Metaphysics* (Englewood Cliffs, N. J.: Prentice-Hall, 1963), Chap. 7.

Chapter 4—Naturalism: Nature as Ultimate

1. Sterling Lamprecht, "Naturalism and Religion," in *Naturalism and the Human Spirit*, ed. Yervant H. Krikorian (New York: Columbia University Press, 1945), p. 18. See the

use of the idea of God by naturalistic emergent evolutionary thinkers in Samuel Alexander, *Space, Time, and Deity,* 2 vols. (New York: Macmillan, 1927); C. Lloyd Morgan, *Emergent Evolution* (London: Williams and Norgate, 1927); Henri Bergson, *Creative Evolution,* trans. A. Mitchell (New York: Random House, 1944).

2. See the excellent collection of essays advocating naturalism in Yervant H. Krikorian, *Naturalism and the Human Spirit* (New York: Columbia University Press, 1944).

3. John Dewey, "Antinaturalism in Extremis," in *Naturalism and the Human Spirit,* ed. Yervant Krikorian, pp. 1-4. See naturalist Morris Cohen's critique of the close equation of science with all knowing in his *Studies in Philosophy and Science* (New York: Ungar, 1949), pp. 48-89.

4. Sigmund Freud, *The Complete Psychological Works of Sigmund Freud* (New York: Macmillan, 1953-1964); B. F. Skinner, *Science and Human Behavior* (New York: Free Press, 1965); *Beyond Freedom and Dignity* (New York: Bantam/Vintage Books, 1972); J. B. Watson, *Behaviorism,* rev. ed. (New York: Norton, 1930); Morton Hunt, *The Universe Within* (New York: Simon and Schuster, 1982).

5. John Dewey, *Philosophy and Civilization* (New York: Capricorn Books, 1963); *Experience and Education* (New York: Macmillan, 1938).

6. George Santayana, *The Life of Reason,* One vol. ed. (New York: Charles Scribner's Sons, 1954).

7. John Dewey, *Experience and Nature* (New York: W. W. Norton and Co., 1929); *The Quest for Certainty* (New York: Minton, Balch, and Co., 1929); Morris R. Cohen, *Reason and Nature: An Essay on the Meaning of the Scientific Method* (London: Kegan Paul, French, Trubner, and Co., 1931); Sidney Hook, *The Quest for Being* (New York: St. Martin's Press, 1960); Roy Wood Sellars, *Evolutionary Naturalism* (Chicago: Open Court Publishing Co., 1922); George Herbert Mead, *Mind, Self, and Society* (Chicago: University of Chicago Press, 1934); Frederick J. E. Woodbridge, *The Realm of Mind: An Essay in Metaphysics* (New York: Columbia University Press, 1926); *An Essay on Nature* (New York: Columbia University Press, 1940).

8. See for examples among analytical philosophers: D. M. Armstrong, *A Materialist Theory of Mind* (London: Routledge & Kegan Paul, 1968); Antony Flew, *The Presumption of Atheism and Other Philosophical Essays on God, Freedom, and Immortality* (London: Elek/Pemberton, 1976); Kai Nielsen, *Contemporary Critiques of Religion* (London: Macmillan, 1971); Richard Rorty, *Philosophy and the Mirror of Nature* (Princeton, N. J.: Princeton University Press, 1979); Bertrand Russell, *The Basic Writings of Bertrand Russell,* ed. Robert Enger and Lester Denonn (New York: George Allen & Unwin, 1961); and J. J. C. Smart, *Philosophy and Scientific Realism* (London: Routledge & Kegan Paul, 1963).

9. John Dewey, "Antinaturalism in Extremis," in *Naturalism and the Human Spirit,* pp. 1-16; George Santayana, *The Life of Reason,* pp. 26-33.

10. John Dewey, *Experience and Nature;* Thelma Z. Lavine, "Naturalism and the Sociological Analysis of Knowledge," in *Naturalism and the Human Spirit,* ed. Yervant H. Krikorian, p. 183.

11. Thelma Z. Lavine, "Naturalism and the Sociological Analysis of Knowledge," pp. 184-185.

12. Ibid., p. 185.

13. Ibid.

14. Bertrand Russell, *Why I Am Not a Christian* (New York: Simon and Schuster, 1957), pp. 6-7; Antony Flew, *God and Philosophy* (London: Hutchinson, 1966), pp. 86-107.

15. Gilbert Ryle, *The Concept of Mind* (New York: Barnes and Noble, 1949); David Armstrong, *A Materialist Theory of Mind* (New York: Humanities Press, 1968); Richard Rorty, "The Mind as Ineffable," in *Mind in Nature,* ed. Richard Q. Elvee (San Francisco: Harper and Row, 1982).

16. John Dewey, *A Common Faith* (New Haven, Conn.: Yale University Press, 1934), p. 43; Samuel Alexander, *Space, Time, and Deity*.

17. Gilbert Ryle, *The Concept of Mind*. See a discussion of Carnap and Neurath in John Passmore, *A Hundred Years of Philosophy* (London: Penguin Books, 1978), pp. 374-386.

18. See the sources cited in note 4.

19. E. O. Wilson, *Sociobiology—The New Synthesis* (Cambridge, Mass.: Harvard University Press, 1975).

20. Julian Huxley, *Religion Without Reservation* (New York: Harper, 1956).

21. See treatments of secularism in Arnold E. Loen, *Secularization: Science Without God?*, trans. Margaret Kohl (Philadelphia: Westminster Press, 1967); E. L. Mascall, *The Secularization of Christianity* (London: Dartmon, Longman, and Todd, 1965); Harvey Cox, *The Secular City* (New York: Macmillan, 1965); and Paul Van Buren, *The Secular Meaning of the Gospel* (New York: Macmillan, 1963).

22. Sidney Hook, *The Quest for Being* (New York: St. Martin's Press, 1934), p. 174.

23. Ibid., p. 175.

24. Jacques Monod, *Chance and Necessity: An Essay on the Natural Philosophy of Biology*, trans. Austryn Wainhouse (London: Collins/Fount, 1974); Manfred Eigen and Ruthild Winkler, *Laws of the Game*, trans. Robert and Rita Kimber (New York: Penguin Books, 1981).

25. C. S. Lewis, *Miracles: A Preliminary Study* (London: Geoffrey Bles, 1947), p. 38.

26. David Hume, *Dialogues Concerning Natural Religion* (New York: Hafner, 1948), pp. 15-25; 35-60.

27. Arthur R. Peacocke, *Creation and the World of Science* (Oxford: Clarendon Press, 1979), pp. 67-68.

28. Samuel Alexander, in his *Space, Time, and Deity*, called for a "natural piety" before this immanent purposive force that emerges from space-time. A good treatment of the probabilities involved in such a teleological assumption is in Richard Swinburne, *The Existence of God* (Oxford: Clarendon Press, 1979), especially pp. 133-151.

29. See this Irenaean position expounded by John Hick in *Evil and the God of Love* (New York: Harper and Row, 1966) and *Death and Eternal Life* (New York: Harper and Row, 1976), pp. 21-54.

Chapter 5—Secular Humanism: Humanity on the Throne

1. Among the useful anthologies of humanist statements are A. J. Ayer ed., *The Humanist Outlook* (London: Pemberton, 1968); Paul Kurtz, ed., *The Humanist Alternative: Some Definitions of Humanism* (Buffalo, N. Y.: Prometheus Books, 1973); Julian Huxley, ed., *The Humanist Frame* (New York: Harper, 1961). *The Humanist*, a journal of the American Humanist Association, regularly publishes articles by secular humanist intellectuals.

2. See the variety of views in books cited in footnote 1 as well as the Christian humanist views discussed by Roger L. Shinn in *Man: The New Humanism* (Philadelphia: Westminster Press, 1968). Corliss Lamont surveys different kinds of humanism in *The Philosophy of Humanism* (New York: Ungar, 1965), pp. 19-29.

3. Surveys of the history of humanism can be found in Corliss Lamont, *The Philosophy of Humanism*; J. Wesley Robb, *The Reverent Skeptic: A Critical Inquiry into the Religion of Secular Humanism* (New York: Philosophical Library, 1979), pp. 1-77; and Jacques Maritain, *True Humanism*, trans. M. R. Adamson (London: Geoffrey Bles, 1941), pp. vii-87.

4. For a more detailed discussion of the Western origins of humanism, see Corliss Lamont, *The Philosophy of Humanism*, pp. 30-34, 60-64, and Jacques Maritain, *True Humanism*, pp. ix-xvii, 1-8.

5. Edwin H. Wilson, "Humanism's Many Dimensions," *The Humanist Alternative*, ed. Paul Kurtz, pp. 15-19; David Tribe, "Our Freethought Heritage: The Humanist and Ethical Movement," pp. 20-27.

6. "Humanist Manifesto I," *The New Humanist,* VI, No. 3 (May/June, 1933); "Humanist Manifesto II," *The Humanist,* XXXIII, No. 5 (September/October, 1973).

7. Jacques Maritain, *True Humanism;* Teihard de Chardin, *The Future of Man,* trans. Norman Denny (New York: Harper, 1964); and Dietrich Bonhoeffer, *Letters and Papers from Prison* (London: SCM, 1967).

8. See Walter M. Abbott, ed., *The Documents of Vatican II* (New York: Herder and Herder, 1966), especially pp. 199-308, 660-668, and 675-698; and also Adrian Hastings, *A Concise Guide to the Documents of the Second Vatican Council* (London: Darton, Longman, and Todd, 1969).

9. Pope Paul VI, "On the Development of Peoples," *Populam Progressio,* Paragraphs 16, 20, 42, and 72. See also Paragraphs 13, 15, 43, and 47 on the growth of the human person in Adrian Hastings, *A Concise Guide to the Documents of the Second Vatican Council.*

10. See *New Delhi to Uppsala, 1961-1968* (Report of the Central Committee to the Fourth Assembly of the World Council of Churches, 1968); Ernest W. Lefever, *Amsterdam to Nairobi* (Ethics and Public Policy Center, Georgetown University, 1979); and Roger L. Shinn, *Man: The New Humanism,* pp. 19-25.

11. See "Humanist Manifesto I," "Humanist Manifesto II," and the anthologies cited in note 1.

12. See a rebuttal to my argument in Paul Kurtz, ed., *Moral Problems in Contemporary Society: Essays in Humanistic Ethics* (New York: Prentice-Hall, 1969), pp. 2-3. Examples of metaphysical naturalistic humanisms can be found in the cited writings of Paul Kurtz; Corliss Lamont, *The Philosophy of Humanism;* Morris Cohen, *Studies in Philosophy and Science* (New York: Ungar, 1949); A. J. Ayer, ed., *The Humanist Outlook,* pp. 1-10; and Antony Flew, *God and Philosophy* (London: Hutchinson, 1966).

13. See for an example Julian Huxley, *Religion Without Revelation* (New York: Harper, 1956).

14. For examples of this view, see Julian Huxley, *Religion Without Revelation,* p. 18; Teilhard de Chardin, *The Future of Man;* Henri Bergson, *Creative Evolution,* trans. A. Mitchell (New York: Modern Library, 1944); and Henri Bergson, *The Two Sources of Morality and Religion,* trans. R. A. Auda and C. Brereton (New York: Macmillan, 1935).

15. A. Y. Ayer, *The Humanist Outlook,* pp. 16-17.

16. See for examples Walter Lippmann, *A Preface to Morals* (New York: Macmillan, 1929); R. M. Hare, *The Language of Morals* (Oxford: Clarendon Press, 1952); Peter Stawson, "Social Morality and Individual Ideal," *Christian Ethics and Contemporary Philosophy,* ed. I. T. Ramsey (London: SCM, 1966); and Paul Kurtz, ed., *Moral Problems in Contemporary Society: Essays in Contemporary Ethics.*

17. For examples of soft naturalisms, see R. B. Braithwaite, *An Empiricist's View of the Nature of Religious Belief;* Ronald Hepburn, "Humanist Religion," in Ronald Hepburn et al., *Religion and Humanism* (London: British Broadcasting Corporation, 1964), pp. 74-82; and Ronald Hepburn, "A Critique of Humanist Theology," in H. J. Blackham, ed., *Objections to Humanism* (Philadelphia: Lippincott, 1963), pp. 29-54; and Julian Huxley, *Religion Without Reservation.* Hard Naturalisms can be seen in Brigid Brophy, "Faith Lost—Imagination Enriched," *The Humanist Outlook,* ed. A. J. Ayer, pp. 189-197; Antony Flew, *God and Philosophy;* Bertrand Russell, *Why I Am Not a Christian* (New York: Simon and Schuster, 1957); and George Santayana, *Reason in Religion* (New York: Scribner's, 1905), chapters 6, 9, 10, and 11.

18. Bertrand Russell, *Why I Am Not a Christian,* p. 7; Sidney Hook, *The Quest for Being* (New York: St. Martin's Press, 1934), pp. 174-175.

19. Morris Cohen, *Studies in Philosophy and Science,* pp. 140ff.

20. See Ronald Hepburn, "A Critique of Humanist Theology," *Objections to Humanism,* ed. H. J. Blackham, pp. 29-54; H. J. Blackham, "The Pointlessness of It All," *Objections to Humanism,* pp. 105-127; and J. Wesley Robb, *The Reverent Skeptic,* pp. 117-129.

21. Sidney Hook, *The Quest for Being*, pp. 68ff.

22. Jacques Maritain, *True Humanism*, p. xvi.

23. Basil Mitchell, *Morality: Religions and Secular: The Dilemma of the Traditional Conscience* (Oxford: Clarendon Press, 1980); Paul Kurtz, *Moral Problems in Contemporary Society*.

Chapter 6—Marxism: History as Autonomous

1. Karl Marx, "Theses on Feuerbach," in Karl Marx and Friedrich Engels, *The German Ideology*, 3rd rev. ed. (Moscow: Progress Publishers, 1976).

2. Roger Garaudy, *Karl Marx: The Evolution of His Thought*, trans. Nan Apotheker (Westport, Conn.: Greenwood Press, 1967), p. 5.

3. Ibid., p. 205.

4. V. I. Lenin, *The Teachings of Karl Marx* (New York: International Publishers, 1930), p. 10.

5. *German Ideology*, p. 618.

6. Ibid., p. 43.

7. Karl Marx and Friedrich Engels, *Basic Writings on Politics and Philosophy*, ed. Lewis S. Feuer (Garden City, N. Y.: Anchor Books), p. 54.

8. *German Ideology*, pp. 37-42.

9. Karl Marx and Friedrich Engels, *Communist Manifesto*, trans. Samuel Moore in 1888, The Great Books, Vol. VII, No. 14 (Chicago: The Great Books Foundation, 1964), p. 8.

10. *German Ideology*, pp. 58-60.

11. Ibid., p. 37.

12. Ibid., pp. 51-58.

13. Ibid., pp. 58-60.

14. Karl Marx, *Capital*, ed. Frederick Engels, rev. and amplified according to the 4th German ed. by Ernest Untermann (New York: The Modern Library, n. d.), pp. 41-585.

15. *German Ideology*, pp. 58-60.

16. *Communist Manifesto*, pp. 17-18; *Capital*, pp. 708-709; Part IV, pp. 342-556.

17. *German Ideology*, p. 60.

18. *Communist Manifesto*, p. 48.

19. *Karl Marx: Selected Writings*, ed. David McLellan (New York: Oxford University Press, 1977), p. 594; *Communist Manifesto*, p. 34; *Basic Writings in Politics and Philosophy*, pp. 386-390.

20. *Communist Manifesto*, pp. 32-34.

21. Karl Marx: Selected Writings, p. 569.

22. Ibid.

23. *Communist Manifesto*, p. 34.

24. Ibid., p. 48.

25. *Karl Marx: Selected Writings*, p. 12-13.

26. *German Ideology*, p. 619.

27. Karl Marx, *Economic and Philosophic Manuscripts of 1844*, ed. Dirk J. Struik, trans. Martin Milligan (New York: International Publishers, 1969), p. 145.

28. Karl Marx, *Early Writings*, ed. and trans. T. B. Bottomore (London: C. A. Watts & Co., 1963), pp. 206-207.

29. Karl Marx, *On Religion*, ed. and trans. Saul K. Padover, Vol. V of The Karl Marx Library (New York: McGraw-Hill Book Co., 1974), p. 54.

30. *German Ideology*, p. 619.

31. *Early Writings*, pp. 126-127.

32. Ibid., p. 157.

33. *Capital*, p. 198.

34. *German Ideology*, p. 36-43.

35. *Economic and Philosophic Manuscripts of 1844*, pp. 106-119.
36. Ibid., p. 111.
37. Ibid., p. 168.
38. *Early Writings*, p. 191.
39. Ibid., p. 193.
40. *Economic and Philosophic Manuscripts of 1844*, p. 147.
41. Ibid., pp. 147-148.
42. Karl Marx, *On Religion*, p. 8.
43. *Karl Marx and Friedrich Engels on Religion* (New York: Schocken Books, 1957), p. 15. A reprint of the 1957 ed. published by The Foreign Languages Publishing House, Moscow.
44. Karl Marx, *On Religion*, p. 35.
45. Ibid.
46. Ibid., pp. 35-37.
47. Ibid.
48. Ibid., p. 36.
49. Ibid.
50. Ibid., p. 94.
51. Ibid., p. 36.

Chapter 7—Nihilism: Affirmation of Nothingness

1. Michael Novak, *The Experience of Nothingness* (New York: Harper and Row, 1970), p. 13.
2. Good historical treatments are in Johan Goudsblom, *Nihilism and Culture* (Oxford: Basil Blackwell, 1980) and Albert Camus, *The Rebel: An Essay on Man in Revolt*, trans. Anthony Bower (New York: Alfred A. Knopf, 1954).
3. Fyodor Dostoevsky, *The Brothers Karamazov*, trans. Constance Garnett (New York: Modern Library, 1943), p. 789; *Notes from the Underground*, trans. Mirra Ginsburg (New York: Bantam Books, 1981).
4. Johan Goudsblom, *Nihilism*, especially pp. 36-47 and 87-202.
5. Amonng good introductions to Nietzsche are: Walter Kaufmann, *Nietzsche: Philosopher, Psychologist, Antichrist* (Princeton, N. J.: Princeton University Press, 1950); R. J. Hollingdale, *Nietzsche: The Man and His Philosophy* (London: Routledge & Kegan Paul, 1965); J. P. Stern, *Nietzsche* (London: Fontana Books, 1978); and Arthur C. Danto, *Nietzsche as Philosopher* (New York: Macmillan, 1965).
6. Friedrich Nietzsche, *Untimely Meditations*, trans. R. J. Hollingdale (New York: Cambridge University Press, 1983), III, 3, pp. 140-142; III, 4, pp. 148-150; I, 1, p. 12, pp. 3-55.
7. Friedrich Nietzsche, *Beyond Good and Evil: Prelude to a Philosophy of the Future*, in *Basic Writings of Nietzsche*, ed. and trans. Walter Kaufmann (New York: Modern Library, 1968), 61-62, pp. 262-266; *The Anti-Christ* in *Twilight of the Idols/The Anti-Christ*, trans. R. J. Hollingdale (Baltimore, Md.: Penguin Books, 1968), 15-18, pp. 125-126.
8. Friedrich Nietzsche, *The Gay Science*, trans. Walter Kaufmann (New York: Vintage Books 1974), V, 343, p. 279.
9. Ibid., III, 125, pp. 181-182.
10. Friedrich Nietzsche, *The Will to Power*, trans. Walter Kaufmann and R. J. Hollingdale (London: Vintage Books, 1968), I, 55, p. 35.
11. Ibid., I, 2, p. 9.
12. Ibid., I, 12, pp. 12-13.
13. Ibid., 1, pp. 7-8; I, 7, pp. 10-11; III, 553-586, pp. 300-322; III, 636, pp. 339-340; III, 850, p. 448; III, 616, p. 330; *Beyond Good and Evil*, V, 199-203, pp. 300-308.

14. Friedrich Nietzsche, "The Four Great Errors," 1-8, in *Twilight of the Idols*, pp. 47-54.

15. Friedrich Nietzsche, *The Will to Power*, III, 602, p. 326.

16. Ibid., I, 3, p. 9.

17. Ibid., I, 22, p. 17.

18. Ibid., I, 23, p. 18.

19. Ibid., I, 22, p. 17.

20. Ibid., I, 28, p. 19.

21. Ibid., I, 29, p. 20.

22. Ibid., I, 30, pp. 20-21.

23. Ibid., IV, 1041, p. 536.

24. Ibid., I, 55, p. 36.

25. Ibid., 954-1002, pp. 500-519; Friedrich Nietzsche, *Thus Spoke Zarathustra*, trans. R. J. Hollingdale (New York: Penguin Books, 1969), "Prologue," 3-4, pp. 41-44; "Of the Higher Men," 1-20, pp. 296-306.

26. Ibid., I, 36, p. 23.

27. See Charles I. Glicksberg, *The Literature of Nihilism* (Lewisburg, Pa.: Bucknell University Press, 1975) and Maurice Friedman, *To Deny Our Nothingness: Contemporary Images of Man* (London: Victor Gollancz Ltd., 1967).

28. Martin Heidegger, *The Question of Being*, trans. William Kluback and Jean T. Wilde (New York: Twayne Publishers, 1958), p. 7.

29. Paul Tillich, *The Courage To Be* (New Haven: Yale University Press, 1952).

30. Karl Jaspers, *Psychologie der Welt—Anschauungen*, 2 Auflage (Berlin: Julius Springer, 1922), pp. 285-304.

31. Franz Kafka, *The Trial*, trans. Willa and Edwin Muir (New York: Modern Library, 1956).

32. Anton Chekhov, *Select Tales*, trans. Constance Garnett (London: Chatto and Windus, 1927), pp. 755-756.

33. Jean-Paul Sartre, *Nausea*, trans. Lloyd Alexander (New York: New Directions, 1964), pp. 221, 243; *Notebooks, 1942-1951*, trans. Justin O'Brien (New York: Alfred A. Knopf, 1965), p. 20.

34. Albert Camus, *Notebooks, 1942-1951*, trans. Justin O'Brien (New York: Modern Library, 1965), p. 20.

35. Albert Camus, *The Rebel*, p. 191.

36. Jean-Paul Sartre, *Existentialism and Humanism*, trans. Philip Mairet (London: Methuen and Co., 1946), p. 28.

37. Friedrich Nietzsche, *Daybreak: Thoughts of the Prejudices of Morality*, trans. R. J. Hollingdale (New York: Cambridge University Press, 1982), I, 95, p. 54.

38. Karl Jaspers, *Tragedy is Not Enough*, trans. Harold A. T. Reicke, Harry T. Moore, and Karl W. Deutsch (Boston: Beacon Press, 1952), pp. 72-89.

39. Soren Kierkegaard, *Fear and Trembling* in *Fear and Trembling/Repetition*, ed. and trans. Howard V. Hong and Edna H. Hong (Princeton, N.J.: Princeton University Press, 1983), pp. 27-123.

Chapter 8—World Religions: The Search for Ultimacy

1. See discussions of the problem of defining religion in Frederick Ferré, *Basic Modern Philosophy of Religion* (New York: Charles Scribner's Sons, 1967), pp. 30-115; Geddes MacGregor, *Philosophical Issues in Religious Thought* (Boston: Houghton Mifflin, 1973), pp. 11-28; Ninian Smart, *The Philosophy of Religion* (New York: Oxford University Press, 1970); *The Phenomenon of Religion* (New York: Macmillan, 1973).

2. John Hick, *God and the Universe of Faiths* (London: Collins, 1973), p. 133.

3. Wilfred Cantwell Smith, *The Meaning and End of Religion* (New York: New Ameri-

can Library, 1964), Chaps. 1-3, 6; pp. 141, 170-173, 342. A. C. Bouquet, *Comparative Religion*, 6th ed. (Baltimore: Penguin Books, 1962); Edward J. Jurji, *The Phenomenology of Religion* (Philadelphia: Westminster Press, 1963); Gerardus van der Leeuw, *Religion in Essence and Manifestation*, trans. J. E. Turner (London: Allen and Unwin, 1964); Joachim Wach, *The Comparative Study of Religions*, ed. Joseph M. Kitagawa (New York: Columbia University Press, 1958); Eric J. Sharpe, *Comparative Religion: A History* (New York: Scribner's 1975); Ninian Smart, *The Phenomenon of Religion*.

4. See the following introductions to the study of world religions: Huston Smith, *The Religions of Man* (New York: Mentor Books, 1958); Wilfred Cantwell Smith, *The Faith of Other Men* (New York: Harper Torchbooks, 1972); Harold H. Watts, *The Modern Reader's Guide to Religions* (New York: Barnes and Noble, 1964); Winston L. King, *Introduction to Religion: A Phenomenological Approach*, rev. ed. (New York: Harper, 1968); Charles S. Braden, *The World's Religions*, rev. ed. (Nashville: Abingdon Press, 1954); Stephen Neill, *Christian Faith and Other Faiths: The Christian Dialogue with Other Religions*, 2nd ed. (New York: Oxford University Press, 1970); Ninian Smart, *The Religious Experience of Mankind* (New York: Charles Scribner's Sons, 1969); *World Religions: A Dialogue* (Baltimore: Penguin Books, 1966); Joseph M. Kitagawa, *Religions of the East* (Philadelphia: Westminster Press, 1960); A. C. Bouquet, *Comparative Religion*; E. O. James, *Christianity and Other Religions* (London: Hodder & Stoughton, 1968); Gerardus van der Leeuw, *Religion in Essence and Manifestation*; Joachim Wach, *The Comparative Study of Religions*; John Clark Archer, *Faiths Men Live By*, rev. Carl E. Purinton, 2nd ed. (New York: Ronald Press, 1958); John B. Noss, *Man's Religions* (New York: Macmillan, 1956).

5. Different types of a relativistic understanding of Christianity in relation to other world religions are expressed in John Hick, *God and the Universe of Faiths* (London: Collins, 1973); *God Has Many Names* (Philadelphia: Westminster Press, 1980); Alan Race, *Christian and Religious Pluralism: Patterns in the Christian Theology of Religion* (Mary Knoll, N. Y.: Orbis Books, 1983); Wilfred Cantwell Smith, *Toward a World Theology* (London: Macmillan, 1980); Stanley Samartha, *Courage for Dialogue* (Maryknoll, N. Y.: Orbis Books, 1982); Raimundo Pannikar, *The Unknown Christ of Hinduism*, rev. ed., (Maryknoll, N. Y.: Orbis Books, 1981); Paul F. Knitter, *No Other Name? A Critical Survey of Christian Attitudes Toward the World Religions* (Maryknoll, N. Y.: Orbis Books, 1985); and Ernst Troeltsch, *The Absoluteness of Christianity* (Richmond: John Knox Press, 1971).

6. See John Hick's treatment of this idea in his *God Has Many Names*, pp. 60-78.

7. This non-conversionist dialogical approach to the encounter with world religions is advocated in Wilfred Cantwell Smith, *Towards a World Theology*; Paul F. Kitter, *No Other Name?*, pp. 205-232; Raimundo Pannikar, *The Intra-religious Dialogue* (New York: Paulist Press, 1978); *Guidelines on Dialogue with People of Living Faiths and Ideologies* (Geneva: World Council of Churches, 1979); and Stanley Samartha, *Courage for Dialogue*.

8. The Vatican II revised view of world religions can be read in the "Declaration on the Relation of the Church to Non-Christian Religions," in *The Documents of Vatican II*, ed. Walter M. Abbott (New York: Herder and Herder, 1966). Good historical sketches of traditional and post-Vatican II Roman Catholic views can be found in John Hick, *God and the Universe of Faiths*, pp. 120-132; *God Has Many Names*, pp. 29-39; and Paul F. Kitter, *No Other Name?* pp. 120-144.

9. Representative exclusivist views are in Harold Lindsell, "Missionary Imperative: A Conservative Evangelical Exposition," in *Protestant Crosscurrents in Mission: The Ecumenical-Conservative Encounter*, ed. Norman A. Horner (Nashville: Abingdon Press, 1968); Peter Beyerhaus, "Mission and Humanization," in *Mission Trends No. 1: Critical Issues in Mission Today*, eds. Gerald A. Anderson and Thomas F. Stransky (New York: Paulist Press, 1974); and "Lausanne Congress, 1974," in *Mission Trends No. 2: Evangelization*, eds. Gerald A. Anderson and Thomas F. Stransky (New York: Paulist Press, 1975).

10. Karl Barth, *Church Dogmatics* 1/2, trans. G. T. Thomson and Harold Knight (Edin-

burgh: T & T Clark, 1956), pp. 1-44, 280-361; Hendrick Kraemer, *Religion and the Christian Faith*, (Philadelphia: Westminster Press, 1956), pp. 340-365; *The Christian Message in a Non-Christian World* (Grand Rapids, Mich.: Kregel, 1938). A more moderate view than the extreme Barthian position, one which asserts that there is general revelation but no salvation outside Christ, is found in Emil Brunner, *Revelation and Reason: The Christian Doctrine of Faith and Knowledge*, trans. Olive Wyon (Philadelphia: Westminster Press, 1948). The classic debate on the issue of general revelation is in Emil Brunner and Karl Barth, *Natural Theology*, trans. Peter Fraenkel (London: Geoffrey Bles, 1946).

11. Karl Barth, *Church Dogmatics*, IV/3, trans. G. W. Bromiley (Edinburgh: T & T Clark, 1962), pp. 870-876, especially p. 874.

12. Examples are Karl Rahner, "Christianity and Non-Christian Religions," in *Theological Investigations*, Vol. 12 (New York: Seabury Press, 1974), pp. 161-178; "Observations on the Problem of Anonymous Christians," in *Theological Investigations*, Vol. 14 (New York: Seabury Press, 1976), pp. 280-294; and Hans Küng, *On Being a Christian*, trans. Edward Quinn (New York: Doubleday, 1976), pp. 89-118.

13. Representative protestants are Stephen Neill, *Christian Faith and Other Faiths;* and Leslie Newbigin, *The Open Secret: Sketches for a Missionary Theology* (Grand Rapids, Mich.: Eerdmans, 1978).